D0948650

PARADOX:

TRUDEAU

AS PRIME MINISTER

PARADOX:

TRUDEAU
AS PRIME MINISTER

ANTHONY WESTELL

PRENTICE-HALL OF CANADA, LTD. *Scarborough, Ontario*

FOR JEANNE

© 1972 by Prentice-Hall of Canada, Ltd.
Scarborough, Ontario

ALL RIGHTS RESERVED
*No part of this book may be reproduced in any form without
permission in writing from the publishers.*

PRENTICE-HALL, INC., ENGELWOOD CLIFFS, NEW JERSEY
PRENTICE HALL OF AUSTRALIA, PTY., LTD., SYDNEY
PRENTICE-HALL OF INDIA, PVT., LTD., NEW DELHI
PRENTICE-HALL INTERNATIONAL, INC., LONDON
PRENTICE-HALL OF JAPAN, INC., TOKYO

Library of Congress Catalog Card No. 72-6554
ISBN 0-13-648667-3
PRINTED IN CANADA
1 2 3 4 5 76 75 74 73 72

F
1034.2
.W47

CONTENTS

ALMA COLLEGE
MONTEITH LIBRARY
ALMA, MICHIGAN

PREFACE

At lunchtime on May 19, 1972, a crowd of political reporters were clustered around the door of the Prime Minister's office on Parliament Hill. The word had spread that he was going to announce his decision about whether to hold a summer election and the newsmen were excited, jumpy, as they always are when a story is imminent. The TV cameramen jockeyed to keep a clear view of the door. Radio reporters fiddled with their tape recorders and edged to the front of the crowd, ready to push their microphones forward to catch the Prime Minister's words. Two press photographers clung precariously to a ledge, hoping for a better picture angle, until a security guard ordered them down for their own safety.

As the minutes went by the tension mounted and the newsment began to clap in slow rhythm to remind the Prime Minister that they were waiting. Actually, he could not hear because he was down the corridor in the Cabinet Room discussing his decision with ministers and some backbench MPs. But soon he came hurrying along, flanked by aides, and the news ran ahead of him in whispers. So it was an anti-climax when he came out of his own door into the middle of the crowd to say cheerfully: "I'm announcing that Canadians can look forward to a prosperous, sunny, election-free summer."

That was the signal to start writing this book. I had been planning it in my mind for months, gathering information, but always some major political event loomed just ahead to make the time inappropriate. With the threat of an early election removed, I could begin to write. And now, seven weeks later, I have finished. This is not an excuse for shortcomings the reader may find. It is an explanation that this book is not history, but journalism, written in the midst of moving events, and against a deadline. I hope it makes up in relevance whatever it may lack in completeness and perspective.

A reporter is constantly picking other people's brains, gleaning facts, snapping up ideas. As I have been a reporter for 30 years, and a political writer for almost 20 of those, I cannot begin to remember all the people who have contributed to my knowledge and shaped my impressions. But here are some to whom I am indebted.

The School of International Affairs at Carleton University kindly made available to me the research assistance of Sheldon Gordon, an M.A. candidate. Sheldon brought me not only information, but also lively opinions: I have accepted some, disagreed with others and am alone responsible for the material and the judgments in the chapter on foreign policy.

For three years I have enjoyed holding seminars on public affairs for graduate division students taking journalism at Carleton. It has been a learning as well as a teaching experience and I am grateful to the students on whom I sharpened some of my ideas.

The *Toronto Star* gave me the time to write the book and permission to draw material from the Ottawa column which I have been writing since 1969. My colleagues in the Ottawa Bureau provided information and encouragement, and the Bureau Chief, Jack Cahill, saved my morale on several occasions during seven hectic weeks by prising my fingers from the typewriter and taking me sailing.

My friend Clyde Sanger read a number of chapters in draft and made extremely useful comments. The Parliamentary Librarian, Mr. E. J. Spicer, and his staff were unfailingly helpful. The Prime Minister's Office and other departments of Government produced all the documentation for which I asked.

Among many books I have used as sources, some have been particularly valuable. On the constitutional issues, there is *Federal-Provincial Diplomacy, The Making of Recent Policy in Canada,* by Richard Simeon (University of Toronto Press). On the FLQ crisis, *Quebec 70, A Documentary Narrative,* by John Saywell (University of Toronto Press); *The October Crisis,* by Gérard Pelletier (McClelland and Stewart Limited); *Terror in Quebec, case studies of the FLQ,* by Gustave Morf (Clarke, Irwin and Company Limited); and *Rumors of War,* by Ron Haggart and Aubrey E. Golden (New Press, Toronto). On foreign policy, *Canada's Search for New Roles,* by Peter C. Dobell (Oxford University Press for the Royal Institute of International Affairs); and *Trudeau and Foreign Policy, a case study of the making of Canadian foreign policy,* by Bruce Thordarson (Oxford University Press). An interesting view of Western alienation is provided in *The Unfinished Revolt,* by Owen Anderson and John J. Barr (McClelland and Stewart Limited).

A final note: when I say this book is journalism, I do not mean that it is an objective recital of facts. It is not human to be objective, without bias. We are all conditioned by inheritance, upbringing, experience. Even the simplest and most straightforward news report represents subjective judgments about which facts to use and in which order to arrange them. In this book I have selected from the facts available to me those which I think significant and interesting, and I have presented them in the order I believe most revealing. So although I have drawn on many sources, including those above, the responsibility for the book is mine.

By Macpherson, May 4, 1971, reprinted with permission—Toronto Star.

PROLOGUE

Pa-ra-dox, *n.* a statement or proposition seemingly self-contradictory or absurd but in reality expressing a possible truth.

Pierre Elliott Trudeau is paradoxical. He seems to be a collection of contradictions, and sometimes they are absurd. But does he in reality express a Canadian truth? This book explores that question.

But first let us establish the nature of the paradox, the contradictions. For after all, every Prime Minister is a controversial figure, praised by his supporters, derided by opponents. If he has a powerful personality, he may even arouse public feelings of love and hate. With every decision, he pleases some of the people and displeases others, and in time, those he has displeased will become a majority and remove him from power — unless he has the wisdom to retire first.

Prime Minister Trudeau is praised and damned, loved and hated, in these entirely normal ways. In the regular course of the political process, he makes friends and enemies, and probably, as the decisions flow, more enemies than friends. But Trudeau is also controversial in quite a different and deeper way. There is disagreement among both his admirers and his critics about what sort of man he is, where he stands in the political spectrum, what his goals are. Even before he became Prime Minister in 1968, John Saywell wrote that he was to many people an enigma: a wealthy socialist, an advocate of state power and of personal liberty, a French Canadian proud of his culture and yet bitterly critical of French Canadian society, and so on.

Trudeau's campaigns to win the Liberal leadership and the general election in 1968 compounded the confusion. There was an extraordinary gap between his style and his content. He wore the costumes and manners of a new era, suggesting adventure, excitement, change. But he spoke as a philosopher who knew there were no magic solutions to anyone's problems. To those who could hear above the shrieks and cheers of his fans, he made clear that he would try to govern by cold reason and cost-benefit analysis, by the painstaking examination of alternative policies and their implications. For me and, I think, for most Canadians, the gap between Trudeau's popular image and what he said was unbridgeable. There were two Trudeaus running, and two were elected.

So in power he continued to be a puzzling political personality. He sought to entrench a charter of fundamental freedoms in the constitution, but suspended civil liberties during the FLQ crisis. He promoted participatory democracy, but took the power to limit debate in Parliament. He spoke of a Just Society and pressed measures to redistribute income, but squeezed the economy and raised unemployment among the poor. He was generous to his opponents on one day and swore at them the next. A man of culture, he could descend abruptly to obscenity.

It is not surprising that commentators have completely different opinions about Trudeau. To Jean-Jacques Servan-Schreiber, the French writer and politician, he is "the first truly modern political figure in the West." But the leader of the Left in Canada, David Lewis, saw him as a throw-back to the divine right of kings in a quip hurled across the House of Commons: "There but for the grace of Pierre Elliott Trudeau, sits God."

To Lubor Zink, the columnist, Trudeau is a socialist, perhaps worse. But Ed Broadbent, a socialist MP and political scientist, describes him as "probably the most able conservative head of government we have had since the Second World War."

I had a flash of recognition while listening to the American political analyst, William Pfaff, describe what he called the New Right in Europe: "Anti-parliamentarian, but democratic. Unideological, but nationalist. Conservative, but innovative. Authoritarian and reformist. Technocratic, meritocratic, paternalistic, pessimistic." Give or take a word or two, I thought, and it's not a bad fit for Trudeau. But to another columnist, Professor James Eayrs, Trudeau is a mere dilettante, a dabbler.

Read Hansard and the press and you will see Trudeau denounced variously as a playboy and an inflexible lawyer, as an overgrown hippie and a constipated constitutionalist. But he has himself warned us not to look for narrow consistency.

"The only constant factor to be found in my thinking over the years has been opposition to accepted opinion," he wrote in the oft-quoted foreword to *Federalism and the French Canadians*. The oldest problem in political philosophy, he said, was to justify authority without destroying human independence, and the best answer he had found was to keep an equal distance from both alternatives. So Trudeau counts himself a pragmatist, a man who rows against the current of public opinion to avoid being swept over the falls of extremism. He steers by no compass of ideology which would show where his true course lies. To chart his progress, and ours, we have to examine not where he points on any single issue, but what he has done on many issues over his years in power.

That is what this books attempts.

Trudeau greeted by angry farmers in Saskatchewan July, 1969. Reprinted with permission—Canadian Press.

NATIONAL DISUNITY

In the great Confederation Room on Parliament Hill, redecorated with second-hand chandeliers and gilt paint, and looking gaudy and somehow unreal, like a movie set, Prime Minister Lester Pearson called the first meeting of the Constitutional Conference to order and began to read from a text:

"There are times in the life of a country when the assurance of good intentions, the discharge of normal duty and acceptance of routine responsibility are not enough. What such times demand is the exercise of courage and decision that go far beyond the needs of the moment. I believe that this is such a time for Canada."

The words were not mere rhetoric churned out by a speechwriter in a florid style judged appropriate for a historic occasion. They came, that Monday morning in February 1968, from the weary and deeply worried elder statesman who had been struggling for five years to hold Canada together. With his minority governments often on the edge of defeat and some of his trusted French Canadian advisers destroyed by scandal, Pearson had sought first to take the measure of the Quiet Revolution in Quebec and then to appease it while arousing English Canada to the reality of the Confederation crisis.

The circumstances had allowed him no grand strategy beyond survival of the federation and his tactics had frequently baffled Canadians and earned him more abuse than admiration. A confused, noisy, sometimes angry constitutional debate had welled up, little understood by most Canadians, resented by many and alarming even to Pearson who had come only reluctantly to acknowledge that the terms of Confederation might have to be renegotiated. But now he knew that the fundamental issues could no longer be avoided, and he went on in his opening statement to the conference: "Here the road forks. If we have the resolution and the wisdom to choose now the right course and to follow it steadfastly, I can see few limits to what we may achieve together as a people. But if we lack the courage to choose, or if we choose wrongly, we will leave to our children and our children's children a country in fragments, and we ourselves would have become the failures of Confederation."

Gathered around the green baize horseshoe table in the Confederation room listening sceptically to Pearson, under the fascinated eyes of the country, were the leading spokesmen for 11 governments, 10 provinces, two languages and cultures and a variety of political theories — the men who if they could not agree on a formula to save Confederation, would have to fight for the power to shape it to their own design.

There was Quebec Premier Daniel Johnson, a dark quick man who could switch in mid-sentence from furious French eloquence to soft Irish charm. He had written a book called *Equality or Independence*, by which he meant that if the French Canadian nation could not secure in its homeland of Quebec the political powers it felt necessary to develop its language, culture and distinctive values, it would have to separate. In speeches and statements he had claimed that his Government needed, at the minimum, exclusive control of social policies and local economic development, guaranteed under a new or drastically revised Canadian constitution. When he reactivated the constitutional committee of the Quebec National (not provincial) Assembly, he said the aim was to create "a new pact, a new alliance between two nations."

Johnson was far from alone in his claim that Quebec, as the homeland of a nation, needed more autonomy than the other provinces, more independence from federal rule — in short, a Special or Particular Status within Canada. This doctrine had become the conventional wisdom in Quebec by 1967 and it was accepted in some measure by many English Canadians in the political capital of Ottawa and the communications capital of Toronto.

The Quebec Liberal Party, at its conference in October 1967, rejected the frank separatism proposed by René Lévesque — causing him to walk out and found a new movement — but received from its official constitutional advisers a detailed blueprint for Particular Status, claiming for Quebec, among other powers, full control over social policy, radio and TV, immigration and manpower, and relations with foreign countries on matters such as education which fell under provincial jurisdiction.

It was so obvious that the proposal was different only in degree from Lévesque's plan for two associated states within a Canadian Union that it was shelved, although not immediately disowned by the Liberals.

The Thinkers' Conference organized by the Progressive Conservative Party in the summer of 1967 also agreed on a fuzzy Two Nations concept of Canada. It was later rejected by the full national party meeting and by the new leader Robert Stanfield. But in the confusion typical of the times, Stanfield went on to welcome as a leading recruit in Quebec, the formidable figure of Marcel Faribault, a constitutional adviser to Premier Johnson and advocate of Two Nations.

The New Democratic Party had written Special Status for Quebec into its election program. And Pearson himself, while never fully accepting the theory, had allowed Special Status to develop in practical ways by permitting Quebec to institute its own Pension Plan, instead of joining the Canada Pension Plan, and to opt out of a number of federal programs.

So Johnson spoke not just for his Union Nationale Government, but for a powerful body of opinion which accepted Special Status in some degree.

On the other side of the horseshoe table was the senior Provincial Premier, Alberta's Ernest Manning who had been almost 25 years at the head of his Social Credit Government. He had already been tagged by an irreverent reporter as the Abominable No-man most likely to refuse constitutional concessions to Quebec. He was concerned, as he said later, that the conference should not become a "Munich" — in other words, should not make cowardly concessions while achieving no lasting peace with Quebec. With him from the West were British Columbia's W.A.C. (Wacky) Bennett, with his toothy smiles, syrupy stories about French Canadian friends and a Chinese Canadian in his delegation to hint what Two Nations meant in his province; Saskatchewan's Ross Thatcher, who had announced that if he had a hundred problems the constitution was number 101; and Manitoba's novice Premier, Walter Weir, already out of his depth and soon to return to his trade of undertaker.

The four Atlantic Premiers were ready to conciliate Quebec if they could, but desperately anxious that nothing should be done to curtail the power of the federal Government on which they relied for so much of their tax revenues and services.

Somewhere uneasily in the middle of these disparate provinces and premiers was Ontario's bluff John Robarts, the man most responsible for bringing them all together around the horseshoe table. He had done business with Daniel Johnson when they were both young lawyers, and as Premiers the two had renewed the acquaintance and held several secret meetings. Robarts was impressed by the urgency of Johnson's arguments for a conference to hear Quebec's claims and by the warning that some action had to be taken to stem separatism. He was angered also by the refusal of the federal

Government to help the provinces meet their growing financial needs by transferring more tax resources to them. As the leader of the largest and richest province, with a substantial minority of French Canadians and historic ties to Quebec, he decided to take the initiative.

He therefore convened his Confederation for Tomorrow Conference of the provinces in November 1967, on the top floor of the still uncompleted Toronto-Dominion Centre, a symbol of the power of Bay Street's bankers and a vantage point from which the visiting premiers could look out over the busy factories, office skyscrapers and luxury apartment buildings of booming Metro, the promised land of the Canadian dream. Pearson and the federal Cabinet had resisted the idea of an open-ended constitutional conference because they could see no basis for agreement and feared that failure could be a mortal blow to Confederation. But the pressure of events during 1967 had forced Ottawa toward the view that some sort of showdown was inevitable, and Robarts' conference showed that most of the English provinces, if far from enthusiastic, were more open to the idea of constitutional reform than the federal Government had suspected.

But as Pearson looked around the horseshoe table at the full constitutional conference three months later and spoke his dramatic warning — "Here the road forks" — he must have wondered just how the eleven Captains of Confederation could keep the show on the road, let alone read the constitutional map correctly and agree on the right fork. If there was one thing Johnson was demanding as the minimum terms on which Quebec would stay in Confederation, it was Special Status; and if there was one thing on which the nine English provinces were agreed, it was that Quebec could not be allowed powers and privileges denied to them, or which would so weaken Ottawa as to balkanize Canada. Who could possibly take the wheel and bring order out of chaos?

The answer might be Justice Minister Trudeau, sitting quietly beside the Prime Minister and destined to succeed him at the Liberal leadership conference two months later.

One Nation or Two?

Trudeau had good credentials in Quebec as one of the intellectual fathers of the Quiet Revolution. He was a powerful opponent of separatism which he had called the *New Treason of the Intellectuals.* He had been a consistent and articulate critic of Special Status which he dismissed as impracticable, a hoax foisted on French Canadians. More power for the Government of Quebec, he argued insistently, could only mean less power for the representatives of Quebec in Ottawa. If, for example, social policy for French Canadians was made in Quebec City and social policy for English Canadians was made in Ottawa, how could Quebec's MPs participate or vote in the House of Commons? And once granted special favors within Confederation, he feared, Quebec's provincial politicians, building their own powers and empires, would constantly demand more authority until the result was effective separation.

So when Pearson allowed Quebec to introduce its own pension plan in place of the Canada Pension Plan, and to opt out of other federal programs. Trudeau did not consider it progress for Quebec, or even a sensible compromise, but a dangerous development, a slide toward Special Status. He entered federal politics in 1965 as a Liberal because he wanted to strengthen the federal Government, encourage it to resist the encroachment of the provincial politicians, and with other MPs, become a strong voice for federalism in Quebec. By 1966, the new men from Quebec, in alliance with Finance Minister Mitchell Sharp and others, had almost turned around the policy of the Pearson Government. At the tax sharing conference that year, they drew the line against yielding any more tax resources, and therefore economic leverage, to Quebec and the other provinces, asserted the federal right to manage manpower training and generally took a tougher line than Quebec had seen in Ottawa for several years.

These views and activities did not of course endear the Quebec MPs to their provincial rivals and to the leaders of

Quebec opinion who were driving for Special Status. Johnson snapped that the MPs were traitors to Quebec, and even the Quebec Liberal leader, Jean Lesage, said Trudeau had separated himself from the great majority of his compatriots by rejecting the Two Nations concept.

At the horseshoe table, Johnson tried to brush away Trudeau's views by saying to Pearson and the Premiers: "Although the adamant few still refuse to admit it, we all know Canada is made up of two nations." He argued that ensuring cultural equality depended not only on bilingualism, but even more on extending the powers of the Government of Quebec as the homeland of the French nation. Trudeau retorted that the same argument could apply within Quebec where there were two nations. He was pointing out that if French Canadians could claim to need a special government within Canada to protect them, so also could English Canadians in Quebec claim to need their own government.

The logic and clarity of his argument had already won over the federal Cabinet, converted the federal Liberal Party and was now challenging Johnson before the national TV cameras. But this was not Trudeau's only asset in those critical and confused months of 1967 and 1968.

He also had a positive and attractive philosophy of Canadian federalism which just might transcend all the quarrels around the table and unite Canadians from coast to coast, French and English, of many political faiths — a formula in short for saving Confederation.

The correct policy, he had argued in closely reasoned articles and lucid lectures, was not to give more power to the Government of Quebec, but more rights to all French Canadians. The object should not be to protect the French language and culture within Quebec alone, but to guarantee them an opportunity to flourish across Canada. The slogan was not the divisive Two Nations, but the ringing One Canada (with two official languages). "It amounts to fighting for the only thing that can make Canada united — to take the fuse out of explosive Quebec nationalism by making sure that Quebec is not a ghetto for French Canadians, that all Canada is theirs," he said.

He argued that French culture would have to learn to compete with English if it was to survive in North America, and he wanted to make it possible for French Canadians to move outside Quebec and enjoy the opportunities of other parts of Canada without losing touch with their language.

Only the national Government could implement such a vision of Canada and that was why he had entered politics in 1965 and won election to Ottawa. But in addition to language rights, he had also been advocating for years a Charter of Human Rights to guarantee such basic liberties as freedom of expression, conscience, religion, assembly and association; security of life, liberty and property; and the right not to be discriminated against on grounds of race, national origin, color, religion or sex.

While he was unenthusiastic about constitutional reform — opening a can of worms, he grumbled — he believed that his Charter could be a statement of human values on which all Canadians could agree, and could thus serve as the secure foundation for a constitution describing the machinery of the state. In a major speech to the Canadian Bar Association in September 1967, he explained that federal-provincial discussion on his proposed charter would prepare the way for constitutional change because "essentially we will be testing — and hopefully establishing — the one-ness of Canada."

Trudeau's design for a Charter of Rights, including language rights, coincided with the report of the Royal Commission on Bilingualism and Biculturalism which had been laboring since 1963 to answer the unofficial question, What does Quebec want?, and officially, "to recommend what steps should be taken to develop Canadian Confederation on the basis of an equal partnership between the two founding races."

When the commissioners had rushed out an interim report in 1965, flashing red lights and clanging with alarm, most English Canadians were hardly listening. "Ten Canadians travelled through the country for months, met thousands of their fellow citizens, heard and read what they had to say," wrote the Commissioners describing their own voyage of discovery. "This experience may be summarized very simply. The Commissioners, like all Canadians who read newspapers, fully expected to find themselves confronted by tensions and conflicts. They know that there have been strains throughout the history of Confederation, and that difficulties can be expected in a country where cultures exist side by side. What the commissioners have discovered little by little, however, is very different. They have been driven to the conclusion that Canada, without being fully conscious of the fact, is passing through the greatest crisis in its history . . . it would appear from what is happening that the state of affairs established in 1867, and never seriously challenged, is now for the first time being rejected by the French Canadians of Quebec."

Alarmist, irresponsible, exaggerated, protested many English Canadians in 1965. But two years later, they knew a national crisis was upon them and were looking for solutions. So when the commission published in 1967 the first volume of its final report suggesting that greater rights for the French language across Canada would help to conciliate Quebec, it was favorably received. The guiding principle of the report was that French and English should be the official languages of the Parliament of Canada and federal institutions, and that all government services — federal, provincial, municipal — should become available in both languages wherever there was a sufficient demand. That meant that in areas of English Canada in which there was a viable minority of French Canadians, they should be able to receive services in French, and in areas of Quebec in which there was a viable minority of English Canadians, they should be guaranteed services in English. Parents were also to have the right to have their children educated in the language of their choice.

Basically, French Canadians outside Quebec were to be granted the rights which English Canadians had always received in Quebec, and there was no design to make everybody speak both languages. As the commission said: "A bilingual country is not one where all the inhabitants necessarily have to speak two languages: rather it is a country where the principal public and private institutions must provide services in two languages to citizens, the vast majority of whom may very well be unilingual."

The report thus put into workable terms the general concept of language rights which Trudeau was advocating as the answer to Quebec nationalism. Together with his Charter of other human rights, it became the central policy thrust of the federal team around the table at the opening of the constitutional conference.

So while Johnson was demanding Special Status for Quebec, Trudeau was proposing Equal Status for French and English Canadians. And while Johnson was talking about more rights for the Government of Quebec, Trudeau was urging that the rights of all citizens should be guaranteed and placed beyond the reach of all governments.

These fundamental differences were not always clear around the horseshoe table. For most Canadians, the debate between the two concepts of the place of French Canadians in Canada was only just beginning and would remain a foggy business. But there were some obviously attractive aspects to Trudeau's ideas. He was talking about One Canada, which was better than two and evoked memories in the West of John Diefenbaker who had used the same slogan. He was a Quebecker who did not want Special Status and who said that his compatriots did not really want it either. He was ready to act on language rights when the B and B Commission had persuaded most people that something had to be done. He was promoting a Charter of Rights — another echo of Diefenbaker — which was hard to oppose in principle, even if it did smack more of the American Revolution than the parliamentary tradition that legislatures were supreme and not to be fettered by tricky constitutions limiting their powers.

The provincial Premiers went along with the federal proposals, without enthusiasm and with considerable reservations. Most of them were already moving to improve the status of French in some way, but they weren't ready to be bound by constitutional guarantees, and they were suspicious of Trudeau's charter. It took all Pearson's skill as a master diplomat to wheedle and bully them to a consensus that French Canadians outside Quebec should have the same rights as English Canadians inside Quebec, and to agree to set up a secretariat and a committee of officials to study this and other issues in preparation for another conference on the road to a new constitution.

Putting the best face on this tenuous agreement, Pearson closed the session by recalling the French woman who, when told that the martyred first Bishop of Paris had walked five miles carrying his head, pointed out: "The distance was not important. It was the first step that counted." Pearson drew the lesson: "Well, the distance is important in this voyage that we have begun, but the first step is even more important. It has been a good step. It may well be that fifty years from now school children will have to say about us, as we had to say about the Fathers of Confederation, 'they built it better than they knew.' "

Perhaps they will. History will tell. But what was only dimly perceived then, but is clear in restrospect, is that the first constitutional conference faced the fork in the road which Pearson had described and chose, however reluctantly and tentatively, the route mapped by Trudeau.

The road to Special Status down which the country had been drifting for several years and which might have led to a gradual accommodation of Quebec's aspirations in an associate states arrangement, was blocked. A new highway was suddenly open which promised to lead to a united and bilingual Canada in which the French would feel as much at home as the English.

The conference had not only taken this route, but had also given Trudeau the opportunity to advertise on TV his charisma and his beautifully simple concept of One Canada. He was well on his way to winning the Liberal leadership in April and, subsequently, asking the country to endorse his vision in the June general elction.

The country proved more than willing to do so. Not only was Trudeau an engaging personality, he was also a leader who was confident he knew how to save Confederation.

It has become fashionable to say that English Canada

voted for Trudeau to put Quebec in its place. But that was never the mood of the campaign. Trudeau made it abundantly clear that his form of federalism would not restrict the rights of French Canadians, but would enlarge them across Canada. He was never more applauded than when he spoke French, even in the interior of British Columbia, and it was not uncommon to see little old ladies who had never spoken a word of French in their lives waving hand-lettered signs which said "bienvenu".

It has been commonly said, also, that Trudeau won election without discussing real issues or making promises. But the biggest issue in Canada has always been national unity and his extravagant promise, the theme of his entire campaign, was that he could deliver it.

English and French Canadians believed him at least enough to give him a working although not overwhelming majority in Parliament. He was free to start work on his program to convert the sketchy and frail agreement of 1968 into a new and secure Confederation.

"Voilà Monsieur Thibaut"

Some initiatives were within his own power to take as head of the federal Government and he moved quickly. On October 17, 1968 he introduced in the Commons the Official Languages bill, saying: "We want to live in a country in which French Canadians can choose to live among English Canadians and English Canadians can choose to be among French Canadians without abandoning their cultural heritage ... Such a country will be able to make full use of the skills and energy of all its citizens. Such a country will be more interesting, more stimulating and, in many ways, richer than it has ever been. Such a country will be much better equipped to play a useful role in the world of today and tomorrow."

The bill sought to implement as far as possible the recommendations of the B and B Commission as they concerned the federal administration. It made it the right of all Canadians to communicate with the Government in the official language of their choice; ordered that all official documents should be published in both languages; provided for federal services to be made available eventually in the minority language in any district in which the minority reached 10 per cent; instructed that all services be offered in both languages to travellers within Canada (as for example on Air Canada and Canadian National Railways and at immigration and customs desks); made both languages official in federal courts and agencies; appointed an Official Language Commissioner, as a servant of Parliament instead of the Government, to oversee and assist with the implementation of the Act and to fill the role of a language ombudsman, guarding individuals against linguistic injustice.

As Secretary of State Gérard Pelletier emphasized repeatedly, "There is no question whatsoever of forcing English-speaking persons to learn French or of imposing the use of English on French-speaking persons." And the man eventually chosen to be a language commissioner was a tactful and witty English Canadian, academic and journalist Keith Spicer, who promptly advised that the best way to learn French was in bed — meaning that he had learnt his impeccable French from his wife. He set about reassuring Canadians that their rights would be protected.

But the national euphoria induced by the Trudeau election campaign was already evaporating. Some of the provinces were perhaps regretting the consensus they had granted to Pearson the previous February, and the more aggressive opposition politicians in Parliament were starting their task of eroding the support which the Prime Minister had built for his policies in all parts of Canada.

The languages bill was never well understood — Trudeau blamed the press for not explaining it — and there were rising fears that everybody was going to be forced to learn French, or at least that nobody would be able to get a good job in the civil service unless he had been raised in Quebec, New Brunswick or some other French-speaking area and therefore had a bilingual grounding. Ukrainians and other "third-force" ethnic minorities feared that the emphasis on

Two Official Languages slopped over to mean Two Official Cultures and downgraded their heritage. Three western Premiers, reacting to these and other pressures, objected vigorously to the bill and threatened to challenge it in the courts as unconstitutional, and the new Justice Minister John Turner finally persuaded the Cabinet that the bill would have to be relaxed in some ways to satisfy the Premiers and prevent a long delay in the courts. Nevertheless, Diefenbaker led a rump of western Tories in voting against the amended bill when it finally came to Parliament.

Despite the criticism Trudeau remained convinced that bilingualism was the only hope for Canada. I talked with him one night in 1969 in his study at the official home of the Prime Minister, 24 Sussex Drive. He was drinking Vichy water on ice before dinner, and he said quietly that if the country ever gave up on becoming bilingual, Quebec would certainly separate, and he'd go off and work in Europe or Washington. "What attaches me to this country is the belief that the French language can have certain rights," he said. "I think it's true for many French Canadians who believe in federalism . . . It's the only view that can make any sense."

Three years later, on a visit to Alberta, he put the point even more sharply by asking Westerners if they would feel that Ottawa was the capital of their country if its working and communicating language was exclusively French, as for so many years it had been exclusively English and French Canadians were expected to accept it.

Meantime, Trudeau was also forcing the pace in the campaign to convert the federal civil service to bilingualism, so that it could offer more attractive careers and life-styles to French Canadians (who, it was hoped, would automatically become federalists) and extend service to French Candians in their own language. Pearson had launched experimental language training for 60 civil servants in 1964, and now it was rapidly expanded. Instead of one-hour-a-day lessons, hundreds and then thousands of bureaucrats trooped off for three-week immersion courses in schools in Ottawa and regional centres.

They took a course called *Voix et Images de France*

which combined film strips with recorded French phrases and — some of them came to suspect as they were drilled for hour after hour by alternating severe and sympathetic teachers — some of the techniques of brainwashing. It was said to be the best system available and it was certainly far superior to the old grammar book method, but it had been devised in France to introduce newcomers to French life as well as to give them the rudiments of the language.

So the Canadian students found themselves learning how to admire the Paris skyline, deal with a French customs officer, and take a ride on the Métro or a bus to the Opéra. The principal characters in the film strip were a smug French family called Thibaut, and at every Ottawa cocktail party, civil servants exchanged stories, sometimes in halting French, about the frustrations of the course and information about the instructors to be sought or feared — particularly the pretty but demanding young women who boasted sweetly, "I can make Deputy Ministers cry." But if it was sometimes hard, it could also be fun and rewarding, at least for those who had the talent, tenacity and opportunity to stick at it for three years.

By 1972, the Thibauts had gone home to France and a new course using Canadian customs and backgrounds was in use. Of 18,000 who had entered training since 1964, 2,500 had graduated as officially bilingual and 9,000 were still studying. That implied a drop-out of 6,500, or a third of the total number of students. But many of those were lost in the early experimental years, while others were out temporarily because of job transfers and might be back to finish the course later. The Government planned to increase classroom capacity to 10,000 in 1972 (with about 2,000 learning English and 8,000 learning French), and the graduation rate was expected to rise to 2,000 a year. The total investment was $30 million in staff and facilities over seven years, but vast sums had been written off in salaries of civil servants while they took the course instead of doing their normal jobs. The question which troubled many people was how well the second language was retained once the course was completed and the opportunities for practice diminished. This was one of the reasons for introducing experimental units in some departments in which only French is used and a graduate can polish his skill among French Canadians who can work entirely in their own language.

The Government also tried to raise the proportion of French Canadians in the public service by active recruiting in colleges and universities. But although French Canadians make up about 27 per cent of the total population, they still fill only 18 per cent of jobs controlled by the Public Service Commission. When the commission made a computer analysis to find out from which universities the executive class of civil servants in Ottawa had graduated, it was found that the highest percentage were from the West and from Saskatchewan in particular.

Language Commissioner Spicer reported to Parliament that of 59,000 appointments to the federal civil service in 1971, command of English only was required for 80 per cent, command of French only for 8 per cent, and command of English and French for only 9 per cent.

But many civil servants were concerned that increasingly the best jobs seemed to be reserved for the bilingual. Trudeau appeared to be pushing men with French names into prominent positions, presumably to advertise to French Canada that careers, status and power were available in Ottawa as well as in Quebec City.

There was a rising wasp-like hum of gossip about alleged injustices to English Canadian bureaucrats and talk of a gathering political backlash against the bilingualism program. Stanfield and other opposition politicians who claimed to support the concept began to suggest that Trudeau was pushing too fast. But journalists who tried to find concrete evidence of injustices had little success and Commissioner Spicer reported receiving only 57 complaints from civil servants — 29 from English-speaking officials and 28 from French-speaking, of which about half were found to be groundless, a dozen concerned language training and only 17 alleged unfairness in job competitions.

Spicer began speaking tours, often in company with MPs, to explain the Official Languages Act and tell people they had nothing to fear, and he appealed: "Wait before setting free rumors, heresy and innuendos." After one hundred years of injustice, he argued, the language pendulum was just returning to centre in Canada.

In Quebec, the pendulum began to swing the other way. Nationalists feared that French could not survive unless it became the only official language, the language which all Quebeckers would use and immigrants would learn as a matter of course, just as English was the only language effectively used in English Canada. They warned that Montreal, dominated by an English Canadian and American business establishment and bombarded by English-language communications from Ontario and the United States, would become an English-speaking city unless drastic action were taken to ban English, in effect, and make Quebec a unilingual French community. Their protests and propaganda exerted considerable pressure on the worried provincial Government which searched for a language policy which would be both effective in defense of French and practical in everyday application in a North American metropolis.

Across the country, the other provinces acted, formally or informally, to improve the teaching of French with the aid of $50 million in subsidies from Ottawa, and to encourage the use of the language in their official institutions.

Ottawa itself ran into severe difficulties in implementing its policies, and three years after approval of the Official Languages Act, it was still struggling to define Bilingual Districts in which services would be available in both languages. Part of the problem was that the first results from the 1971 census showing distribution of language groups in Canada outdated much of the planning which had been based on the 1961 figures. In May 1972, the best that Pelletier could announce was that bilingual districts should be defined and announced within another year.

But if progress toward an officially bilingual Canada was slow and often painful, there was progress. And while there was danger that a political backlash might explode, not only the Government but the three opposition parties in the Commons remained committed to the concept in principle, if not always in their political tactics.

The Language of Dollars

The fundamental question about whether Trudeau's policy was really a solution to the problem of national unity came from quite another and unexpected source — the B and B Commission. Although its first report had proposed official bilingualism and provided the blueprint for implementing Trudeau's theories, its third volume published in 1969 suggested almost rudely that this was mere tokenism. In a study of the use of language in the factories and offices of Quebec, the commission said: "Official equality of language has very limited significance if it is not accompanied by equality of economic opportunity. Unless a language can flourish in the world of work, legal guarantees of its use by government services, courts and schools will not be able to ensure its long-term development. Formal linguistic equality is of little importance to those living under a system that always places them in inferior social and economic conditions. Such a partnership is not only unequal, but may in the long run imperil Confederation; the fate of the two cultures and the two dominant languages of Canada, within two distinct societies, ultimately depends on their positions in the world of work and the economy at large."

The report went on to document a dismaying picture of French Canadians almost as a servant class in a colonial society. It should have been no great surprise in Ottawa where everyone knows that if he wants his house cleaned, his elevator operated, his snow shovelled or any menial labor performed, it will probably be done by a French Canadian from Hull just across the river. But the commission set it out in cold and unforgiving figures. The average income of Canadian men of British origin was $1,000 a year more than that of men of French origin. In Quebec, the heartland of the French Canadian nation, the situation was worse: those of British origin averaged $5,918; those of French origin,

$3,880. Those in Quebec who did not bother to learn French and could speak only English earned more than the French who could speak both languages.

"There is little reason to suppose that the free play of economic forces will in itself bring about real equality of opportunity for Francophones or lead to a strengthening of their language and culture in Canada," said the report. "Left to themselves, the current pressures are more likely to lead to the opposite result."

Part of the problem in Quebec was that industry and commerce were largely owned and controlled by English Canadians or U.S. corporations, so English was the language of money and management. The commission urged a vigorous campaign by the Quebec Government to compel business to accept French as the normal language of work, and it proposed special measures to encourage the growth of French-owned enterprises. For the public service in Ottawa, it recommended unilingual units in which French only would be used — just as English is the only language used in the vast majority of federal offices.

These proposals were a far and radical cry from the limited program of bilingualism in some official institutions which had been first proposed. There was at once a shout of rage and alarm in English Canada, raising questions about how far the country was really prepared to go toward equality of language and opportunity in the federal service.

Less obvious but equally important was the fact that the commission's analysis of socio-economic problems in Quebec and the drastic action needed to solve them raised questions about the powers and resources the Quebec Government would need to carry through such reforms — powers and resources which were not needed in the English provinces because they faced no similar problem of protecting language and culture against the attack of economics and international business. In short, the report provided new ammunition for the old battle about Special Status — except that Special Status no longer existed as a popular option. It had been defeated by Trudeau the year before, and those who talked about more power for the Province of Quebec were edging toward René Lévesque and his emerging separatist party.

Less than a year after Trudeau had seemed to build a national consensus on his program for unity, the debate was starting again in a new and sharper form. What had gone wrong? The new report from the B and B Commissioners was not a change of heart, a sudden discovery that official equality of language would not be sufficient to satisfy the aspirations of French Canada. In their first report they had specifically warned that language did not go to the heart of the division in Canada. The basic issue, they said, was the degree to which the two societies, French and English, were to be allowed to determine their own affairs within Confederation — in other words, the degree of independence which Quebec could enjoy in setting its own priorities and managing its own destiny. To ignore this fundamental political issue in favour of simple language rights, said the commissioners, ". . . would not only constitute an error; it would likely mean that Quebec would not listen to us." But Trudeau had largely ignored the issue. In fact the commission's secretary, a senior public servant who had drafted much of the report, was so dismayed at Trudeau's narrow interpretation of it that he went off to Quebec and ran as a Conservative candidate as a sort of protest. He was buried by the Trudeau landslide, but came back to Ottawa to help implement those of the commission's recommendations which had been accepted.

Constitutional Merry-go-round

All this is not to say that Trudeau was preoccupied with language and other civil rights to the exclusion of ideas for making political and structural changes in the system of government prescribed for Canada in the British North America Act of 1867. Despite his earlier reluctance to open what he called the constitutional can of worms, he took with him into the Prime Minister's Office a task force of constitutional lawyers and senior officials to review the BNA Act. They included Carl Goldenberg, the soft-talking, pipe-smoking and hugely successful labor arbitrator from Montreal; Al Johnson, who had been a financial adviser to the old CCF government in Saskatchewan and moved to Ottawa to be the energetic assistant deputy minister in charge of federal-provincial fiscal relations; and Barry Strayer, a cool and competent law professor from the University of Saskatchewan. The team set about reviewing the BNA Act clause by clause and preparing reform proposals for a Cabinet committee which Trudeau chaired. Trudeau also ordered that the abandoned CN station in central Ottawa, an impressive example of railway monolithic architecture, should be converted into a permanent conference centre. The booking hall was skilfully converted into a conference room, handily connected to the CN's Château Laurier Hotel on the other side of the road by a tunnel through which Premiers could duck if they wanted to avoid reporters.

How seriously all this was intended is open to a slight doubt. Trudeau once remarked that constitutional conferences were essentially an exercise in convincing some people that no national agreement on reform was possible and that real problems would have to be solved more pragmatically. "Convince what people," he was asked. "Claude Ryan," he quipped in reply, naming the editor of Quebec's small but influential nationalist daily, *Le Devoir*. Ryan was a powerful advocate of constitutional reform and an old adversary of Trudeau. A senior policy adviser to Trudeau took much the same tack when he said in a private conversation that as the provinces had insisted on opening the constitution against federal advice, Ottawa was now going to recapture the initiative by pouring out proposals until the provinces tired of the game and called for a halt.

These may have been flippant remarks rather than a serious reflection of Trudeau's attitude on taking power, but they proved a reasonably accurate forecast of coming events. Some of the provinces were already preoccupied with more pressing problems than the constitution and impatient to talk about matters in which they were deeply interested — matters such as a greater share of national tax revenues.

When they came to Ottawa in February 1969 for their first constitutional conference under Chairman Trudeau, the premiers were in a mood for a showdown. The federal Government had persisted with the medicare program which many of the premiers regarded as a direct encroachment upon their constitutional jurisdiction, and the new government was proving even tougher than the old in refusing to yield more tax resources. "If you need more revenue, raise your own taxes," the new Finance Minister, Edgar Benson, told the provincial Treasurers. Adding injury to insult, he imposed a special income tax to finance Ottawa's share of medicare costs in such a way that the provinces got no part of the revenue. Ontario spluttered that it was effrontery," "unacceptable" and another example of "unjust federalism," and Premier Robarts said darkly that Trudeau was endangering Confederation. In Quebec Premier Jean-Jacques Bertrand, who had succeeded on the death of Johnson, frothed about "a fiscal crisis." It was not an atmosphere in which much progress on constitutional reform could be expected, and the provinces simply ignored an elaborate federal proposal that they should share with Ottawa the power to appoint Senators to create a new instrument of federalism on Parliament Hill, a sort of standing federal-provincial conference. It was hardly mentioned again during constitutional negotiations, perhaps to the relief of Trudeau who had never been enthusiastic about the plan. "I rather fear that it is going to be hard to sell to the federalists," he said before the idea was put to the Premiers. "If the provincialists don't want it either, we certainly don't . . ."

He met the provincial attack instead with the well-tried federal tactic of allowing the rich provinces and the poor provinces to discover the extent of their differences and to counter each others' best arguments. He was full of sweet reason as he opened the session. Ottawa was ready of course to consider constitutional curbs on its spending power so that more taxes would be left for the provinces. Perhaps the federal Government should get out of hospital insurance, or tax equalization payments to the poor provinces, or regional economic development? He was looking for guidance, he told the premiers, and then sat back with a smile playing around his mouth to watch the provinces slug it out. He knew that the Atlantic provinces, so heavily dependent on federal power to tax the rich provinces and send them subsidies, would be bound to oppose any idea of curtailing federal taxing powers, and sure enough, Newfoundland's Joey Smallwood came to his rescue. Almost as if he had been primed by federal experts, Smallwood, always a brilliant propagandist, pulled out a raft of figures designed to show that the poorest fisherman in the farthest outport of his impoverished island paid taxes for government services at a higher rate that the burghers of rich Ontario, and the rate would go even higher if Ontario insisted on reducing the federal ability to pay subsidies to Newfoundland. After two hours of inconclusive debate among the provinces, Saskatchewan's deputy Premier, David Steuart, said disgustedly: "We can hardly agree on the time of day around here," and the provincial fiscal revolt fizzled out.

That did not mean, however, that constitutional talks were back on the rails. The sad truth was that almost no advance had been made in the ideas and propositions put forward at the original meeting a year earlier. The Continuing Committee of federal and provincial officials had met four times and collected briefs from the 11 governments hoping to find some common ground. But when it was all boiled down to a 68 page private summary for the heads of government, it showed that while most governments had only platitudes to offer, those which had substantial ideas — Ottawa, Quebec, Ontario and New Brunswick — were often in sharp disagreement. There was no emerging consensus, and Prince Edward Island's clear thinking and outspoken young Premier, Alex Campbell, told the conference bluntly: "Once the Continuing Committee of officials makes recommendations I shall devote the time required to consider specific constitutional reforms. Until that stage has been reached . . . future sessions such as this are little more than a means to reaffirm our belief in the need to preserve and foster Canadian unity."

Not even that belief in unity was as clear as Trudeau had hoped. Funerals which mark the passing of one leader and the inheritance of his power by another are a natural occasion for preliminary political negotiations, and the Trudeau Government sought to take the measure of the new Premier of Quebec immediately after the burial of Johnson. The impression was formed that Bertrand was a mild man more interested in solving Quebec's economic problems than engaging in constitutional polemics, and it was even hoped that he would drop the more outspoken nationalists from his Cabinet and quickly come to terms with Ottawa. Even if Bertrand did toy with such ideas, the intense pressures within his Union Nationale party and the still rising tide of nationalism among Quebec intellectuals left him no room for maneuver. The constitutional conference was postponed from December 1968 to February 1969 to give him time to prepare, but when he arrived at the table he was in the same position as the Premiers who had gone before him. "Men may come and go, but the reality of Quebec endures," he said quietly, and proceeded to set out the case for Special Status in eloquent and unyielding terms. In response to the iron rule of democracy, he began, the Ottawa Government must identify with the English majority in Canada, regardless of the language or cultural background of the Prime Minister of the day — a cool dismissal of Trudeau as a captive Uncle Tom. He went on: "If there is a crisis in Canada, it is not because our country is made up of individuals who speak different languages; it is because Canada is the home of two communities, two peoples, two nations between which relations need to be harmonized.

"The important thing for French Canadians from Quebec is not to be allowed, as individuals, to speak their mother tongue even in regions of the country where it has little chance of being understood. What they want is the opportunity to live together in French, to work in French, to build a society in their image and to be able to organize their community life so that it will reflect their culture. And this cannot be achieved unless the Government of Quebec has powers proportionate to the responsibilities it is expected by its population to shoulder. Without Quebec, there might still be French minorities, but French Canada would no longer exist."

If the English provinces were becoming more interested in money than the constitution, it was clear that Quebec was still more interested in Special Status than in equal language rights. And when the conference was closing with the exchange of cordial platitudes, Bertrand again reminded all that the real problems had not been touched: "We should be looking in much greater depth at the division of powers (between Ottawa and the provinces) . . . It (is) clear that there are considerable and basic differences between the point of view of Quebec and that of most other provinces."

When the premiers returned in June 1969 to meet in private session away from the TV cameras and newsmen in the hope there would be more discussion and less posturing, Trudeau was ready to discuss some of the basic issues. His task force had produced papers on how to divide taxing and spending powers. But while they were generally acceptable to the provinces as far as they went, they did not go very far.

Instead of dividing taxing powers between Ottawa and the provinces, Trudeau proposed that all governments should share them equally: that is, both levels of government would tax personal incomes and corporate profits and sales to the limit acceptable to the voters. This meant that the provinces would be able to levy sales tax indirectly at the manufacturing level instead of directly and most unpopularly at the store counter, so it was better than nothing.

Trudeau had always claimed to be a strict constitutionalist who believed that Ottawa should stay out of provincial jurisdictions and he went some way to support this with his proposal to curb the federal spending power. Although successive postwar governments in Ottawa had always piously conceded that health and welfare services were primarily matters of provincial jurisdiction, they imposed their own policies by offering bribes which the provinces could not afford, financially or politically, to refuse. For example, when Ottawa wanted to introduce a hospital insurance program, it announced that it would pay half the cost to any province which chose to use its power to introduce a scheme which met Ottawa's standards. The provinces immediately came under pressure from their voters to accept the federal offer because they were already paying their taxes to Ottawa to finance half the cost. The provincial governments had to accept Ottawa's terms, despite the fact that it was a matter within their jurisdiction. And they had to find 50 per cent of the cost of the plan from their own revenues, which sometimes distorted their priorities, compelling them to spend money on hospitals which they would have preferred to spend on, say, education.

The Pearson Government's plan for medicare, offered as part of the 1965 election program, was the last straw for the provinces. Led by Ontario in open revolt, they were persuaded only with great difficulty to swallow the federal offer, and Trudeau, when he came to power, promised, "No more medicares." His proposal to the June 1969 constitutional conference was that the federal spending power should be curtailed to the extent that Ottawa would not be empowered to spend money in areas of provincial jurisdiction unless a national consensus of provincial governments wanted a federal plan. Even then, any province which objected could opt out and take cash instead. There were curious and probably impractical administrative features about the federal plan but as it proposed in principle to limit federal spending power, the provinces were interested. Nothing final was decided behind the closed doors, but the mood was reasonably co-operative.

Tensions between Ottawa and Quebec seldom relax for long, however, and now, behind the scenes, they were mounting again toward another confrontation. Bertrand and Trudeau had already clashed over the site of the new federal airport north of Montreal. It was placed in such a way as to transfer the economic benefits of the development to Ontario, alleged Bertrand, making the familiar claim that only the Quebec Government could be trusted to serve Quebec. Trudeau retorted that the Premier must be stupid or off his rocker and added insultingly: "Mr. Bertrand is falling into the sterile kind of anti-federalism that so characterized Mr. Duplessis (the former and much criticized Union Nationale Premier)."

Within his own party and Cabinet, Bertrand was coming under quiet but sharp criticism. He was admired for his sincerity, but feared to be a weak leader, lacking the style and skill to be something more than a competent Premier, to be a spokesman for the French Canadian nation, their champion in jousts with Ottawa. His Cabinet was increasingly paralyzed by divisions which he was not a powerful enough personality or leader to resolve.

To the annoyance of some of his colleagues, he had quietly dropped Quebec's claims to conduct its own foreign policy toward Paris and the French territories in Africa, which had been a great embarrassment to Ottawa. But in October 1969, perhaps by accident, perhaps by design, this old issue flared again when France's junior Foreign Minister, Jean de Lipkowski, arrived in Quebec to try to restore the flagging relations. He rudely refused an invitation to pay his diplomatic respects to Ottawa. Trudeau was enraged at this renewal of what he called "The Battle of the Red Carpet" and let the French Ambassador know of his displeasure. Quebec City watched with malicious amusement.

A few days later, there was a new outbreak of terrorist violence in Montreal, and Trudeau's concern about the rising nationalist-separatist turmoil in his own province now turned into white anger. He was due to speak to Quebec Liberals and he went that Sunday to Montreal with a few notes but no text which might inhibit him from speaking from the depth of his determination. Knowing what to expect, his staff assembled a team of transcribers and translators to catch his unrehearsed words and rush out an English and French text. There was no holding Trudeau that night, and attention focussed on his spectacular threat to close down the French-language CBC if it served as a vehicle for separatist propaganda and to abolish the Company of Young Canadians if it assisted revolutionaries. But the guts of his speech was in his advice to the Quebec Liberals to choose a strong federalist to lead them in the coming provincial election — a sign that he had given up on Bertrand — and in his prophetic reassurance to the people of Quebec who feared the growing violence of separatist extremists in the FLQ and associated front organizations: "You can count on us. We shall not allow the country to be divided, neither from within nor from without . . . I tell you again that no crisis will find us absent anywhere in Canada, especially in Quebec."

It was not a hopeful augury for the third full session of the constitutional conference which convened in December 1969. The heads of governments met for the first time in the new conference centre in the old Union Station, and Regional Economic Expansion Minister Jean Marchand looked around and quipped that as Confederation had begun with railways, he hoped it wouldn't end right there with railways. "All aboard," retorted Trudeau, and the conference was off to its first attempt in two years' labor to come to grips with Quebec's real concern — social policy.

The federal Government had put out a working paper in which it argued (a) Ottawa had to retain the right to make direct payments to individuals, as for example in the case of family allowances, in order to redistribute wealth, influence economic policy, build a sense of national community and provide for portability of benefits when Canadians moved from province to province; (b) It had to retain control of unemployment insurance because it was an economic rather than a social instrument; (c) It should gain paramount power over old age pensions in order to ensure portability, instead of legislating in the field only with the consent of the provinces.

As soon as the conference opened, Bertrand brushed aside Trudeau's protests that it had been agreed to forgo opening statements and set out to show that the federal position flew in the face of Quebec's frequently stated desires. Not just his Government, he insisted, but past governments and all parties in Quebec agreed that the province must control "social security, including all social allowances, old age pensions, family allowances, health and hospitals, manpower placement and training." But Bertrand now went beyond the traditional argument that these social instruments were necessary to preserve and direct the development of French society to advance a new claim. A strong-minded actuary named Claude Castonguay had recently completed an intensive study of social security in Quebec and emerged with the conclusion — presented in a provincial white paper — that all services should be integrated into one family plan for reasons of efficiency. Family allowances, student grants and loans, medical aid and hospital insurance, social assistance and old age pensions, child services, housing, workmen's compensation, unemployment insurance and vocational training and other agencies and services could and should be woven into one co-ordinated program directed to the basic unit of Quebec society, the family. This of course implied that some federal services would have to pass under provincial control. But as Bertand pointed out, the federal Government was not only "refusing to hand over to Quebec the programs for which we have frequently asked and concerning which we have been given legal priority by the constitution, but for all practical purposes it wants to get its hands on certain programs which are now under provincial jurisdiction. In our opinion, this is doing things backwards."

While some of the English provinces sympathized with Bertrand's views, they were not driven by the same cultural imperatives and were aware that many of their voters still expected national social policy to be directed from Ottawa. The new face at the conference, the young NDP Premier from Manitoba, Ed Schreyer, a former federal MP, even chided Trudeau for being so backward in coming forward to declare federal responsibility.

It was painfully clear when the conference ended that two years of constitutional talk had sharpened rather than reconciled the basic differences, and that Quebec stood alone in Confederation. "We won't come to any rapid conclusions," said Ontario's Robarts wearily. "It's just not possible with the great variations of opinions among governments. Some of our differences may never be reconciled and we may, in fact, never be able to reach agreement."

In that mood of discouragment, the focus of federal-provincial negotiations turned in 1970 from the abstractions of the constitution to such immediate issues as prices for Prairie grain, freight rates and the federal plan for tax reform. Some minds, however, were turning back to the idea that if the heads of governments could not yet agree on what to put into a new constitution, they could perhaps work out a way to patriate the old one. It was a familiar puzzle which had been attempted many times before and an answer had nearly been found in the so-called Fulton-Favreau formula (named after two federal Justice Ministers) which had been devised in the early Sixties and turned down only at the last moment by Quebec. The BNA Act uniting the former British colonies in Confederation in 1867 and specifying the form of federal government and the powers to be allowed to the federal and provincial governments had of necessity been passed by the British Parliament. And although Canada had long since achieved full effective independence, the constitution remained embarassingly at Westminster, where Canada had to apply for action every time it wanted a change made. This was not because the British Parliament wanted to be bothered — it was anxious to get rid of the nuisance of having to legislate on Canadian request — but because the Canadians could never agree on a formula for amending the BNA Act at home. The provinces, for example, could not dream of allowing the federal Parliament to take sole charge of the constitution and make what changes it might please, for then they might lose some of their cherished rights, such as Quebec's rights to the French language. But any formula which said that all the provinces would have to agree with Ottawa before changes could be made would put the constitution into a straitjacket and make change almost impossible, for there would always be somebody to object or hold out for concessions. The trick therefore was to find a formula which would make change reasonably possible within guarantees satisfactory to all, and then the Canadian Constitution could finally come to Canada.

While Robarts and some federal experts began to think along these lines, political events were developing in Quebec. The provincial Liberals chose as their new leader Robert Bourassa, a highly-educated young technocrat who had served quite recently as an adviser to the federal Finance Department on tax reforms, and who sold his bungalow home on the Rideau River to Paul Hellyer when he left Ottawa to enter Quebec politics. He had something of Trudeau's style in politics, but Ottawa of course was keenly interested in whether he was a genuine federalist. When he ducked a crude but revealing test question — if elected, would he fly the Canadian flag over the Quebec Assembly — some federal ministers growled that he was soft-centered, an incipient nationalist with suspect advisers, and not to be trusted. Trudeau and Marchand at last persuaded Bourassa to make a low key but public confession of his federalism, and had to be satisfied with that.

Premier Bertrand waited for Bourassa to install himself as Opposition leader and then judged the moment right to call an election for April. I had been to see Bertrand in his office in the Assembly in February, when the campaign was already unofficially underway, and he talked frankly of his campaign strategy.

It was the time of the Winter Carnival and he came in wearing a tartan blazer with the Jolly Snowman symbol on the breast pocket and a matching tie, looking for all the world like a small town mayor, or perhaps the chairman of the local chamber of commerce, and talking an old style of Quebec politics. He and the Union Nationale were going to take the nationalist middle ground, with Lévesque and his Parti Québécois separatists on one extreme and the Trudeau-Bourassa "centralizers" on the other. "We are going to settle some of the problems this year, no doubt. It will be — and I think I'm right when I say that — somewhat like a referendum." He was confident that Quebeckers would vote again, as they often had in the past, for Special Status, the concept of a Quebec which was neither fully committed to Canada nor separatist.

The view from Ottawa was quite different. Trudeau was confident that the separatists could not do very well, and he was supported by Liberal polls which showed him to be by far the most popular politician among French Canadians.

But it was feared that the Créditistes might run strong, particularly if the national leader, Réal Caouette, decided to leave Ottawa and lead the provincial party. A car dealer from Rouyn and an orator who could weave dazzling spells with social credit monetary theory, Caouette was a convinced federalist, encouraged by the fact that the Queen had chatted to him charmingly in French when on a visit to Ottawa, and by the discovery on his first visit to France that living standards, as measured by the number of private toilets in his hotel, were not as high as in Canada. But if he entered the Quebec race and the vote split four ways — between Union Nationale, Liberals, Separatists and Créditistes — there was no telling what the result would be. In the event, Caouette stayed in federal politics, but Ottawa still had nightmares about a weak minority government in Quebec City unable to face up to the growing unemployment, declining business confidence and rising unrest in the streets.

What happened on election day was that Bourassa and the Liberals won a comfortable majority. The Union Nationale was almost wiped out, and the Créditistes did less well than expected. Lévesque lost his seat in Montreal, but the PQ separatists collected 24 per cent of the total vote, which included, they were quick to point out, about 30 per cent of the vote by French Canadians. It was on the face of it a victory not only for Bourassa but also for Trudeau. Quebec had elected the strongest federalist party running in the campaign, rejecting both Bertrand's Special Status and Lévesque's separatism. A deeper and more disturbing truth, perhaps, was that provincial politics were now polarizing between federalists and separatists. The middle ground was disappearing, but Trudeau seemed not to care. He liked people to stand up and be counted, he said, sending a shudder through the old hands in Ottawa to whom the name of the game of federal-provincial negotiations had always been to avoid confrontations and final decisions from Quebec in case you got the wrong one.

But now the scene appeared set exactly to Trudeau's design to bring the constitutional negotiations to a brilliant conclusion. Bourassa was more interested in economics, in making jobs, than in haggling over minor points of the BNA Act, and that was fine by Trudeau. The two men had a private meeting soon after Bourassa took office and Trudeau assured him that despite his reputation as a rigid centralizer, he was in fact anxious to be flexible in meeting any reasonable and precise request from Quebec for reform of the constitution. What Trudeau did not want was a continuation of the long-drawn negotiations in which every proposal or concession by Ottawa could be met by a new demand from Quebec, with never a final settlement in sight. Trudeau told Bourassa in so many words: "Tell us what package of reforms you must have to persuade your voters to accept a new constitution and we'll do our best to satisfy you." Bourassa repeated the familiar formula: Quebec must be assured the power to shape its own society. The two leaders thereupon agreed to concentrate their efforts in this area.

Trudeau quietly recruited to his personal staff Bob Bryce, one of Ottawa's most respected and knowledgeable mandarins, who had announced his retirement as Deputy Minister of Finance. He asked him to work out how Ottawa could integrate its programs with Quebec's desire for control of social policy. Bourassa, at his end, had taken into his Cabinet, as Minister for Social Affairs, Claude Castonguay whose White Paper on social policy had been quoted by Bertrand at the constitutional conference and who knew precisely what powers he needed to carry through his plans for a co-ordinated social security program.

While this was going on behind the scenes, the constitutional conference was dragging on its weary way. The heads of the governments met for a closed door session in September 1970, but made little progress. Manitoba's Schreyer said in exasperation that maybe the thing to do would be turn over the whole set of problems to a commission of experts for 18 months, and Saskatchewan's Thatcher, who had never concealed his boredom with the whole process, suggested that as the constitution was really of interest only to Ottawa, Quebec and Ontario, perhaps they could negotiate to their hearts' content and then tell the others what they had agreed. It was then that Robarts made public the idea of going back to the problem of patriating the BNA Act, and Trudeau agreed because it offered at least some chance of success.

In October came the FLQ crisis which further polarized the already explosive politics in Quebec and made it more urgent than ever to achieve some success in constitutional negotiations, to show that peaceful change was possible. Federal Justice Minister Turner was dispatched across the country to sell the provinces on a formula for amending the BNA Act which, if accepted, would make it possible to bring it home from Britain. The formula proposed that most changes would need the approval of the federal Government, plus each of the provinces with 25 per cent or more of the population (meaning Ontario and Quebec could each veto any change of which it did not approve), plus two Atlantic provinces and two Western provinces.

By the time the conference resumed, again behind closed doors in February 1971, the prospects for agreement looked brighter than they had for three years.

For one thing, some of the old premiers who had become bogged down in the tired cliches were gone, retired or defeated. There were younger and more flexible men to join Bourassa at the table. Robarts, attending the last conference before his retirement, watched them with interest, and when we went to have a drink in his suite after the conference, he remarked admiringly about the newcomers: "They aren't hung up on the old shibboleths. They just say, Why not?"

The new flexibility had become apparent that day at a difficult moment around the horseshoe table. B.C.'s Bennett was standing on the pride of his great province and objecting to one feature in the amending formula. If Ontario and Quebec were going to hold a veto on change, B.C. should have some recognition and not be just one of four western provinces, any two of which could consent to change. He demanded that the formula should be changed to say that the two western provinces giving consent should contain at least 50 per cent of the western population. That meant that B.C. and one other province could agree to a change, but if B.C. disagreed, it would have to be outvoted by all three Prairie provinces.

The other western provinces were not happy at the idea of granting this distinction to British Columbia, and Trudeau and Turner were dubious about adding a feature which would make the formula more rigid. The whole idea was in danger. Then one of the relative newcomers, Manitoba's Schreyer, stepped in and said he thought that the Prairies could make the sacrifice to meet Bennett's demand if it were essential to agreement. The next problem was with the Atlantic region. If British Columbia was to be granted senior status in the West, should not the East have a similar arrangement? After all, proud Nova Scotia was being placed by the formula on an equal footing with tiny Prince Edward Island. But Nova Scotia's new Liberal Premier, Gerald Regan, turned quietly to Newfoundland's Smallwood and they agreed they could forgo equal status with British Columbia. Prince Edward Island's Campbell agreed and Regan looked across the table to New Brunswick's young Conservative leader, Richard Hatfield, who gave his consent.

So a tentative private deal was made on the formula to amend the constitution. Trudeau called it a breakthrough, and it certainly seemed to mean that the BNA Act would soon be brought triumphantly from Britain to Canada, a popular symbol of the country's new unity and maturity. But it was not to be that simple. Bourassa was not quite committed. "We shall see," he kept saying to reporters. "On verra, we shall see." He was in fact demanding a price, and the price was familiar: an agreement on social policy. Castonguay was pressing his idea of an integrated social security plan, and the communique from behind the closed doors of the February conference noted that there should be little difficulty in fitting Ottawa's family allowances and old age pensions into the Quebec scheme. Unemployment Insurance was already being adjusted. The remaining problem was with Castonguay's proposed General Social Allowances Plan, a sort of guaranteed income scheme, and Trudeau and Bourassa dined together to argue about costs and over how many years the plan might be phased in.

The objective now was to tidy up this substantial detail so that a package of constitutional agreements could be approved by the heads of governments when they met in Victoria, B.C., in June to help British Columbia celebrate its 100th birthday as part of Confederation. Ottawa and Quebec both prepared their final offers, but no agreement had been made when Trudeau and Bourassa set out for Victoria. It was clear to the federal experts that this was going to be a make-or-break bargaining session and they knew the odds on success were no better than 50-50. There was concern not only over Quebec and social policy but also over Ontario's reluctance to accept even a limited guarantee of language rights in a new constitution. The new Premier, William Davis, who had succeeded Robarts, was committed to making practical progress in developing the use of French in the province, but reluctant to be bound by any constitutional formula which might impose legal obligations he was not ready to meet in every detail.

The Victoria conference opened with a ceremonial parade through the city to the provincial legislature building on the handsome harbor. With Premier Bennett acting as an enthusiastic parade marshal, leaping in and out of his Buick to make last minute arrangements, Trudeau led the way in a magnificent gray-green Cadillac, while PEI's Campbell was allotted a yellow Mustang considered appropriate to the size of his tiny province. The quaintly Victorian chamber of the legislature where the talks were to be held was smotherd in flags and flowers for the official opening of the conference before the TV cameras and reporters. As always, the opportunity for publicity brought out the worst in the politicians and the gaiety and goodwill of the occasion quickly gave way to partisan backbiting in the opening statements.

Speaking to the folks back home in the ridings, Bennett belittled the importance of the constitution and managed to insult Quebec by suggesting that it was somehow robbing the taxpayers of British Columbia. Schreyer launched into a bitter attack on Trudeau's economic policies. Alberta's Harry Strom protested that Canada was not bicultural but multicultural and implied that French could have no preferred status in his province. And Saskatchewan's Attorney General Darrel Heald, subbing for Premier Thatcher who had stayed home to fight and lose his election, raised the perennial problem of freight rates. Once again it was PEI's Campbell who cut through the self-serving oratory: "This is, I understand, a constitutional conference. I am here not only to discuss constitutional change, but in the hope of changing the constitution. Let us to the task."

When the conference went into closed session, the atmosphere was still difficult. The working document before the heads of governments was called the Constitutional Charter, a grand title for a grab bag of items salvaged from previous conferences and on which there seemed to be hope of agreement. There were, for example, the tattered remnants of Trudeau's proud Charter of Human Rights, now reduced to a few of the most elementary political freedoms of thought, conscience, religion, opinion, expression, assembly and association. The section on language guarantees was restricted in scope and limited to a few consenting provinces; the West had more or less opted out and even where there was agreement, it was far short of ensuring equality of French and English. The provinces were to have a voice in appointing judges to the Supreme Court of Canada, one of the so-called "institutions of federalism," and there was a motherhood clause in which all governments committed themselves to reducing regional disparities, but guaranteed nothing in practice. Then there was of course the famous amending formula as negotiated in February, some proposals to tidy up out-of-date clauses in the BNA Act, and finally, the competing proposals from Ottawa and Quebec on social policy.

When the bargaining began, it was soon apparent that Bourassa was unsure of his ground on some issues. He hesitated, procrastinated and several times excused himself to go to the phone and take advice, presumably from Cabinet colleagues back home in Quebec. To the other Premiers, it seemed that he was not so much a head of government as a spokesman for a collective leadership — a collective which was divided on some major matters. No official record of the exchanges around the table was published, but there were plenty of revealing, if not perhaps entirely accurate, leaks.

Trudeau wanted a clause in a new constitution making it clear that foreign relations were a federal responsibility and putting an end to Quebec's adventures abroad. "I'll have to think about that," said Bourassa and Trudeau dropped the clause from the draft agreement with a resigned shrug and the tired remark, "But Robert, you've had since last year to think about it."

When Bourassa said he could not guarantee to provide provincial services in English in bilingual districts in Quebec in which more than 10 per cent of the population spoke English, Ontario's Davis exploded: "If you can't sell English rights in your province, how do you expect us to guarantee services in French in Ontario?"

Bourassa was also unready to guarantee education in the language of the parents' choice, and an Atlantic delegate complained: "I felt like a bridegroom who had finally decided to go to the altar with the girl who's been asking you for years to do the right thing by her, and when I turned round to put the ring on her finger, she'd gone."

When it came to social policy, both proposals were based on an adaptation of Section 94A of the BNA Act. Under this clause, years before, the provinces had granted to Ottawa the right to legislate for old age pensions, which were a social matter and therefore primarily a provincial jurisdiction. The precise meaning of the clause was arguable, but it appeared to give paramount powers to the provinces. That is, Ottawa could set up a pension plan, but if a province also wanted to set up a plan, its legislation would take precedence.

Ottawa now proposed to bring under this clause, in addition to pensions, family and youth allowances and allowances paid to persons undergoing vocational training. This meant that if Quebec or any of the other provinces decided to set up its own scheme of allowances — as Castonguay intended — and its legislation clashed with Ottawa's, the provincial plan would take precedence.

In Ottawa's terms, it was a substantial concession. Although the provinces were acknowledged to be primarily responsible for social policy under the BNA Act, the federal

Government had grown accustomed since the Second World War to setting the pace of development with national plans. It claimed the right to make direct payments such as family allowances to all citizens under its general responsibility, to manage the economy, redistribute income and create a sense of community across the country. Now it was willing to compromise to the extent of acknowledging provincial primacy, although the offer was not quite as good as it seemed at first glance. The federal formula made no mention of money. If Quebec legislated in such a way as to exclude federal family, youth and vocational allowances, would Ottawa simply keep its cash at home, leaving Bourassa with no extra funds to increase provincial allowances while trying to explain to his voters why they were no longer getting cheques from Ottawa? That would be an empty constitutional victory for the provinces and would do nothing for Castonguay's dream of an integrated system of social security. French Canadians would simply be paying federal taxes but getting no federal benefits, at least until Ottawa and Quebec gave in to the inevitable political pressure and made some arrangement beyond that specified in the federal offer.

The federal experts who had worked out the proposed compromise on social policy knew that this was a critical issue, the climax of more than three years' constitutional negotiations to try to arrange Confederation to Quebec's satisfaction. So they watched anxiously to see how Bourassa and Castonguay, who was at Victoria as part of the Quebec delegation, would react. They began to suspect the worst on the second night of the conference when Bennett loaded the entire conference aboard a provincial ferry steamer for a cruise through the scenic Straits of Juan de Fuca.

Optimists were suggesting that the cruise could be a repetition of the famous sea-borne meeting in Charlottetown, P.E.I., in 1864 when the politicians from Ontario and Quebec sailed into the harbor in their yacht, invited the Maritimers aboard and persuaded them that Confederation might be a good idea. But while the Canadian yacht in Charlottetown was heavily loaded with champagne which is said to have greatly helped the negotiations, Bennett is a non-drinking man and there was no liquor aboard his ferry, except the bottles which delegates with foresight smuggled aboard. While most of the voyagers divided their attention between the new Mrs. Trudeau in a becoming orange pant suit and the extravagant, snow-capped mountains in the evening sun, the federal experts were watching Castonguay. Up and down the deck he marched, with an aide on each side, the three heads bowed in conversation and — depressingly — their faces getting longer and grimmer by the minute.

The fact was that however generous Ottawa might think its proposal on social policy, it was far short of what Castonguay was asking in the new Quebec proposal before the conference. This suggested placing most federal social allowances under Section 94A and therefore making them subject to provincial primacy. Any provincial plan to pay family allowances, manpower training allowances or a guaranteed income supplement to the aged would automatically absorb any federal plan in those areas; and any federal plan to pay youth and social allowances, unemployment insurance and regular pensions to the old and disabled, would be allowed to operate only to the extent that it did not clash with a provincial plan. Wherever a provincial plan replaced a federal plan under these arrangements, the province would automatically receive from Ottawa the amount of money which would have been spent under the federal plan.

This was far more than Trudeau was prepared to surrender. In addition to the economic argument that Ottawa must retain some powers to tax and spend and redistribute income, and the social argument that it had a duty to establish at least national minimums for social security, there were political factors involved. The federal Parliament could hardly be expected to go on levying taxes to send the money to Quebec and the other provinces to spend, and it would certainly not be enthusiastic about innovating social programs if they could be taken over at will by the provinces. Trudeau also thought it important that French Canadians should continue to get some cheques direct from Ottawa to remind them that they had a federal Government and that not all good things flowed from Quebec City. So while Ottawa's offer was too little for Bourassa and Castonguay to accept, Quebec's proposal was too big for Trudeau to swallow. In a bid to win support for his proposals, Castonguay conducted a private briefing for the other provinces. There was admiring interest in his concept of an integrated social security system. Some of the provinces were coming around to Quebec's view that they would be better off running their own show, designed to meet their own local needs and priorities, than trying to operate a patchwork of programs in an uneasy partnership with Ottawa, which might change the rules at any moment. But the Atlantic provinces were keenly aware as usual that they really couldn't afford to bite the federal hand that kept them solvent with subsidies.

The heads of governments trooped into the legislative chamber at 10 a.m. for the third and final day of the conference. Clause by clause, line by line, word by word they worked through what was left of the constitutional charter, now known as the Victoria Charter, seeking final agreement. Again they pondered the riddle of social policy, and Ottawa insisted that the charter could go no further than its offer. The Quebec draft dropped from sight and was never officially published at Victoria, although bootleg copies circulated among the press. The conference could have ended right there in disagreement, but all parties at the meeting were desperate for some sort of agreement. Who, after all, wanted to walk out and announce that the long effort to find a new basis for Confederation had failed? Lunch was sent in to the meeting, pastries followed at supper time, and Bennett steadfastly refused permission to smoke in the legislative chamber, an agony for some of the delegates. Outside the meeting, newsmen wiled away hour after hour speculating on what was happening behind the closed doors.

Finally, at 11.30 p.m., after thirteen and a half hours of talk, the conference ended, and Trudeau met the press, with deep dark circles of fatigue under his eyes and a yellow daisy drooping from his lapel. He put the best interpretation he could on events, but it was apparent that nothing had really been decided. The Victoria Charter had been saved as far as possible — with its token political and language rights, federal offer on social policy, amending formula and so on — but none of the governments were finally committed to it.

The heads of the eleven governments were going home to reflect on the total package for 12 days until June 28, consult their colleagues and public opinion, and decide if it were acceptable. There would be no more deals, no more negotiations, but if all decided to accept, the Charter would take effect. Canada would be able to bring the constititution home from Britain and begin to make changes. But more important would be the tacit acknowledgment by Quebec that solutions were possible within Canada, that it had decided that its future lay in a new Confederation rather than in separatism.

The federal experts knew that Bourassa had not got what he wanted in the Charter and that he would have a tough job persuading his Cabinet and his voters that he had won enough on social policy to justify acceptance of the amending formula. They hoped that he would realize that he had won all he could in the circumstances and that he would think it better tactics to stand and fight for the Charter against the nationalists and separatists, rather than reject the Charter and enter a new period of uncertainty. It was a doubtful proposition, and on the ferry back to Vancouver that day, a reporter was surprised to see a smile on the face of Gordon Robertson, the Secretary of the federal Cabinet who had served as head of the Continuing Committee of federal-provincial officials through the years of constitutional negotiations and whose work was now obviously in peril. "Glad to see you have something to smile about," said the reporter. "Well, it beats crying," replied Robertson.

When he got back to Quebec, Bourassa encountered the predictable storm of opposition from the nationalists and crypto-separatists in the patriotic societies, the unions, the press, the opposition parties, among the intellectuals — and in his own government. Unfairly, they argued that Quebec was being confronted with an ultimatum: accept the Charter within 12 days, or else . . . It was not an ultimatum but simply a deadline for decision after long and open-ended discussions. But the critics were quite accurate in pointing out that the federal offer on social policy would not grant to Quebec the degree of independence which it had always claimed to need to develop its own society and protect its culture.

Bourassa did not go quite that far when he finally rejected the Charter. He said that he could not accept it because the social policy clause was ambiguous, which it was if only because it left open the matter of what would happen to federal funds displaced by provincial legislation. He left the door open for clarification in future negotiations, but Trudeau was apparently not interested. "That is the end of the matter," he said, and began to wind down his own staff of constitutional advisers and the secretariat which had been set up to serve the constitutional conferences.

The highway which Trudeau had seemed to open at the first constitutional conference in February 1968 had come to a dead end. There was no constitutional guarantee for the French language across Canada, no Charter of human freedoms to express the fundamental values of Canadian society and serve as a foundation for a constitution. The Quebec Government was where it had always been, demanding a degree of social autonomy, a status which Ottawa was unwilling to grant.

The Wrong Fork?

Trudeau's concept of One Canada with two official languages which had entranced the country in 1968 had not delivered the unity he promised. Having chosen the fork in the road which Trudeau had recommended, the constitutional conference had ended in failure, and it was a time to recall Pearson's warnings: "If we choose wrongly, we will leave to our children and our children's children a country in fragments, and we ourselves would have become the failures of Confederation."

Confederation did indeed seem closer to break-up after the failure of the Victoria conference than ever before. Bourassa the federalist had not been able to make a deal with Ottawa. The Union Nationale representing the old nationalist and Special Status position had been almost destroyed by the polarization of Quebec politics. The real opposition to the Liberals, the alternative to federalism, now seemed to be the Parti Québécois and separatism.

But until the day of separation, and probably not even then, nothing will ever be quite final in constitutional negotiations between Ottawa and Quebec. So despite Trudeau's statement that matters were at an end, at least for some time, talks resumed almost immediately under a new guise. If no constitutional formula could be found for dividing responsibilty for social policy, perhaps an administrative arrangement could be worked out. Trudeau and Bourassa thereupon exchanged letters in September and welfare experts of both governments began intricate negotiations. While Quebec wanted to talk family allowances and manpower policies, Ottawa concentrated upon the allowances first, having always regarded manpower training and movement as an economic rather than a social issue.

By March of 1972, 9 months after Quebec had rejected Ottawa's "final offer" at Victoria, Trudeau was ready to formalize a new proposal on family allowances in a letter to Bourassa which he repeated to the other provinces and published.

The formula was complicated — it took some 2,000 words to explain — but the essence was: "Where the federal Parliament and a provincial legislature have each established a scheme for the payment of family allowances and the provincial law relating to such a scheme seeks to ensure an integrated system of allowances with the province, provision will be made for the federal scheme to be modified by a federal-provincial agreement so that the amount of monthly benefits, the levels of income at which the reduction of full benefits commences and the rates of reduction to be applied will accord with the standards of the provincial scheme." In brief, Ottawa was willing to let a province decide who among its citizens should receive federal allowances and in what amount — subject only to low minimum national standards and Ottawa's right to mail out its own cheques to the grateful voters. "Acceptance of a plan along these lines would represent, as you will appreciate, a very important change so far as the federal Government is concerned," wrote Trudeau.

"For the first time, a federally financed and adminstered program, legislated by Parliament, would be subject to modification to accord with a provincial program . . . What is contemplated here is a major adjustment in the federal approach to an important income security payment established by Parliament more than 25 years ago. It would introduce a degree of flexibility in relation to provincial conditions that has been hitherto unknown. It would permit provinces that so wished to move toward an integrated system of family allowances within their boundaries, while still maintaining certain general standards for payments to poorer families. I think the plan would meet the basic requirements necessary for the government of Quebec to establish the integrated system of family allowances that it wishes to introduce." While the offer covered only family allowances and made some provision for youth allowances, Trudeau conceded that "the principles involved are clearly capable of extension to other income support programs." And while it would be only an administrative arrangement which could be revoked at any time by Act of Parliament, Trudeau said, "if a constitutional guarantee were needed, this could be contemplated . . ."

If this showed that Trudeau was not as rigid in his federalism as critics alleged, it also raised questions about why it had not been done long before and whether now it might not, tragically, be too late to arrest Quebec's drift toward separatism. Offered to René Lévesque when he came to Ottawa as a Minister in the Lesage Liberal Government asking for greater control over social policy to develop the Quiet Revolution, it might have been enough to maintain a faith in the possibilities of federalism and keep his thoughts from separatism. Offered to Premier Johnson when he first proposed constitutional redivision of powers, it could have been the Equality which he sought as an alternative to Independence. Offered to Premier Bertrand, it could have been the lever he needed to quiet the nationalists in his divided Cabinet. Offered to Premier Bourassa at Victoria, it could have been enough to win acceptance for the Charter.

Now it was touch and go if the formula could be translated into administration in time to prevent a blow-up. When the federal budget in May 1972 raised old age pensions, Castonguay was outraged that Quebec and the other provinces had not first been consulted. Here was Ottawa again pouring unco-ordinated cash into the social security system and undermining his efforts to create an integrated system. If there were money to spare, Castonguay wanted to spend it on people between the ages of 60 and 65 who were in need but still not eligible for the basic old age pension. His anger was not altogether rational: Ottawa was inescapably responsible for old age pensions, at least until some new arrangement could be negotiated, and was under moral and political pressure to assist the aged. But Ottawa's unilateral action seemed almost the last straw, a final frustration, and Castonguay decided to resign from the Bourassa Cabinet in protest. One or two other important ministers were prepared to leave with him. Even if they had not immediately joined the Parti Québécois, they would have been saying quite clearly that Quebec could not achieve its aspirations within Trudeau's Confederation. All that prevented — or perhaps postponed — this crisis was the coincidence of an outbreak of revolutionary labor violence across Quebec. Castonguay and others thought it would be unfair to weaken the Government at such a moment and withheld their resignations. Bourassa was so severely shaken, however, that he announced that he was re-examining his whole attitude toward Ottawa, suggesting that he would take a much stronger line in future.

In June, the angry Castonguay brushed off a personal plea from federal Health and Welfare Minister John Munro and revised the Quebec Pension Plan. The result was that it no longer conformed with the Canada Pension Plan in force in all other provinces. Quebec was going its own way and the chances for an agreement on social policy seemed lower than ever. Then, on July 3, Munro decided on a last effort, and flew secretly to Quebec City to have a private talk with Castonguay at his home. He found the Quebec Minister in a different mood, relaxed and co-operative, and returned to Ottawa elated, sure that he had the makings of an agreement. Castonguay was willing to compromise on the Quebec Pension Plan if Munro could persuade the other provinces to make changes in the Canada Plan. But more important, Castonguay indicated that when Munro's Family Income Security Plan to change family allowances passed Parliament, Quebec would probably accept the new scale of payments with minor modifications. But just at this moment of hope, a new difficulty appeared. As the Commons was about to approve Munro's FISP bill in the last minutes before adjourning for the summer, Independent MP Paul Hellyer refused unanimous consent, arguing that it was clumsy legislation and no answer to the real problem of poverty. Family allowances remained under the old law, far removed from Castonguay's priorities, and it would be fall before a new attempt could be made to revise the scheme.

Meanwhile, the old Union Nationale, renamed Unité-Québec and striving for a new image to recapture public interest, reaffirmed its traditional policy of Special Status-Two Nations in a new Canada which would be ". . . a federation of states within which Quebec has one voice equal to the rest of Canada."

But the man whom Ottawa had long regarded as the Grey Eminence behind the Throne in Quebec City, the civil servant who was constitutional adviser to several Premiers and kept the strain of nationalism pure and constant through so many propositions to the constitutional conferences, had already departed. Resigning as deputy minister of Intergovernmental Affairs, Claude Morin allowed a few months to pass and then joined the Parti Québécois, saying: "After several years, after four Premiers and after having explored every conceivable type of federalism — co-operative, decentralized, profitable and God knows what — I believe I can identify one fact: never under this political regime can Quebec really free itself."

With recruits of this calibre, the Parti Québécois began to look more than ever like the real opposition to the provincial Liberals. And as it drew closer to power and responsibility, it seemed to moderate some of its attitudes, firmly disengaging from any idea of revolution and talking less about separatism and more about reform along the lines of social democracy in European countries.

Lévesque had not backed away from the goal of independence, but he had always recognized that it could be only a limited independence. In his original proposal in 1967, he had suggested that the declaration of sovereignty would be followed by negotiations with English Canada to establish a monetary union, a common tariff policy, and co-ordinated fiscal policies, which could lead to other areas of co-operation in a "Canadian Union" — "an association without which it would be, for one as well as the other, impossible to preserve and develop on this continent societies distinct from the United States." A wry footnote was added when a constituent assured federal minister Jean Chrétien that while he was a supporter of Lévesque, he would be glad to work for the return of the Trudeau Government in the federal election. When René came to negotiate independence and a new deal for Quebec, he explained, it would certainly help to have a French Canadian Prime Minister on the federal side of the table.

The prospect that Trudeau might wind up negotiating exactly what he had been elected to prevent, the separation of Quebec, still looked remote to English Canadians in 1972. But not as remote as it would have seemed in 1968 if anybody had dared to mention it. That was because English Canada's own attitudes to Confederation were rapidly changing.

2

THE CHANGING CONFEDERATION

A major shift in the balance of federal and provincial power within Confederation was already well advanced when Trudeau became Prime Minister in 1968. "We have entered a period in which power is flowing away from Ottawa toward the provinces," wrote Paul Fox, the historian and editor, in a study for the Ontario Advisory Committee on Confederation. He was one of many observers who saw a trend which ran deeper and broader than Quebec's demands for Special Status. The English provinces also were seeking a new relationship with the federal Government, but as there was no consensus on what form it might take, it was clear that difficult years lay ahead. The basic question was whether Confederation could be adjusted to accommodate the aspirations of the 10 provinces, or whether it would break under the strain.

The roots of the problem go back to 1864-67 when Confederation was being designed and negotiated into existence. The chief architect, John A. Macdonald, was frank about the way in which he would have preferred to organize the new country of Canada. "I have always contended that if we could agree to have one government and one parliament, legislating for the whole of these peoples, it would be the best, the cheapest, the most vigorous and the strongest system of government we could adopt," he said during the Confederation Debates in 1865. "But, on looking at the subject in the conference, and discussing the matter as we did, most unreservedly, and with a desire to arrive at a satisfactory conclusion, we found that such a system was impracticable."

Macdonald went on to explain that Quebec feared that in a simple union under one government, its language, religion and traditions might be attacked. It would be difficult also to impose a unitary State on the English-speaking colonies which had their own laws and traditions.

The solution negotiated by the Fathers of Confederation was a federal system which, said Macdonald, " . . . would give to the general government the strength of a legislative and administrative union, while at the same time it preserved the liberty of action for the different sections . . ." But in fact, the balance of power was tilted heavily to the central government, as Macdonald clearly wanted.

"All the great subjects of legislation" were reserved for the central government, he noted with satisfaction. Provincial legislation could be disallowed by the central government, but even so the powers of the provinces were defined in strictly local terms. In Macdonald's words, "Each province will have the power and means of developing its own resources and aiding its own progress after its own fashion and in its own way. Therefore all local improvements, all local enterprises and undertakings of any kind have been left to the care and management of local legislatures of each province."

In terms of political power, this did not mean much a century ago when the role of government in affairs was small. The provincial governments were to be no more than glorified county councils, as one of the Fathers put it. Ottawa even took over all their public debts — along with the major taxing powers, of course.

So here was a prescription for confusion: a sort of make-believe federation in which all the real power lay with the central government. And the story of Confederation, almost from July 1, 1867, has been one of struggle by the provinces to enlarge their power at the expense of Ottawa. They might have given up except that when constitutional disputes were referred to the supreme legal authority in Britain, the decisions of the learned Law Lords tended to favor the provinces. To some authorities in Canada, that was a tragic reversal of what the Fathers had intended; to others, it was a wise legal reflection of political realities. It matters little now. The fact is that the provinces were recognized as substantial powers within Confederation and any lingering hope that they would wither away and leave the federal Government supreme has long ago vanished.

With the depression of the Thirties, however, most of the provinces were in no position to flex their constitutional muscles. Some of them were almost bankrupt and forced to turn to Ottawa for help. Then came the Second World War and the federal Government assumed broad powers with which to direct the national effort. Canadians, at least English Canadians, became more and more accustomed to paying their taxes to Ottawa and looking to the national government for leadership. French Canadians in Quebec, meanwhile, raised the walls of their ghetto a little higher to resist as best they could the encroachments of the federal Government.

Ottawa emerged from the war with the prestige of victory, an energetic civil service with experience in planning on a grand scale, and a zeal for social and economic reform. Throughout the Western world, governments were assuming responsibility for managing their economies so as to avoid the massive unemployment of the pre-war years, and planning for social security on a scale previously undreamed of.

Certainly it had never been dreamed of by the Fathers of Confederation, and here lay one of the inherent contradictions of Confederation. The little local matters which had been left to the provinces were now becoming the great subjects of legislation: education, social and cultural life, urban renewal in the exploding cities, highways, regional economic growth and other matters. Maneuvering around the constitution, the prestigious federal Government moved into all these areas, using its spending power (as we have seen in the previous chapter) to bribe the provinces to accept shared-cost programs.

This spending power arose from Ottawa's control of tax sources, and this was another contradiction in Confederation. In 1867, the federal Parliament was given the broad power to raise money by any mode or system of taxation. The provinces were granted what were then only minor sources of revenue: direct taxes, which meant primarily the property tax.

With the introduction of income taxes, however, direct taxes became the great sources of revenue. But Ottawa contrived to scoop in most of this, and the provinces had only the leavings — plus payments and subsidies from Ottawa, some of which were dependent on them doing as they were asked.

For fifteen years after the war, the system seemed to work well enough. The federal Government maintained its political prestige by saving — or appearing to save — the economy from relapsing into depression, promoting rapid economic growth and launching a series of social security plans such as family allowances, old age pensions and hospital insurance. But as the public demands on the provinces grew, they became more and more frustrated by Big Brother in Ottawa who was hogging all their taxes and constantly invading their jurisdictions and upsetting their priorities.

When Quebec began its Quiet Revolution in 1960 and burst out of its ghetto to demand a new deal, Ontario and some of the Western provinces were not far behind. But Quebec was talking dramatically in terms of constitutional reform, differences of language and culture and the threat of separation, and this tended to overshadow the more pragmatic claims of the other provinces which were interested mainly in money. But in a democracy the power to tax and spend is the essence of the power to govern, so the English provinces really wanted much the same as Quebec: Power.

When Pearson became Prime Minister in 1963, he tried to meet this rising turmoil with what he called "Co-operative Federalism." This meant much closer relations between the federal and provincial governments, and the number of conferences between heads of governments, departmental ministers and officials mushroomed.

Soon there were literally hundreds of meetings a year and the federal-provincial conference was becoming, in effect, a new level of national government. The Cabinets of the eleven governments first worked out their policy proposals; then they met in Ottawa, usually in private, to negotiate a consensus if they could; finally they went to Parliament and the legislatures to have the agreement ratified, and because it was a delicate treaty approved in advance by the eleven governments, it could not be amended. This was indeed a far cry from the masterful federal Government and weakly provinces which the Fathers of Confederation had envisaged.

One of the important instruments of the new federalism was the Tax Structure Committee set up in 1964. The idea was for each of the 11 governments to work out its spending and revenue needs, according to agreed guidelines, and then to bring them all together to form a picture and projection of the national finances.

It was supposed to show where the real priorities lay and to indicate which level of government should have first claim on available tax revenues. But what it actually showed to everybody's dismay was that everybody's needs were rising. The study predicted that to meet their needs governments would have to take a rapidly rising share of the Gross National Product — the value of all the goods and services produced in the country. This of course was highly alarming to conservatives in all parties who worried about how much money could be diverted from private to public purposes without fatally damaging the private enterprise economy.

But the study did show beyond doubt that the needs of the provinces, and the municipalities which they controlled, were growing much faster than Ottawa's needs. If no new programs were added, the provincial-municipal deficit would be $2.5 billion in 1971-72, while Ottawa would have a small surplus of $323 million.

There were many ways of looking at these forcasts. From the point of view of the provinces, they proved beyond doubt that it was time for the federal Government to cut back on spending and to turn over more money to them. Ottawa could do this either by increasing grants and subsidies or by reducing its own taxes so that the provinces could raise theirs without annoying the taxpayers. The federal Government, however, had no intention of cutting back on spending plans. Pearson had come to power on a program of social reform and had promises to keep, notably a national medicare plan. He was in the uncomfortable position of a Prime Minister at a time of transition, still trying to play the leadership role expected by English Canadians while seeking a new balance with the provinces. The federal Government was reluctant also to yield any more tax room to the provinces for fear of losing its power to manage the economy by tax policy, and Trudeau and others, as mentioned in the previous chapter, were determined to stand firm against Quebec and stop the drift toward Special Status.

The stage was set for a federal-provincial showdown, and it came when the 11 heads of government met in October 1966 to try to work out a new tax sharing agreement. The Premiers arrived armed with copies of the Tax Structure report and briefs explaining how Ottawa should go about correcting the situation. Quebec wanted 100 per cent of personal and corporate income taxes, among other things. Manitoba suggested a $1 billion transfer from federal to provincial revenues. Ontario was militant in demanding more tax room. Pearson met them with a program — thrown together at the last minute and not understood by even the federal experts when they tried to explain it to newsmen at a private briefing — which offered some additional cash to the provinces but nothing like what they thought they needed. Finance Minister Mitchell Sharp told them bluntly that the federal till was empty and that if they wanted more money they would have to raise their taxes.

The principle was sound: the politicians who wanted to spend money should accept the responsibility of imposing taxes and accounting to the voters. It was realistic also to face the fact that federal spending would continue to rise and that there was not much room to make concessions to the provinces. But the Premiers could see only that the federal Government was occupying the major tax fields, squandering the money on fancy schemes such as medicare and telling them that in order to meet their inescapable needs, they would have to add their taxes on top of federal taxes — which would be politically unpopular and possibly damaging to the economy.

The Premiers were enraged, and after a week of confused and often bitter argument, the conference broke up without agreement or even a final communique. Ottawa could enforce its proposals because it had the major taxing power and was in the saddle. But federal-provincial relations were in a desperate state.

It was then that Premier Robarts of Ontario first mentioned the idea of a conference to discuss the future of Confederation. He was concerned, as we have seen, by the rising tide of nationalism in Quebec, where his friend Johnson had recently become Premier. But it was also his view that if Ottawa and the provinces could not agree on national priorities and how to share tax revenues, it was time to go back to first principles and look at the division of responsibilities in the constitution. The Centennial Year of 1967 was an appropriate time to do this in a spirit of goodwill, and one of the consequences already discussed was to encourage the federal Government to review the BNA Act.

So when Pearson — with Trudeau at his side — faced the provincial Premiers in the Confederation Room in February 1968, the issues at stake were not only Quebec's place in Confederation, but also the relationship between the English provinces and Ottawa, the balance of power within Confederation and the structure and the very existence of Canada.

This was the critical situation which Trudeau inherited when he became Prime Minister two months later. We have examined his approach to national unity, proposals for constitutional reform and attitude to Quebec. Now let us look at his relations with other regions of Canada.

A Pass Mark for DREE

When the ten provincial Premiers met in Toronto in November 1967, to discuss Confederation for Tomorrow, the problem of regional disparity — the economic gulf between the rich provinces and the poor — came suddenly to national attention and into the forefront of politics. The leaders of the four Atlantic provinces drove home the argument that if Canadians who spoke French were not getting a fair deal, neither were Canadians in the underdeveloped regions of the country.

Slow growth and poverty in the Maritimes and Newfoundland were an old and seemingly hopeless story in Canada, but now it was seen in a dramatic new context. It was a threat to national unity, just as Quebec's discontents were a threat. And instead of trying to explain it in the language of statistics, Joey Smallwood peered into the TV cameras and talked eloquently about babies: the right of the Canadian baby born in a remote outport on the North East coast of Newfoundland to have the same education and opportunity to serve his country as the baby born in Montreal or Toronto.

Trudeau took up the issue and made it one of his major themes in his election campaign: "If the underdevelopment of the Atlantic Provinces is not corrected, not by charity or subsidies, but by helping them become areas of economic growth, then the unity of the country is almost as surely destroyed as it would be by the French-English confrontation." Standing in a windswept shopping plaza in St. John's, Newfoundland, one campaign day, he promised to organize a massive transfer of resources from the rich provinces to the poor, much as the United States had poured its Marshall Aid dollars into postwar Europe to bring about a miracle of economic recovery.

It was the sort of vision needed to confront a dire problem which had resisted all modest solutions. Diefenbaker had made a small start and Pearson had expanded federal aid. But in 1968, personal income per capita in the Atlantic region was still only $1,843 — about $1,200 less than in Ontario. Unemployment was 7.3 per cent compared with the national average of 4.8 per cent.

The average industrial wage was $90 a week, compared-with $120 in British Columbia. Every year, thousands of Maritimers left their homes to move west to the promised land of Toronto and beyond in search of jobs and the affluent life.

Other regions of Canada also suffered from slow growth. Quebec east of Trois Rivières was depressed. Across the north of Ontario and the Prairies there was unemployment and industrial stagnation. Every province, in fact, had at least a pocket of poverty and despair.

A few weeks after he won the election, Trudeau sent his friend and close political adviser, Jean Marchand, to organize an attack on the problem. Marchand was a former president of the Confederation of National Trade Unions in Quebec, a small, somewhat frail and gray man, but with a fiery Gallic style and a commitment to social reform. As his Deputy Minister, Trudeau gave him Tom Kent, a tall, thin, cool English intellectual, a journalist who had written the social reform program for Pearson and served as his right-hand man when he became Prime Minister.

An odd couple in some ways, Marchand and Kent had worked together before the election in the Department of Manpower and Immigration, and they were a top team in Ottawa, combining political muscle in the Cabinet with intellectual capacity and a zeal for social planning and change. They also had almost a free hand at the federal Treasury: when Trudeau froze the budgets of most departments, he exempted their new Department of Regional Economic Expansion.

DREE — the dreary acronym formed by the initials of the new bureaucracy — came into existence on April 1, 1969 and brought under one roof a dozen programs and agencies touching on regional development which had previously been scattered through many departments: Agricultural and Rural Development; the Fund for Rural Economic Development (Fred, son of Arda, as civil servants called it); Maritime Marshland Rehabilitation; the Area Development

Agency; the Atlantic Development Board; Prairie Farm Rehabilitation; Canada NewStart and others. The new strategy had three main thrusts.

GROWTH CENTRES: "The priorities of growth in our modern society lie primarily in industrial and urban development and it would not make any sense for us to work against the forces of change," said Marchand, and DREE chose, in co-operation with the provinces, 23 Special Areas for assistance. Federal funds poured into these towns and cities to provide them with the services and amenities likely to attract a new industry looking for somewhere to settle.

Saint John, New Brunswick, which calls itself Canada's First City and is proud of its Loyalist traditions, got an $8 million system to deliver 80 million gallons of clean water a day, help with a thruway to untangle the snarl of trucks and tourist traffic, a high school complex and other facilities. The Sept Iles-Port Cartier area of Quebec received $9 million in grants and loans to construct storm sewers, pave streets and relocate a trailer park to prepare for new housing. In St. John's, Newfoundland, a new $1.4 million elementary school opened in December 1971 under the program. At Lesser Slave Lake, Alberta, $200,000 in loans helped to open an industrial park.

Expenditure on these and hundreds of other projects in the Special Areas of Newfoundland, Nova Scotia, New Brunswick, Quebec, Manitoba, Saskatchewan and Alberta was estimated to reach $163 million in grants and loans in 1972-73. This was a massive injection of federal funds into community improvements which would normally be paid for by the province and the municipality.

INDUSTRIAL INCENTIVES: To encourage industry to move into areas of slow growth in all 10 provinces, or to expand or modernize plants already there, generous subsidies were offered. A fortunate company qualifying for all possible assistance could collect up to 35 per cent of the capital cost plus $7,000 for each job to be created. The payment formula was designed to offset the cost to the company of moving into an

underdeveloped area rather than settling around an industrial centre such as Toronto, or even moving to the United
States.

Marchand reported to a Commons committee that by
February 1972, 239 incentive offers had been accepted in the
Atlantic region, creating 9,800 new jobs; 671 offers had been
accepted in Quebec, creating almost 30,000 jobs; on the
Prairies, 214 offers created 8,150 jobs. The total of these incentive subsidies was expected to top $187 million in
1972-73.

SOCIAL ADJUSTMENT AND RURAL DEVELOPMENT: This was
a patchwork of programs to assist disadvantaged rural people
— the uneducated and untrained — to adjust to the opportunities of industrial society, and to encourage rural communities to make the most of their resources. For example,
ARDA included schemes to help marginal farmers to improve their soil and water and to establish Indian-run businesses on reservations. FRED provided for comprehensive
planning and development of rural regions, notably the entire province of Prince Edward Island. NewStart experi-
mented with basic education and other techniques to assist
adults entering regular employment and starting a new way
of life. The Manpower Corps offered on-the-job training to
people who lacked work experience. The Newfoundland
Resettlement Program moved families from small isolated
outports to larger communities with better services. Prairie
Farm Rehabilitation offered technical advice and assistance
to farmers and Indian reservations.

DREE inherited these programs from earlier efforts at
regional development but continued to operate them —
mostly in partnership with the provinces — with growing
resources. Federal constributions were rising to $132 million
in 1972-73.

When DREE entered its fourth year, 1972-73, with a
total budget topping $500 million, there could be few criti-
cisms of the scope of its effort and the resources available. Dr.
Stephen Weyman, President of the Atlantic Provinces Economic Council, told a Commons committee that the new

department ". . . represents the first attempt by any Canadian government to come to grips with regional disparities in a comprehensive way. Before DREE all federal regional programs were unco-ordinated or ad hoc in nature and too limited in scope to do much more than scratch the surface of a deep-rooted problem that has been with us virtually since Confederation".

But Dr. Weyman saw room for much improvement, and critics were beginning to press for evidence that the effort and investment were paying off. Marchand replied that it would take 15 years to reduce regional disparities significantly and he cautiously refused to commit himself to the specific targets proposed by the Atlantic Development Council, his own independent advisory board. But he did claim to see encouraging signs of progress. Earned income per person in the Atlantic region was 64.9 per cent of the Canadian average in 1953-68 and rose to 68.5 per cent in 1969-70. The unemployment gap closed from 168 per cent of the Canadian average to 1.38 per cent. Capital investment climbed from 54.3 per cent of the average to 96.1 per cent. But it was also true that the actual numbers of unemployed in the region jumped from 65,000 in 1968 to 80,000 in 1972.

The apparent contradiction explained a good deal about DREE's problems. For while it was striving to stimulate regional economic expansion, broad government policy was directed toward slowing down the national economy to fight inflation. In brief, the gap between the rich and the poor narrowed partly because conditions were worse in the rich provinces. Marchand's efforts to some extent merely prevented the national recession from hitting the poor regions as disastrously as it would have done without DREE.

There were other criticisms. Many of the biggest incentive payments went to foreign firms — $6 million to IBM, for example — and this was offensive to some nationalists. But as long as government policy welcomed foreign capital and enterprise, DREE obviously could not refuse it.

A study made by Dr. David Springate, while a graduate student at Harvard, suggested that some grants were mere windfalls for large, wealthy companies, and others tended to encourage enterprises which were only marginally economic. Opposition critics worried that the whole program might be on the wrong track of propping up, instead of changing, a fundamentally faulty economic structure in the Atlantic region.

Some of the most thoughtful commentary on DREE came from the Atlantic Provinces Economic Council. "As long as the department remains highly centralized with all important decision-making firmly entrenched in Ottawa, so called joint planning and co-ordination of federal and provincial development efforts will be little more than bargaining for available funds," said president Weyman, and the Council urged decentralization so that the people of the regions who knew most about local problems could play a greater role in planning their own future.

Meanwhile, Professor William Y. Smith, of the University of New Brunswick, president of the Atlantic Development Council, gave an end-of-first-term assessment: "I am a college professor. If you said to me, 'How do you mark DREE?' I would say I would not give him honours by any means. I would probably give him a pass — C Plus or B Minus, something of that order. But we are hoping for better performance in the future."

Losing the West

The scene was Regina, Saskatchewan, and Trudeau had climbed onto the back of a truck to try to talk to 700 angry, shouting farmers who could not sell their wheat. "Our P.E.T. is a Pig," said one sign waving over the noisy crowd. "Hustle grain, not Women," said another with calculated insult. A woman shrieked, "Good Lord, he's nuts," and a small boy was hurling grain at the Prime Minister.

The next day in Saskatoon, it was much the same. The farmers had driven into town on their tractors, like an armored regiment on the march, and someone had piled grain mixed with stinking pig manure on the curb outside the hotel in which Trudeau was meeting the farmers' leaders.

The newsmen watching it happen on those hot days on the Prairies in July, 1969 talked about Western Alienation which became one of the cliches of politics in the Trudeau era.

The alienation of the West within Confederation is hardly a new phenomenon. Some observers trace it back to Louis Riel and the Metis rebellion against the authority of Ottawa, although that seems to stretch history. But certainly the West has several times expressed its frustration with the political process by creating its own parties: the Progressives, Social Credit, the CCF. Even when Westerners have voted for national parties, they have usually chosen the Opposition, with the result that they not only lacked a voice in Government but also had a great many voices crying against the Government in Ottawa, and telling them how shamefully they were being treated. The Pearson Government elected in 1963 had seven MPs from British Columbia, but only three from the Prairies; after the 1965 election, there was one from Manitoba and none at all from Alberta and Saskatchewan. It was the political folklore of the period, with just a touch of truth, that as far as the federal Government was concerned, Canada stopped at the Lakehead.

This bleak tradition and unhappy recent history seemed open to change for a brief period in 1968 when Trudeau won election with national support. Trudeaumania ran as strong in the West during the campaign as in any part of Canada and British Columbia elected 16 Liberals; Alberta, 4; Saskatchewan, 1; Manitoba, 5. The West's problems and dissatisfactions with Ottawa remained, but for the first time in several years there seemed to be an atmosphere in which they could be discussed in reasonable terms and perhaps resolved.

But already, in 1968, a natural disaster was falling on the Prairies, changing the mood of the region to one of resentment, fear and finally anger. The bottom fell out of the world wheat economy. Bumper crops in the Soviet Union, India and elsewhere produced a glut and international trade slumped from 2 billion bushels a year to 1.6 billion. Canada's exports fell, the elevators were jammed and farmers piled their unsaleable grain in the open.

Farm income dropped disastrously and men with assets in land and machinery worth hundreds of thousands of dollars found themselves in the paradoxical position of having no ready cash to pay their bills and jingle in their jeans. The flow of money through the Prairie economy slowed, and retail sales fell 10 per cent in Saskatchewan. Even the University of Saskatchewan accepted wheat in place of cash for tuition fees.

Trudeau was not to blame for a world wheat crisis, but it was a situation which could be turned against him, and in December 1968, he gave his enemies their opening. At a Liberal Parter dinner in Winnipeg, he was asked, "Mr. Prime Minister, I would like to know how and when you are going to sell the Western Canadian farmers' wheat?" He began his 500 word reply with a rhetorical question: "Well, why should I sell the Canadian farmers' wheat?" and wrenched out of context, it became a political catchphrase, the evidence of Trudeau's arrogance and lack of concern for the West. But the complete answer included these passages: "There are various ways in which the State does intervene to help the farmer in distress. But every time there is a drought in another country and we sell more, or every time the other countries produce more and they don't have to buy as much from Canada, or every time that our produce is not competitive with produce of other countries, which perhaps sell different kinds of wheat which are cheaper and of which you can produce more per acre, it's all of Canada's problem because the wheat is so important to the Canadian economy.

"But it is first and foremost the farmer's problem. He makes his representations known, believe me, through his members of Parliament. We hear them every day and that is right. But I think we all realize that, as in the case of other sectors of the economy, the alternative is for the State to be the producer, to own the land, to own the wheat, to hire the farmers and to pay them a wage, and then it will be our problem to sell it and market it. But if we want to have something of a free economy, we can assist — as we do politically — the farmer in various ways; we can also perhaps encourage or hopefully prod sometimes the Wheat Board . . . In cases where we cannot sell it (wheat), we make it part of our external aid program . . . You know, these are forms — ways — in which the Canadian Government can help the problem when there is a great problem. But basically, unless you take the view that the Government should step in and own the farms and hire the farmers, I think we all share the responsibility and we will have to do the best we can all together."

It was not a decisive or particularly enlightening answer, but neither was it offensive. It might have appealed to the West where the pioneer spirit of rugged self-sufficiency blends with a tradition of community co-operation. But it was never seen in that light, probably because the region was looking for comfort from Ottawa but half expecting a rebuff from the mistrusted Easterners.

But what should have shone through was Trudeau's candid admission, in the course of the same answer, that he was really a stranger to the West and only just beginning to learn about its problems. "The PM's like most Easterners," complained Dave Thomson, the young Albertan in charge of Trudeau's Western region desk in Ottawa. "He thinks of the Prairies as a field of waving wheat with some oil in the far corner." He set out to educate Trudeau in the summer of 1969 by organizing a tour in which the Prime Minister hopped by helicopter from the rocket research station at Churchill, Manitoba, to the spanking new mining community at Thompson, Manitoba, to dairy farms outside Winnipeg, to a potash mine in Saskatchewan, to the oil and gas industry around Edmonton and to meet irrigation farmers at Taber, Alberta.

It was a crash course to teach the basic lesson that the Prairies were far more than a great big farm with an occasional oil well gushing wealth. And Trudeau was exposed at his town hall meetings and casual encounters to some other of the West's suspicions and resentments: the bilingualism policy which seemed to emphasize French at the expense of the cultures of the other ethnic minorities in the Prairie mosaic; Ottawa's apparent preoccupation with Quebec and the constitution when the West urgently needed help; the traditional complaint about tariff policy to protect

Eastern industry which meant that Westerners had to pay perhaps $250 million a year in higher prices for imports while selling their own primary products on the free world market; the national energy policy which forbade Alberta to sell its oil to the great refineries in Montreal but guaranteed no alternative market in the United States; Air Canada's decision to move its overhaul base from Winnipeg to Montreal, another step in the concentration of modern, high-technology industry in the East.

But always the problem of wheat overshadowed everything else. The provincial Premiers wanted to talk about wheat when Trudeau called upon them. The press asked about it. He visited farms out on the prairie and sat in the kitchen to talk with the neighbors about their problems. How much wheat did they have in store? What condition was it in? How much was their land worth, and what was the investment in machinery? Were they desperate enough to want the Government to buy their farms and get them out from under their debts? If not, precisely what did they want from Ottawa?

When he faced the angry mobs in Regina and Saskatchewan, he told them, when he could make himself heard: "I see your problem better, but I will be frank with you — I don't see the solution yet. . . . I am not going to pacify and satisfy you by saying now we will give you $200 million." He had to weigh their needs against those of the Indians, the Metis, the Maritime fishermen and the urban poor, he insisted.

It was honest and courageous, but not tactful. The farmers — both the militant minority of angry demonstrators and the quieter majority who stayed at home — knew very well that there were no simple answers to their problems while wheat was in a world slump. They were looking for short-term financial assistance and long-term reassurance that this French Canadian Prime Minister in charge of the faraway Eastern Government really cared about them. What they got was an interrogation, a reminder that they were not as badly off as some other Canadians and a refusal to play politics in the familiar way. The brief honeymoon of 1968 was over and disenchantment deepened.

But back in Ottawa, Trudeau moved swiftly to seek a solution to the underlying problems of the wheat economy. The Canadian Wheat Board had customarily been one of the many responsibilities of the Minister of Trade and Commerce. Now Trudeau placed it under the direct charge of a Minister without Portfolio, Otto Lang, who had a clear mandate to write a new federal policy for the grains industry.

Lang was 37, a pudgy and intense law professor with unbounded faith in the power of reason and in his own capacities. The son of a school teacher in Humboldt, Saskatchewan, he decided early on a political career and that the best entry was through law. He won a Rhodes Scholarship to study at Oxford, became Dean of Law at the University of Saskatchewan in his thirties and was active in the provincial Liberal Party. He was one of the few party leaders strong enough to refuse to knuckle under to the dictatorial methods of the Liberal Premier, Ross Thatcher, and the two men fell out. Lang retired from local politics for a period — although his mother-in-law and a brother-in-law were members of Thatcher's majority in the Legislature. Lang ran for office for the first time in the 1968 federal election and was the only Liberal elected in Saskatchewan. That more or less guaranteed him a seat in the Cabinet, and the wheat crisis gave him the opportunity to show what he could do.

Lang set up the Grains Group, a small task force, to study problems of production, marketing and transportation of wheat and other grains. It was composed of experts borrowed from the Departments of Agriculture, Trade and Commerce, and Transport, and the co-ordinator was an old friend, colleague and think-alike of Lang's — Rod Bryden, who taught both corporation law and urban planning at the University of Saskatchewan, was a brilliant organizer and came to Ottawa as a sort of trouble-shooter for Lang.

From Lang and the Grains Group and the Wheat Board over the next few years came a series of policies designed to make basic changes in the wheat economy. Operation Lift in 1970 paid farmers to take land out of production for a year with the aim of cutting into the huge stockpile of one billion bushels which was clogging the system.

The forage program in 1971 gave farmers a cash incentive to switch into grassland to meet the growing market for beef. A new forecasting system helped farmers to diversify into barley, rapeseed and other crops when the market looked strong. As the world wheat trade recovered, Canada's increased sales effort brought rising orders which began to tax the old railway system of moving grain from the farms to the ports, and a sophisticated computer program was introduced to make maximum use of equipment and speed the flow. In 1972, the farmers got their dream of a two-price system, under which they were guaranteed $3 a bushel for wheat used in Canada, although they still had to meet the world price of about $1.95 in export markets. Canada's exports hit an all-time high of 704 million bushels in 1971 and when they were climbing toward 800 million bushels in 1972, Trudeau announced that the Government would finance the purchase of 2,000 new railway cars needed to move the wheat to market.

As protection against the lean years which were bound to occur, Lang proposed in 1971 a program to stabilize farm income. For every $1 the farmers paid into a fund in good years, Ottawa would put in $2. Then in any year in which receipts for grain fell below the five-year average, the fund would make up the income. It would have evened out Prairie farm income, but it was not well received by farmers and after fierce and protracted opposition in the Commons, Lang withdrew it to think again.

Three years after Trudeau faced the angry farmers in Regina and Saskatchewan, the wheat economy was returning to full prosperity, mainly because of the upswing in world demand but aided by some imaginative policies in Ottawa. The Trudeau-Lang record on wheat was far from perfect, but it was better than that of most federal governments.

Alberta went almost from rags to riches with the major oil strike at Leduc in 1946. Over the following years, $3 billion from royalties, leases and land rentals flowed into the provincial treasury in Edmonton, along with the taxes from business enterprises which flourished in the long boom. Calgary called itself the Oil Capital, and the Husky Tower, named in honor of the U.S. oil company, dominated its changing skyline.

The market for the oil was always in the United States. There was no pipeline to carry it east of the Ottawa river and it was cheaper for the refinery complex in Montreal to use supplies from Venezuela and the Middle East. Anyway, it was anticipated that oil would eventually be found in the Gulf of the St. Lawrence or off the Atlantic Coast.

Canada's consistent policy had been to push and prod Washington to allow more Alberta oil into its rich market, and sales had risen more or less steadily. But when the U.S. discovered vast new reserves in Alaska, and the giant tanker Manhattan prepared for an experimental voyage through the Arctic ice to see about bringing it out, Alberta's future seemed suddenly in doubt. Would the United States close its market? Would the pipelines dry up?

A few days before going to Washington on his first trip to meet President Richard Nixon in March 1969, Trudeau invited Alberta Premier Harry Strom to Ottawa. The two men talked through the afternoon in the living room at 24 Sussex Drive, and oil and gas were the top items on the agenda. Strom impressed on Trudeau the importance of a free energy market in which Alberta's oil and gas could flow to the United States, and he left a detailed brief with the Prime Minister.

Trudeau had this paper with him when he met Nixon in the oval study at the White House and he argued as persuasively as he could that despite the Alaska discovery, the United States would still need Canada's energy. Nixon told him that he was going to announce the next day the appointment of a Cabinet task force to study oil import policy, but he was receptive toward Trudeau's sales pitch, and they issued a communique in which they affirmed " . . . agreement with respect to our community of interest in the expansion of energy movements across our border." At a press conference in Washington's National Press Club, Trudeau was explicit: "We have a continental oil policy of sorts," he said, and the objective was to make it work better in new circumstances.

In Canada, the debate soon became hopelessly confused. Nationalists were convinced that Nixon was trying to bully Canada into some sort of continental energy treaty and warned Trudeau not to surrender resources. The Alberta Government and industry leaders worried that the Ottawa Government was too nationalistic and would not push for an open market in the United States. In fact, Trudeau's policy throughout was to sell as much oil as possible and to obtain entry into the protected U.S. market for Canada's uranium. The National Energy Board, an independent authority set up by the Diefenbaker Government to safeguard resources for the future, finally cut off natural gas sales in 1972 when known reserves reached the danger point — leaving roughly 30 years' supply for Canadian needs.

Soon after Peter Lougheed became the Conservative Premier of Alberta in 1971, he visited Ottawa and spent a day in private talks with Trudeau and some of his closest advisers. He suggested in a public speech that because oil and gas were so vital to the province, Alberta should have an advisory voice in making national energy policy, and Trudeau accepted this.

Lougheed also spoke strongly against the growing forces of regionalism in Canada and promised to co-operate more closely with the federal Government.

So the record suggested that Trudeau faithfully followed the traditional Canadian policy toward Alberta's major industry — despite rising opposition from nationalists — and had reasonable working relationships with the Governments of the province.

"British Columbia is not alienated from Ottawa; it just hopes that Ottawa is not too alienated from British Columbia." This quip, coined in Vancouver, explained something about the province which is part of the West but so unlike the Prairies. It indicated the enormous self-confidence with which British Columbia regarded its future. It suggested that as the West Coast province went bustling about its affairs, Ottawa was a remote influence rather than a daily concern.

British Columbia was rich and paid taxes to Ottawa, rather than drawing subsidies. It had no French Canadian population, so the issue of bilingualism was irrelevant. Its trade and increasingly its cultural ties were with the United States and across the Pacific, rather than with Eastern Canada.

Its attachment to Ottawa was based less on a realistic assessment of the political and economic advantages than on custom and sentiment — the remembrance of values shared in simpler times, of battles fought together. That was probably why British Columbians soured on Trudeau within a year or two of voting so enthusiastically for him. He seemed to be discarding the ties of tradition — the Monarchy, Parliament, the British heritage, even good manners — without having much to offer in return except unemployment and pre-occupation with Quebec.

Trudeau's attitude toward traditions has been wildly distorted — he treated them with disinterested tolerance rather than hostility — and this raises the issue of the influence of Premier Bennett on public opinion in his province. He was a masterful but often malicious politician who seldom missed an opportunity to attack the federal Government and misrepresent its leaders and their policies. When Trudeau in exasperation called him a bigot, it was foolish but understandable. If British Columbia failed to understand Ottawa, to the point of alienation, it was at least as much the fault of Bennett as of Trudeau.

But even if it is conceded that Trudeau made sincere efforts to understand the West and meet its problems, it remains a cold fact that the alienation of the region grew stronger during his period of office. There was talk about Western separatism and when it was dismissed as being of no importance, one had to remember that the same thing was being said in Quebec ten years ago. Federal politicians of all parties worried about the strength of Western regionalism and the loosening ties of Confederation. Owen Anderson, an executive assistant to Premier Strom in Alberta, and John J. Barr, a political scientist, journalist and aide to Strom's Minister of Education, even published in 1970 a book with the threatening title, *The Unfinished Revolt*, in which they said: "Perhaps no one who is not a Westerner can really understand the kind of helpless anger Westerners have felt for the past decade or so as they have tried, and failed, to get a hearing for their unique regional perspective."

Barr wrote in his essay: "Why should Westerners be bitter to discover that Quebeckers basically want to run their own affairs and control their own destiny? Isn't that what Westerners have wanted and fought for? . . . Now that we know there are not two solitudes in Canada, but many, we can all stop pretending that this is a united nation, or indeed a nation at all, in the modern tight-knit nation-state sense of the word. It is really a collection of fairly parochial regions held together by a tenuous sense of shared consciousness and a fear of American or other outside domination — but each area pursuing its own identity and its own sense of destiny."

There was at least one member of Trudeau's Cabinet who agreed. James Richardson was heir to a business empire based in Winnipeg, involving the grain trade, insurance and investment dealing. While still a young man in 1968, he had a seat on every blue-chip board of directors that interested him: the CPR, Hudson's Bay, International Nickel and others. But the biggest board of all was in Ottawa — the federal Cabinet.

He had been interested in politics since his student days, but never active until 1968 when he decided to run and chose Trudeau and the Liberals as the vehicle. He arrived in Ottawa fresh from the executives suites and the executive jets which fly business tycoons between Winnipeg, Toronto, New York and Montreal, convinced that the West had no problems in Confederation which could not be solved by common sense and hard work. Experience soon changed his mind. Although Trudeau appointed him to the Cabinet as Manitoba's voice, he soon discovered that he carried little weight. It was partly because he was naive, an innocent abroad in politics. But it was also because the West was outnumbered in Ottawa. The three Prairie provinces elect 45 MPs; Ontario returns 88. British Columbia has 23 members; Quebec 74.

Richardson began to develop radical ideas about what was wrong with Confederation. There was first of all the economic imbalance which tended to concentrate development of modern, manufacturing industry in the East and to reduce the West to the status of a colony supplying raw materials and a captive market. And then there was the political imbalance which meant that Ottawa would always be more interested in Ontario and Quebec than in the West, because that was where the votes and the politicians came from. Richardson could see no solution short of what he called Reconfederation — a whole new structure for Canada. This would involve either a reorganized Parliament in which the regions would have more equal voices, or, more likely, drastic decentralization of power from the centre to the regions. What would satisfy the West, he argued, would probably satisfy Quebec also.

Richardson won a few concessions by way of dispersal of federal activities: a new $16 million federal Mint in Winnipeg rather than Ottawa; a request to the Canada Development Corporation to base itself in Vancouver, instead of in Montreal or Toronto; more directors from the West appointed to Crown Corporations and federal purchasing policies to give Western suppliers a fairer chance of winning orders. But there was no sign of headway on the idea that power structures and not policies might be at the root of Western alienation and the greatest threat to Confederation.

Anger in Ontario

Premier Robarts of Ontario was talking about Reconfederation as early as 1967, but he was not thinking so much about radical changes in the structures of Confederation as better federal-provincial co-operation. He was sore about his defeat at the tax sharing conference the previous year and angry about the federal medicare proposals. He was worried about separatism in Quebec and concerned that federal tax reform, then in the works, would turn out to be a plot to grab more of the existing revenues and, with them, the political power to spend and innovate.

Robarts felt sure there had to be a better way to run Confederation and was quietly optimistic when Trudeau became Prime Minister in 1968. They liked and admired each other and had good personal communication. In the constitutional conferences, Trudeau even went some way to meet Robarts' views when he promised "No more medicares" — that is, no more shared-cost programs without provincial consent, which was a curb on the spending power of the federal Government.

But on current issues, Trudeau was tough. He refused to compromise on the existing medicare plan and forced Robarts to eat crow by accepting it. He would not offer Ontario an acceptable tax share or set up the sort of consultative machinery which Robarts thought could co-ordinate fiscal policies. When Ontario's experts ran the proposals in the federal White Paper on Tax Reform through their computer, they calculated that they would enrich Ottawa by hundreds of millions of dollars a year, and therefore make the provincial Governments poorer. When Trudeau tightened the squeeze on the economy in 1969, he publicly blamed Ontario for not controlling its economy better. And when the federal measures slowed the economy, Ontario suffered unemployment and tighter provincial revenues.

By 1971, Ontario was back in Ottawa renewing the demand for a voice in national economic decision-making through some form of fiscal co-ordination. But this time there was a threatening tone. "We warned in early 1970 about excessive federal tax drag in Ontario, but the federal Government was apparently not prepared to listen," said Treasurer Darcy McKeough to one of the regular meetings of federal and provincial finance ministers. ". . . Similarly, we warned the federal Government at the end of 1970 that the business community was in a cash flow squeeze and that action would be required to head off a decline in private investment in production facilities. Events proved this judgment to be correct . . . If these meetings have not been able to help avoid these massive problems in fiscal policy co-ordination, then clearly they have to be reconstituted in a manner that will realize the objectives they were designed to achieve."

The alternative, said McKeough, was that Ontario would make its own economic policy. Federal experts could quarrel with McKeough's analysis of events, but they could not argue with the fact that Ontario had grown the muscle to make its threat stick. McKeough claimed that Ontario's independent actions in 1971-72 to stabilize the provincial economy — the heart of the national economy — were comparatively more important than the federal budget policies. "Ontario was obliged to implement expansionary economic policies to offset the effects of contractionary federal fiscal policies which we opposed and had no part in designing."

It was a quietly dramatic moment in the history of Confederation. The largest and richest province was saying that it no longer recognized Ottawa's right to make national economic policy. It wanted to co-operate, but if it disagreed with federal policy, it would use its own economic power to reverse it.

Breaking with B and B

One of Trudeau's most far-reaching but least noticed national policy initiatives was his program to promote multiculturalism. "Although there are two official languages there is no official culture, nor does any ethnic group take precedence over any other," he proclaimed to the Commons on October 8, 1971, just before flying to Winnipeg to speak to a congress of Ukrainian Canadians.

About one-third of Canadians are of British origin, one-third French, and one-third belong to some 30 other ethnic groups, a vigorous and growing "third force" in the national community. While virtually all these third-force Canadians speak English or French, many take great pride in their distinctive cultures and seek to retain their native languages.

Trudeau announced a variety of grants and special projects to assist ethnic minorities in preserving and strengthening their cultures, saying: "A policy of multiculturalism within a bilingual framework commends itself to the Government as the most suitable means of assuring the cultural freedom of Canadians. Such a policy should help to break down discriminatory attitudes and cultural jealousies.

National unity, if it is to mean anything in the deeply personal sense, must be founded on confidence in one's own individual identity; out of this can grow respect for that of others and willingness to share ideas, attitudes and assumptions. A vigorous policy of multiculturalism will help create this initial confidence. It can form the base of a society which is based on fair play for all."

The Royal Commission on Bilingualism and Biculturalism had recognized, in its fourth report, the rights of ethnic minorities and recommended measures to assist them, but it insisted: "Although we should not overlook Canada's 'cultural diversity' this should be done keeping in mind that there are two dominant cultures."

The Commission related biculturalism directly to its concept of two founding societies in Canada, the French and the English. It suggested that the other ethnic groups, while maintaining their heritages, should find their places within this basically bicultural country, and it rejected multiculturalism.

So although Trudeau claimed that he was accepting the commission's recommendations for aid to the minorities and going a little further, he seemed to some observers to be ambiguous if not downright deceitful. He was in fact rejecting biculturalism and, therefore, the whole concept of a Canada composed of two founding societies, or Two Nations.

Trudeau's policy was generally well received by third-force Canadians and went some way, particularly in the West, to correct the impression that the federal Government was interested only in Quebec and French Canadian culture.

The reaction in Quebec was, naturally, the reverse. Premier Bourassa protested to Trudeau about this departure from the philosophy of the B and B Commission, and such a distinguished and moderate observer as Guy Rocher, vice-president of the Canada Council, said: "This step will accelerate the retreat of French Canadians living in Quebec. We will have an even greater tendency to isolate ourselves in Quebec. Outside of Quebec, I am nothing more than any other member of ethnic minorities. French Canadians have not yet understood the repercussions of this policy. I am now on the same footing as a Ukrainian, a German, etc. But I repeat, this is not a superiority complex; it's an historical reaction. The Canada to which I belonged no longer exists when I look at it as a French Canadian from Quebec . . . Now my image of Canada is that there is one cultural nation which is Quebec, and then there is a multicultural nation which is outside Quebec . . . this image is based on the concept of Two Nations. It's a very strange step for him (Trudeau) to have taken!"

Meetings and Money

In his general relations with the provinces, Trudeau rapidly enlarged the machinery of consultation which Pearson had set up and called "Co-operative Federalism." He established a special division within the Cabinet Secretariat to co-ordinate federal policies which concerned the provinces, and the number of federal-provincial committees and conferences grew at an extraordinary rate. By June 1970, there were 57 formal committees involving Cabinet ministers or deputy ministers, and over 400 made up of lesser officials. Gordon Robertson, the head of the Cabinet Secretariat suggested wryly: "At times one could be led to wonder whether it is not the very plethora of meetings that has provided the occasions for the disagreements and the wide reporting of them. A Canadian Parkinson could probably demonstrate that the number of federal-provincial disputes in any one year varies in direct proportion to the number of federal-provincial meetings multiplied by the cube of the number of federal-provincial co-ordinating agencies in respective governments."

Under the constitution, the provinces have complete control of the municipalities, and Trudeau was careful not to encroach upon this power by dealing directly with the cities on urban problems. But after long and tortuous negotiations, there was agreement in 1972 to establish a national council on which the three levels of government would meet for the first time to co-ordinate urban policies. This would be yet another new mechanism of government in Canada.

Trudeau also proved willing to transfer federal revenues to the provinces on a rising scale. Total federal payments in grants, subsidies and contributions to shared-cost
programs rose dramatically from $2.3 billion in 1969 to an
estimated $4.3 billion in 1972.

To an important extent, Ottawa was taxing the citizens
of the rich provinces to pass the wealth to the citizens of the
poorer provinces. For example, equalization grants designed
to ensure that all provinces could afford a basic level of
public services were being distributed in this proportion in
1972-73: $214 for each person in Prince Edward Island;
$213 in Newfoundland; $164 in New Brunswick; $135 in
Nova Scotia; $102 in Saskatchewan; $74 in Quebec; $59 in
Manitoba. The prosperous provinces of Ontario, Alberta
and British Columbia needed no equalization payments as
their tax revenues were already above the national average.
This meant that while all governments collectively were
taking an increasing share of the gross national product, the
percentage of the wealth actually spent by Ottawa was falling
and the percentage spent by the provinces and their municipalities was rising rapidly.

Thus the shift in the balance of federal and provincial
power which was strongly under way when Trudeau took office in 1968 continued and probably accelerated under his administration. But no constitutional formula was found to
recognize the new realities and relieve the stresses and strains
which were evident in English Canada as well as in French.
As the Joint Committee of the Senate and Commons on the
Constitution of Canada reported in 1972, "Constitutional
reform is not for Quebec alone nor is it desired by Quebec
alone. We found substantial discontent in the West, the
Northwest Territories and the Atlantic Provinces, and resi-
dents of Ontario also expressed their displeasure with some
parts of the constitutional picture. We also encountered feelings of dissatisfaction from many groups — native peoples,
some ethnic groups, French-speaking Canadians outside Quebec, and the young generally."

After four years, therefore, Trudeau's version of federalism had not satisfied either French or English Canada. He

had responded energetically to the problems of language, regional disparity and alienation, but had tried to tinker with the old constitution when a bold new vision of Confederation might have enthused the country. When the tinkering failed, debilitating doubts about the future remained and national unity was weaker rather than stronger.

3

THE POLITICS OF PARTICIPATION

"Come Work with Me" invited Trudeau's striking mod posters in 1968, and Participatory Democracy became one of the catch phrases of the general election campaign. He called on Canadians to plug in to Ottawa, to play their role in government, and millions of people responded to the idea that they could somehow join with this brilliant new political personality in making the decisions which would transform Canada. Yet barely a year later, Parliament was rocking to angry cries of "Heil Hitler" as Trudeau cut off debate in the House of Commons, and it was the wisdom of the day that the Prime Minister was contemptuous of Parliament, arrogant toward his critics and greedy for personal power.

Trudeau certainly wielded more power more effectively than any predecessor. He doubled the size of the Prime Minister's personal staff, thereby extending his political reach and control, and he expanded the Privy Council Office through which he directed the vast administrative machine of the federal Government, with its $16 billion budget and 225,000 civil servants. But at the same time, Trudeau made Parliament a more effective forum for scrutiny and criticism in some ways, and he deliberately opened himself and his Government to public pressure.

He came to office after a period of minority governments in Ottawa — three between 1962 and 1968 — when there was much criticism about weak leadership in Ottawa in comparison with the growing confidence of the provinces. There was also concern about declining respect for Parliament and a rising interest among the young in the politics of protest and confrontation. He felt he was elected to give strong leadership to Parliament and to the people, to restore political stability and confidence in democracy, and he was frank about what he was doing.

"In our system everybody is growing stronger. The unions are growing stronger, multi-national corporations are growing stronger, the universities are growing stronger, academics are growing stronger, you know, the press is growing stronger, the media is growing stronger," he told Tom Gould of CTV who was questioning his use of power in an interview in 1971. "The only one you wouldn't want to grow stronger is the government of the country . . . If this is what you want, I can have six people in my office. I won't be able to follow any of the complex subjects which are being discussed in this government or in this country and you will have a lousy, weak-kneed government. And if that's the kind of a thing you want, you had better elect somebody else. I just don't understand this absurd criticsm of the Executive being too strong. I have tried in every way to strengthen the Parliament . . . but I have not tried to weaken the Executive and I don't apologize for that."

When Trudeau became Prime Minister, his aides analyzed his responsibilities and requirements in his different roles as leader of the Government in Parliament, head of the federal administration, chief of the Liberal Party, public personality and private man. The idea was to organize his time so that he could keep on top of all the jobs, and the breakdown of his duties is a convenient framework in which to look at the ways in which Trudeau followed through on his promise of participatory democracy.

Parliament: Myth and Reality

The House of Commons is unquestionably the heart of Canadian democracy, but it is also the subject of a great many myths. It is essential to separate fact from romantic fancy to understand what the situation was before Trudeau came to power and what changes he made in the parliamentary system.

It was a myth long before Trudeau came to Ottawa that MPs exercised any effective day by day control over the Prime Minister and the Cabinet. There was a classic period of parliamentary government in Britain more than a century ago when MPs were sufficiently independent to defeat one government and appoint another to achieve a change in policy. But strong national political parties, as they were organized, were able to discipline the MPs they helped to elect, and Cabinets were soon in full control of affairs.

From the earliest days of Confederation, a Canadian government with a majority of supporters in the Commons was effectively its own master. It could force through whatever legislation it pleased and MPs could not add a comma or cross a *t* unless the responsible minister gave his gracious consent. A government backbencher tempted to be critical or obstructive in the House knew that he would risk his chance of promotion to Parliamentary Secretary or Minister. In extreme cases, the party machine might disown him, withhold campaign funds and run an official candidate against him in the next election, virtually assuring his defeat. If he had serious objections to government policy, he was expected to make his views known only in the privacy of the party caucus so that the public would not see cracks in party unity or know that the wisdom of the Cabinet was open to question.

When the opposition parties held up a bill for too long, the Government simply introduced a motion to end debate and had it passed by its obedient majority. This power of closure dated back half a century in Ottawa, although it seldom had to be used.

The only real rein on Government in these circumstances was public opinion. Ministers who faced election every four or five years dared not become too unpopular, individually or collectively. So, while opposition members might not be able to change government legislation, they could hold it up to public ridicule and contempt in the hope that the voters would decide to remove the Government from office at the first opportunity.

The passing of power from the Commons to the Cabinet was not, however, the end of the evolution in the parliamentary system. Political observers began to comment on the way in which power was passing from the Cabinet to the Prime Minister. "The post-war epoch has seen the final transformation of the Cabinet Government into Prime Ministerial Government," wrote the British parliamentarian, R. H. S. Crossman, in 1963, commenting on the trend at Westminster, the Mother of Parliaments, as Prime Ministers took personal command of powerful party machines and growing government beaureaucracies.

In Canada, Denis Smith, a Trent University political scientist, generally agreed with Crossman and went even further. He told a Conservative Party thinkers' conference in 1969 that the political security of Canadian Prime Ministers is greater than that of their British counterparts, because they are chosen at national party conventions in a glare of publicity and owe their position to public support rather than to colleagues in Cabinet or Parliament.

Smith called his paper *President and Parliament* and remarked of the modern Canadian Prime Minister: "He is virtually as immovable as an American president during his term of office." The comparison was taken up by Trudeau's critics who cried that he was gathering so much power into his own hands that he was becoming a president. This was a thoroughly misleading catchphrase because in fact a parliamentary Prime Minister has more power than any U.S. president.

A president controls the executive branch of government, but has limited influence over the Congress, which usually regards itself as a rival authority and frequently refuses to approve the president's policies. A Prime Minister has control of the Executive and a majority to enforce his wishes in the Commons. Trudeau has joked in private that he is not interested in the congressional system precisely because it would reduce his power.

This has been a sketch of the real state of the parliamentary system when Trudeau came to power. The Prime Minister controlled the Cabinet. The Cabinet controlled the Commons, which was not so much a place for reasoned debate as a political battleground. The Senate was supine. But change was in the wind.

The public seemed to be fed up with the repeated crises of unstable minority governments, with filibusters which held up action on urgent problems, with excessive and sometimes degrading partisanship in debate. When the Pearson Government was defeated more or less by accident in a vote in the Commons in February 1968, the Parliamentarians were thrown into hysterical excitement and many were convinced that the Government would have to resign. But when Prime Minister Pearson took to television to explain the reality behind the rigmarole, the public response was to tell MPs to stop playing games and get on with the nation's business. NDP leader Tommy Douglas complained that it was hard to know if the Government was ruling by divine right or the news service of the CBC, and it is clear in retrospect that this was a significant event in the history of Parliament. Able to see and hear their political leaders on TV, the public were less willing to leave day by day decisions to their elected MPs. A Prime Minister could appeal over the head of Parliament directly to the public, and Parliament would feel the public reaction within hours.

There had been no major changes in the rules of the Commons from 1867 to 1962. But then there were changes, hesitant and experimental, in 1962, 1964 and 1965 as MPs came reluctantly to the conclusion that something had to be done to speed up the flow of business in a society in which Big Government was becoming ever more responsible for regulating and improving the quality of life.

Trudeau was elected partly because he promised to speed up change in the system, to make it more democratic. His performance must be judged, however, not against some idealistic concept of Parliament which never existed, but on how well he succeeded in pushing an imperfect and hidebound institution into the last third of the twentieth century.

The political difficulties of bringing about change were illustrated by one of his first moves. He thought it absurd that every Cabinet minister should sit in the House for an hour or so every day during Question Period on the off-chance that a member of the Opposition might want to ask him a question. He wanted his ministers to spend more time at their desks or in Cabinet committees, and so he set up a roster system under which each minister was supposed to be in the House three days a week, instead of five. It was tactlessly done, without the courtesy of consulting the Opposition, but it was hardly a major step: a similar system had been in use in Britain for years. Nevertheless, there were indignant protests in the Commons and some criticism in the press: the Government was treating Parliament with contempt and trampling on the rights of the Opposition to question and challenge its activities.

Trudeau in fact was doing rather better by the Opposition than had been customary. He volunteered $195,000 a year in public funds to the leaders of the opposition parties to enable them to hire some 20 full-time and five part-time researchers to help document their criticisms of his Government. His original view was that as the Government had the resources of the civil service, it needed no independent research, but his own backbenchers complained that while that might satisfy Cabinet Ministers, it did nothing for them, so he provided $130,000 for researchers attached to the Liberal caucus. While not perhaps a major reform, it was unprecedented for a Government to be encouraging critical analysis of its policies. This was in addition to a rapid expansion of nonpartisan research facilities in the Parliamentary Library. By the end of 1968, a special all-party committee was ready with proposals for radical changes in the rules and procedures for examining and authorizing government spending, and debating the approving legislation.

One of the traditional powers of Parliament was to

withhold supply — that is, to refuse to vote money for spending — until grievances had been redressed. The Opposition could take advantage of supply debates to raise every sort of complaint and sometimes try to wring concessions from the government by prolonging debate for so long that there was an embarrassing shortage of money with which to pay the civil service. In extremes, the government could be forced to go to the country in an election if Parliament refused to provide money. But this was all a time-consuming business, and political debate under the formal rules of the House was not an effective way to scrutinize the routine details of government spending. Even when the House was spending about 50 days a year on this type of business, it still amounted to only about 200 hours of discussion on the detailed estimates of dozens of departments and agencies.

At the recommendation of the all-party committee, the House agreed — although the Conservatives were reluctant — to take all this business of supply out of the full House and put it before 16 special committees of MPs. These small committees of about 20 members could proceed less formally than the House and call ministers and officials to give evidence and be questioned. MPs could begin to acquire expertise in a particular branch of government spending, such as defense or agriculture. The committees were instructed to report on the estimates with recommendations by a certain date, so there could be no question of holding the Government to ransom. However, 25 days in each session were reserved for the opposition parties to bring before the full House any problem they wished and, when they desired, to force a vote and try to defeat the Government.

There are clear advantages in the new system. More time is better spent in examining spending: the Government calculates that committees spend 500 hours each year on this business. The full House meanwhile has more time to deal with debates on general issues and on legislation.

Another big change made by agreement in 1968 was to give detailed examination to nearly all bills in committee instead of in the full House. Again the idea was to encourage MPs to develop expertise, call expert witnesses if they wished and spend more time on detail than would be possible in the House. Of course, the full House continued to debate the principles of every bill and could refuse or accept amendments proposed by the committee.

In addition to sending bills to committees, Trudeau also extended the practice of stating government policy in a tentative way in White Papers. Papers were produced on tax reform, Indian affairs, social security, farm policy and a number of other issues and most were sent to committee for study before the Cabinett finally decided on policy and approved legislation. In this way, MPs were invited to advise the Government before it became committed to a position. The White Papers also stimulated broad public discussion, and scores of expert witnesses were invited to appear before parliamentary committees to give their opinion on public policy.

Between October 8, 1970 and February 16, 1972, to use a convenient period for which statistics are available, 21 committees of the Commons were organized and held over 900 meetings. They called 2,751 witnesses and the verbatim record of their proceedings ran to more than 30,000 printed pages. All this represented an extraordinary increase in the activity of Parliament. MPs were more involved than they had ever been in the study of public issues and they had more influence on the final decisions of Government. Outside experts and organizations representing special interests had also been drawn into the decision-making process to an unprecedented degree.

But it was not an unqualified success. Because the Opposition could no longer hold up supply, much of the drama — even it had often been phoney drama — was lost from the House. With public issues being explored in committee before they came to the House in legislation, the press and therefore the public lost interest in debates. On most nights now, there was only a handful of bored members in the chamber going through the routine of business, and in the press gallery there might be one or two reporters from the Canadian Press news agency filing stories which they knew would not get much space in the next day's papers. Some ministers conceded that it was easier to steer their spending estimates through committee when they could take along officials to answer questions than it was when they had to stand on the floor of the House and face an Opposition in full cry. There was talk of again adjusting the rules so some estimates, at the choosing of the Opposition, could come back for consideration before the full House.

A more subtle and serious criticism was that the Government never really thought through the philosophy of switching so much business to committees. In the parliamentary system, as we have seen, the Cabinet is normally in full control of the Commons. As committees were always considered mere shadows of the House, the Government insisted upon being in control of them also, appointing the chairman and maintaining a majority of members. When Trudeau increased the number of committees and gave them more authority to call witnesses and undertake investigations, it was assumed that they would also become more independent — more like congressional committees in Washington. But sometimes when committees tried to exercise such independence, ministers rudely rejected their advice or ordered the majority of government members to stick to the party line.

What developed in fact was an awkward mixture of the parliamentary and congressional systems, and Government House Leader Allan MacEachen quietly ordered a detailed study of the workings of the committee system by a special unit within his department. He hoped to make recommendations to Cabinet to put the committee system on a more rational and better understood basis, spelling out the rights and powers of members of the committees and the relationship of the committees to the House and the Government.

While these substantial changes in ways of handling business were going on in the background of Parliament, mostly by agreement between Government and Opposition, public attention and criticism focussed on more dramatic but basically less important issues.

Like most new Prime Ministers, Trudeau came to office with a long program of legislation in mind and impatient to get on with the job. He was intrigued — as Pearson had been before him — with the idea of carefully planning the work to be expected of each session of Parliament and then sending bills through the mill according to a fixed timetable. The Opposition would have an opportunity to debate and oppose each bill, but after a specified number of days, it would come to a final vote. In the British Parliament, Government and Opposition were usually able to agree on time limits for business, but in Ottawa, Oppositions — Liberals equally with Tories and New Democrats — had never contemplated such co-operation. They preferred to wage non-stop guerilla warfare against the Government, with deliberate obstruction as a major weapon. The goal was seldom to help govern the country but usually to make the Government look bad by preventing it from carrying through its promised program.

The Liberals on the special committee on procedure in 1968 sought to change this state of affairs. Over the objections of Opposition members on the committee, they proposed a new rule — 16A — which would have created a Standing Committee of House Leaders of all parties charged with working out a timetable for House business, and — here's the snag — giving the Government power to impose a timetable when no agreement was possible. "The Canadian people are impatient for reform," said Trudeau. But it soon became clear that they were not so impatient as to give the Government quite that much power to manage the Commons. When Conservative Leader Stanfield denounced the proposed rule as "The Juggernaut of the Just Society," he was supported by the press and by public opinion. After days of debate, and attempts to negotiate a compromise, the Government backed down. If Stanfield would accept the plan to send estimates to committee, about which he was not too happy, the Government would send 16A back to the procedures committee for another look at the whole problem of a parliamentary timetable.

The deal was made just in time for MPs to go home for Christmas, but Trudeau managed to spoil the atmosphere of agreement by a childish remark which he immediately regretted. The Opposition had been drawn into a trap, he suggested. While they had concentrated all their fire on 16A, they had allowed the Government to put through the really important changes in the handling of estimates and legisla- tion. "I'm extraordinarily happy," he gloated. There was a large element of truth in what he said, which made it all the more wounding. As we have seen, when the Opposition gave up their power to withhold supply, they surrendered a tradi- tional right to demand redress of grievances, and the whole balance of Parliament changed.

Trudeau meanwhile had really given up nothing. His idea of programming the work of Parliament had not been defeated but merely sent back to committee for another look. By the summer of 1969, the Liberal majority on the commit- tee was ready to propose another rule in place of the rejected 16A.

This was Rule 75 and it was in three sections. Section A provided that when House Leaders of all parties agreed on the time to be devoted to a bill, the House would make an order to that effect without debate. The significance of this was that MPs would be made subject to agreements arrived at by their party leaders. Independents, individualists, eccen- trics and natural rebels, of whom there are some in every Parliament, would not be able to frustrate the majority by insisting as private members on their right to talk. Section B provided that when a majority of the House leaders agreed on a timetable, there would be only a two-hour debate to allow dissenters to state objections before the agreement was made a rule of the House. Section C was where the trouble arose, for it provided that when a majority could not agree, the Government could introduce motions to impose its own timetable and force it through. Once again there were cries of tyranny and dictatorship, and it was now that the Opposi- tion began to shout "Heil Hitler" at Trudeau, the participa- tory democrat of a year before.

Rule 75C was far less severe than the proposed 16A. It provided a minimum of one day's debate on each stage of a bill coming under a timetable, which meant in practice that the bill could not be passed into law in less than 10 days. Nevertheless, the Opposition supported by the media argued that this was a new and drastic form of closure, a denial of free speech, the gagging of Parliament, and vowed to oppose it all through the hot Ottawa summer if necessary. With his talent for accurate but tactless remarks, Trudeau replied that this was "a stupid filibuster," and said: "They (the Opposition) do not have to govern, they have only to talk. The best place in which to talk, if they want a forum, is of course Parliament. When they get home, when they get out of Parliament, when they are 50 yards from Parliament Hill, they are no longer Honorable Members — they are just nobodies."

That was good for provoking some more angry debate, but the Government was finally convinced that Canadians had become bored with the whole subject, and got up its courage to use the old form of closure to force approval of the new form, Rule 75.

The episode cost Trudeau goodwill among observers who came to suspect his intentions, and gained him little. Rule 75 is not an effective way of timetabling Commons business and its closure provision was used only once in the following three years — to cut off the seemingly endless debate on tax reform. While the Government was better organized than most in laying its list of proposed bills before Parliament at the start of each session, it made no serious attempt to put them through according to a plan agreed with the Opposition or imposed by the Liberal majority.

One measure of Trudeau's impact on Parliament — and of Parliament's impact on Trudeau — is the rate at which bills were debated and passed into law.

In the four sessions 1960-63, when John Diefenbaker was Conservative Prime Minister, first with a majority and then with a minority government, Parliament sat for 457 days and passed 158 public bills — an average of less than three days for each new law.

In the five sessions 1963-68, when Pearson was head of two minority Liberal governments, 252 bills were passed in 680 days — a little more than three days for each new law.

In the first three Trudeau sessions, from 1968 to '72, when he was heading a majority government and Parliament was under radical new rules, 187 bills were passed in 595 days — a little more than three days for each law. And to these days in the full House must be added the hundreds of hours of committee scrutiny.

These statistics are only a rough guide to the business of Parliament, which includes many activities other than passing legislation. But they do indicate that under Trudeau's rules, there was more rather than less debate on legislation, and that the Opposition was far from throttled. In 1971, for example, the Opposition was able to hold up the Prairie Farm Income Stabilization Bill until the Government decided that the wisest course was to withdraw it and think again.

When Trudeau grumbled about obstruction he sounded much like all the Prime Ministers who had gone before. It was not he but Diefenbaker who said in 1962 when his Government was being talked to a standstill by the Liberals: "Governments propose and Oppositions dispose. There is only one way in which a Government can carry through its legislative program if an Opposition has its eye on certain objectives desirable for the Opposition but not desirable for the effectual operation of Parliament, and that is through the medium of closure."

Parliament's work on legislation is for the most part a plodding, painstaking business, and attracts little attention from the media and the public. The daily excitement is generated by the Question Period when the opposition members have 40 minutes in which to confront the Prime Minister and his Cabinet and, in theory, call them to account.

The Question Period has become something of a myth in its own right within the larger myths about the parliamentary system. It is talked about as an ancient institution, the historic forum which distinguishes our democracy from that of the United States, the essential guardian of our liberties. But the truth is that the Question Period as we know it is a development of the last 30 years. One has only to look at a pre-war Hansard to see that the Question Period was a brief and, by modern standards, controlled affair. MPs usually gave written notice of their questions, except in circumstances of genuine urgency or emergency, and Ministers gave carefully prepared replies.

This is still the way the institution operates in Britain. When the Speaker has approved the form and precision of the question and printed it on the Order Paper and the Minister has given his considered reply, the basic facts of the situation and the nature of the issue should be established. The skill and political infighting then come in supplementary oral exchanges on the floor of the House, with the opposition member probing for more information, or attempting to demonstrate the weakness in the Government's position, and the minister judging how much he should reveal or what mistakes he must confess. As Diefenbaker, a student of British Hansard, has said, "They tear ministers apart on supplementary questions."

A different form has developed in Ottawa. Members still submit written questions and get prepared answers, usually in writing. But the daily exchanges in the House are almost entirely oral. Opposition members ask whatever questions they like in whatever form they can get past the Speaker — very often more accusative than enquiring.

Ministers seldom have notice of questions, but their staffs brief them on matters in the news which are likely to be raised by the Opposition and they go into the House armed with a folder of answers to anticipated questions. For example, Trudeau had as his Legislative Assistant Joyce Fairbairn, an attractive blonde who was the belle of the Parliamentary Press Gallery for several years before she gave up being a reporter and went to work for the Prime Minister. Journalists who know what is likely to make news and how best to present it to the public are in demand as aides to ministers. But when a minister's staff fail to brief him properly, or he has not done his homework, he can be caught by the Opposition and made to look foolish as he waffles, promises lamely to answer on another day, or is harassed into damaging admissions.

At its best, the Question Period is a curb on the Government and a goad to better performance. The knowledge that they can be made to answer for their actions undoubtedly deters ministers from doing those things they should not do; and the fear that inaction can be exposed by questioners encourages them to do those things they should do. At its worst, the Question Period becomes a savage political battleground on which there is small regard for manners, decency or political responsibility. Insults are exchanged, characters impugned, insinuations planted in Hansard and in the press. The most that can be said for the institution on these occasions is that oral violence may serve as a substitute for the physical violence with which political disputes were resolved in earlier times. In the British House of Commons, members speaking from the opposing front benches are not allowed to step across lines marked on the floor, and the lines are two sword's lengths apart. Swords were already out of style when the Candian House of Commons opened in Ottawa, but the principle holds.

It was Trudeau's intemperate outbursts in the Commons, usually during a Question Period flare-up, which did the most damage to his reputation as a Parliamentarian. I have already mentioned the notorious occasion on which he scorned the opposition MPs as "nobodies". Once he snapped about a "goddamned" question from Stanfield. Worst of all, he replied to opposition goading by mouthing words which the Opposition took to be "Fuck off". Trudeau insisted that he had said nothing, but agreed that he was thinking the sort of thoughts which might be expressed by the phrase "fuddle-duddle" — a polite substitute for "Fuck off" and a tacit admission that the words were in his mouth if not on his lips. It was well established elsewhere, in any event, that Trudeau, for all his culture, could be vulgar in language. He could also be humorous. When a reported once asked him if he had again mouthed "Fuck off" in the House, Trudeau retorted. "No, but I want you to."

There was a good deal of hypocrisy about the shocked reaction in the House to Trudeau's bad language. MPs who swore heartily in private claimed to be outraged to hear the Prime Minister swear in public, although Fuck, once a forbidden word, was in common use among young people and in movies and novels. It has to be remembered also that Trudeau was daily subject to insult and provocation in the House, and the Opposition were never more delighted than when they could goad him into losing his temper. The real cause for concern was that it proved so easy to provoke him. It was not his language which was shocking, but the fact that he used it when he knew that he should not. It suggested a man who was not always in control of himself.

These Question Period excitements were of course rare. Most days, the exchanges were neither good nor bad, but simply boring. Stanfield opened with a loaded question about what his advisers considered the most newsworthy topic of the day; Trudeau dodged or returned a barbed answer. Then other opposition members went through the motions of grilling the Government and the ministers went through the weary motions of replying. A considerable amount of time was wasted by members trying to twist the rules of order so that they could say things the Speaker thought they should not say, and the level of wit was schoolboyish. Strong words might be exchanged, but with winks and nods and chuckles across the floor. The members of the club were in fact performing a form of guerilla theatre mostly for the benefit of the Press Gallery who they knew would carry it hot to the public, as if the words were important, the debates fierce, the issues real.

On many days, therefore, the Question Period did more harm than good to the democratic process. It trivialized complex issues by reducing them to an exchange of partisan comments or personal insults between the Prime Minister and the Leader of the Opposition.

When the Ottawa reporter for The Wall Street Journal described the Question Period for U.S. readers, his incredulous editors ran it on the front page under the heading: Canadian Politicians Scream, Hiss and Boo for 40 Minutes Daily. And Charles Lynch, probably the most widely read political columnist in Canada, noted indirectly the way in which stylized daily conflict diverted attention from reality when he began a piece in March, 1972 by saying: "With both Prime Minister Trudeau and Opposition Leader Stanfield out on the hustings taking part in the election campaign that isn't, the House of Commons was able to get down to serious business."

Trudeau was dutiful in his attendance at Question Period but obviously found it boring on many days. He became restless and irritable, gave curt answers to questions and showed his contempt for opposition members who were too partisan or personal for his taste. But the truth was that the Question Period often was boring, even from a seat in the Press Gallery. Newsmen helped to preserve the myth that it was a lively and vital institution because it happened to suit their purpose, providing in a simple and stylized form daily conflict between personalities over current issues.

Perhaps the only man who found that the Question Period demanded his full attention every day was the Speaker. He had to intervene between Opposition and Government in the heat of the exchanges to preserve order, without losing his essential reputation for impartiality. Too many errors in judgment and he could easily be destroyed. Trudeau was fortunate to have Lucien Lamoureux in the chair, a man who combined knowledge of the rules with a ready wit and an even hand. But he retired from the chamber after the Question Period in a lather of sweat to take a shower and change his clothes.

Lamoureux was elected as a Liberal but became an Independent to emphasize his neutrality. He let it be known that he wished to be relieved of his responsibilities to his constituents in Cornwall so that he could concentrate on his many duties as Speaker. There is no easy answer to the problem of how to give the Speaker permanency in the chair without the responsibilities of the ordinary member. But one of the serious complaints that can be made against Trudeau's attitude to Parliament is that he had not, at the time of writing, tried to meet Lamoureux's difficulties. As a result, the House was in danger of losing a first-rate Speaker.

THE BACKBENCHERS. The Question Period was particularly frustrating for government backbenchers. The Speaker generally recognized opposition critics, and even when a government supporter did get a chance to ask a question, his party leaders did not expect him to be accusative or too persistent.

The realization that they were expected to be seen when their votes were needed to support the Government, but not heard from much, came as a shock to many of the bright new Liberal MPs elected in the Trudeau sweep of 1968. They had accepted the invitation on the posters to "work with me"; many of them had an idealized vision of Parliament and they wanted to participate. But they soon discovered that all the action and decision-making was in the bureaucracy and the Cabinet. Even their weekly meetings with the Prime Minister and other ministers in the private party caucus were of little value because they usually were not shown legislation until it was about to be introduced in the House and it was too late to make changes Caucus meetings tended to be a steam-valve for frustrated Liberals who wanted to hear themselves talk, which was useful but not particularly satisfying for able and ambitious MPs, many of whom had been successful executives in private life.

Even when a member did have a pertinent point to raise in caucus, Trudeau was capable of cutting him down with a withering comment. Thus Phil Givens, a former Mayor of Toronto, arrived in Ottawa as an MP expecting to tackle city problems, but found to his dismay that Trudeau regarded the municipalities as primarily a provincial jurisdiction — as, strictly speaking, they are, under the constitution. When Givens complained in caucus, Trudeau told him he'd got elected to the wrong place and should be in a provincial legislature. Trudeau later apologised for that smack in the face, but Givens decided in time that he was right, resigned from the federal Parliament and got elected to the Ontario Parliament.

Within a year of the great Liberal election victory in June 1968, the bloom had worn off for many backbenchers and a few were dangerously disenchanted. Wives too were grumbling about the difficulty of finding homes in Ottawa at prices they could afford on an MP's salary, about husbands who had to stay in the Commons night after night, about the difficulties of learning French to uphold the Government's crusade for bilingualism.

Barney Danson, a successful manufacturer of plastic-making machinery in Metro Toronto and the MP for York North, wrote to Trudeau suggesting a special two-day weekend caucus on The Role of the Backbencher, and Trudeau warmly approved. With the regular caucus chairman, Gerald Laniel, an insurance broker MP from Valleyfield, Quebec, Danson set up private seminars on the role of MPs in the Commons, in caucus, in relation to the Cabinet and the civil service and as representatives of constituents. Bruce Howard, a realtor MP from Penticton, B.C., gave a booster address in which he tried to stake out a new role for the back-bench MP: "Why lament the day when the MP was a big man in the community? When he was the giver of jobs, the dispenser of patronage, and in times of trouble, the Fixer? There's still some of that left, but each year the growing bu-reaucracy and Crown Corporations take more and more from the role of the MP. That's good. It's like automation. This kind of automation frees the MP for more important roles.

"Now there should be time for the MP to do his real job as leader in his community. Time now to motivate and ac-tivate. Time to get in on the revolution that has just begun. We know now that real social reform will not come merely because we pass a law. We know, for instance, that unmotivated people can be cleared from a slum area into something new and make that a slum area too. We know that we can spend lots of money on regional disparity but achieve little if people aren't motivated to use that money correctly . . . We've had nine months to learn about the problems of our areas and the government facilities to solve them. We have three months (of summer recess) ahead of us. They need us in One Potato, New Brunswick, and Dis-traught, Alberta. Three months, the long hot summer. Long enough for a riot. Long enough for a revolution. What will it be for the MP in search of a role? Who's for Revolution?"

It was splendid rhetoric and the idea of realtors,

brokers and plastics manufacturers leading a revolution of the poor and powerless was intriguing. It may even have given the disgruntled Liberal MPs something to think about during the recess and it certainly pleased the officers of the Liberal Party who wanted the boys to go home, get involved and get re-elected.

But it did nothing to improve the parliamentary role of the backbencher. However, when Trudeau had asked Laniel to be caucus chairman, he had given him a free hand to reform the organization, and Laniel took the task seriously.

The caucus was extensively reorganized and set up committees to parallel committees of Cabinet. A statement of Operating Principles was adopted, and the key section of this backbenchers' charter said: "At least a month before the opening of a session (of Parliament), General Caucus shall meet for the purpose of studying the forthcoming legislative program, discussing it with Cabinet and making whatever recommendations it deems appropriate to the government . . . Before a final decision is made on a bill and before its final drafting, the minister responsible shall discuss the bill in general terms with the Caucus committee concerned and a subsequent detailed discussion will be held upon the first reading (when a bill is presented in Parliament and printed, but before it is debated).

"No bill shall be submitted for Second Reading (general debate in the Commons) until such consultation has taken place or has been renounced by common agreement. A similar procedure shall be followed for major changes relating to government policies for which no legislation is required." Trudeau enforced these rights of backbenchers by insisting that Ministers could not bring proposals before Cabinet for final approval without certification that they had been discussed in caucus.

The plan was far from watertight. Some Ministers resented the requirement to consult with backbenchers and sought ways to avoid it. There were even suggestions that it was somehow unparliamentary to reveal details of legislation to caucus before introducing it to the Commons. John Roberts, an energetic young MP from York-Simcoe, commented sceptically: "We now have regional caucuses, ad hoc caucuses, subject matter caucuses and a national caucus which is so busy hearing reports from subsidiary caucuses at the beginning and the Prime Minister's summing up at the end, that it has little time for anything in between, other than exhortations from the House Leader and the Whip to attend the votes in the Commons."

Some experienced MPs complained specifically that the new caucus was so busy with organization and legislation that members had lost the opportunity to air the complaints they were hearing from back home in the riding so that the Prime Minister and the Cabinet could understand the political mood of the country. The new rules were subsequently relaxed to allow more general discussion.

But Trudeau was at least making some effort to involve his backbenchers in decision-making and that was a decided change in the style of parliamentary government. If the system of participation did not always work, the fault sometimes lay with the MPs themselves. One of the most enterprising of the 1968 crop of Liberals was David Anderson, who had been a foreign service officer and Canada's official spy, or intelligence officer, watching Communist China from Hong Kong, before he won election from Esquimalt-Saanich on Vancouver Island. Making imaginative use of his influence as an MP, Anderson ran a one-man campaign against polluting laundry detergents and conducted a long, legal guerilla campaign against the U.S. Government's plan to ship oil from Alaska down the British Columbia coast, risking a disastrous oil spill.

Anderson's initiatives were not always welcomed by his colleagues in Parliament who preferred more conventional methods, and he was slapped down on a couple of occasions. But when he left Ottawa in 1972 to become Liberal Leader in British Columbia, he suggested that backbenchers had mostly their own inertia to blame for relative lack of power. It was not until 1970, for example, that caucus asked and received from Trudeau the right to elect its own chairman instead of having one appointed by the Leader.

It was in 1970 also that Trudeau took another step to

assist backbenchers by appointing an Independent Committee on Parliamentary Pay and Allowances. It was headed by Norbert Beaupré, a tough-minded business executive who bossed 19,000 employees of the Domtar business empire and knew a thing or two about salary levels in private business. Labor lawyer Marc Lapointe and Arthur Maloney, a distinguished former Tory MP, were the other members of the committee.

The idea of more pay for MPs always provokes snarky comments in the press and upsets taxpayers who grumble about politicians voting themselves fat raises. Politically, a Prime Minister is wise to turn a deaf ear to the pleas of his supporters and do nothing. But most people who knew the circumstances of the average backbencher in 1970 were convinced that something had to be done. The pay of $12,000 plus $6,000 in tax free allowances for expenses did not cover unavoidable costs and many members were exhausting savings and going into debt. I surveyed about 50 MPs of all parties at that time and concluded that the expenses of the average member were $8,700 a year. This meant he was dipping into his pay and actually netting less than $10,000 a year on which to live. In some large and remote ridings, expenses were much higher, Gustave Blouin, whose Manicouagan riding covered 300,000 square miles in Quebec, had to rent a light plane at $85 an hour to visit some constituents, and owed $21,000 to the banks.

"My personal savings have been completely dissipated," reported Robert Thompson, the former Social Credit leader who became a Conservative MP. Jack McIntosh, Mayor of Swift Current, Saskatchewan, before he become a Tory member, told me: "If I did not have another source of income, I could not have remained an MP."

Faced with stories such as these, the Beaupré committee recommended that MPs' pay should be jumped from $12,000 to $23,000 and then to $25,000, and that there should be a reasonable expense account instead of a fixed, tax-free allowance. The scheme was sensible but too complicated and too generous to explain to a suspicious public. In April 1971, Trudeau proposed instead to raise salaries from $12,000 to

$18,000 and the tax-free allowance from $6,000 to $8,000, and the House approved by 149 votes to 30. It was not a good solution because it maintained the fixed, non-accountable allowance for expenses, and it mocked the Government's plea to unions to exercise restraint in pay claims to help fight inflation. But it certainly eased the burden on many MPs and encouraged them to do a better job.

The contributory pension plan for MPs was also made markedly more generous — too generous, according to critics, although allowance had to be made for the fact that politics is a high-risk business and surprisingly few members survive more than two or three general elections. When they give up or are defeated, they have to try to resume an interrupted career and many find it difficult. Even with a handsome parliamentary pension, it is doubtful whether they catch up with income and benefits lost during the political years.

Another way in which Trudeau helped his own supporters was by enlarging the Cabinet, and raising the number of Parliamentary Secretaries who assist ministers and are paid an extra $4,000 a year. But with all these appointments, plus some 20 committee chairmen hoping for promotion and pay, the officers of caucus, the Whip and his assistant and other functionaries, more than half of the Liberal majority in the Commons had duties which tied them in some way to the Government. This tended to reduce their independence as MPs and raised serious questions about the proper relationship between the executive and the legislature. MPs were gaining more influence in caucus and in committees of the House. But could they be expected to restrain the Cabinet, or even defeat it in an emergency, if they were dependent on the Prime Minister for extra pay and position?

The question illustrated one of the problems of participatory democracy when it was married to the parliamentary system, and it has yet to be answered.

While most efforts at reform have been focussed on the Commons because that is where real political power resides, the Senate also underwent substantial change during the Trudeau years. At Confederation, it was intended to serve as an Upper House to which solid and reliable citizens from all the provinces could be appointed to keep an eye on the un-ruly Commons. But it decayed into a rest home for faithful party members appointed by Prime Ministers grateful for ser-vices rendered. The succession of Liberal Prime Ministers from the Thirties on stuffed it with Liberal Senators, and when Diefenbaker led the Conservatives back to power in 1957, he could only begin to redress the balance by appoint-ing Tories as vacancies occurred. Pearson resumed the prac-tice of appointing Liberals, but chose several younger men who were willing to try to breathe life into the old place.

These men in their 40's and 50's were beginning to make an impression on the Red Chamber when Trudeau became Prime Minister. His first appointment was Paul Mar-tin, the veteran minister he had defeated for the Liberal leadership and whom he now sent to be Government Leader in the Senate. Martin recovered from the shock of defeat and went bravely to work in the Senate to write a new chapter in his career. He encouraged young Senators to organize com-mittee studies in areas where the Commons had not ven-tured, approved funds for committee staff and research while the Commons was still hesitating, and bugged Trudeau to make good appointments to the Upper House.

If one had to name four areas of critical concern and in-terest in our rapidly changing society, they might be the con-trol of science and technology, the persistence of poverty amid affluence, the role of the mass media and the problem of achieving high employment without inflation.

All were the subject of major Senate studies and reports, while none received much attention from the Commons. The criticism could be made, of course, that the Govern-ment did not act on Senate recommendations. But the real value of such studies, by Senators, Royal Commissioners or other forms of official inquiry, was not in the solutions they proposed, but in the light they threw on problems and the public interest they aroused. Action comes later.

Trudeau made 25 appointments to the Senate. The vast majority were faithful Liberals, but one was Social Credit, another CCF-NDP and several of indeterminate political backgrounds — the first non-partisan appointments in years and among the very few made since Confederation. He sent four women to the Upper House, a labor leader and a member of the National Indian Brotherhood.

The Senate still has a long way to go to capture public esteem, but its reputation probably improved more than that of the Commons during the Trudeau years.

The East Block Machine

The executive headquarters of the Government are in the East Block on Parliament Hill which is appropriately decorated with blind lookout towers, empty turrets and fearsome gargoyles. Built at the time of Confederation, it set a precedent for federal construction projects by costing scandalously more than expected and proving hopelessly inadequate for its purpose of housing all the principal departments of State, which sprawled all over the capital.

The East Block is where the Prime Minister has his offices, gathers his chosen political staff around him, and directs the affairs of the bureaucracy through the mandarins of the Privy Council Office. Today, these two elite staffs of the PMO and the PCO occupy half the entire building, and they have overflowed from the elegant, high-ceilinged Victorian chambers into a warren of cubicles in the attic.

As I have noted, there was a clear trend toward concentration of power in the hands of the Prime Minister long before Trudeau came to power. But Trudeau accepted power more openly than most of his predecessors and carefully organized to use it. Observers who used to complain about indecision and inefficiency in the East Block now worried about excessive strength and direction.

Prime Ministers managed to run things more or less out their hip pockets until the Second World War. They called Ministers to Cabinet meetings without agendas so that they could control what subjects would be discussed, and no official minutes were kept of decisions. "After a meeting few knew precisely what had been decided; there could be no confidence that all relevant information had been available or considered; and the accurate transmission of decisions, if it occurred at all, was a happy accident," said Cabinet Secretary Gordon Robertson in 1971 in a lecture to The Institute of Public Administration of Canada.

Those haphazard days ended in 1940 when the war demanded a sudden expansion of government activities and Prime Minister W. L. Mackenzie King could no longer carry all the information in his head and all the power in his hands. The Cabinet was organized into committees and a small secretariat was set up in the Privy Council Office to serve the central War Committee. By 1945 there were 10 officers in the secretariat, and peace brought new economic and social responsibilities and the need for more expert advice and co-ordination of policies. Cabinet committees proliferated and the secretariat continued to grow.

When Pearson became Prime Minister in 1963 he undertook a major reorganization of the Cabinet system. Nine Cabinet committees were set up and provided with specialized services, but even this tighter system did not succeed in controlling the government — particularly the growth of spending.

The Cabinet continued to make decisions without much idea of the final cost, where the money would come from and which programs would have priority. By 1968, Pearson realized that serious financial difficulties lay ahead and he set up in January a new and powerful Cabinet committee on Priorities and Planning to keep spending commitments under control. Trudeau had been Parliamentary Secretary to Pearson before he entered the Cabinet in 1967. He was familiar with the atmosphere of financial strain and, in fact, there was a severe crisis which rocked the Canadian dollar during the race for the Liberal leadership. So it was not surprising that when Trudeau became Prime Minister in April 1968, almost his first major act was to reorganize the Cabinet to tighten control over government planning and operations.

He swept away the old clutter of committees and set up new ones with increased authority to deal with the five principal policy and problem areas: External Affairs and Defence; Economic Policy; Social Policy; Science, Culture and

Information; and Government Operations. The committees were scheduled to meet regularly and ministers were freed from some duties in the Commons so they could be sure to attend. All matters had to be routed through the committees on their way to full Cabinet. To speed up the flow of business, it was provided that the appropriate committee would make a decision on each issue, and unless a minister registered an objection, the decision would be automatically confirmed by full Cabinet without discussion. In effect, the Cabinet was to operate in five sections, and the full body was a sort of court of appeal.

Trudeau's new organization included four co-ordinating committees which meshed with the five policy committees. The committee on Legislation and House Planning sought to fit policy decisions into a coherent program to be presented to Parliament.

The committee on Federal-Provincial Relations tried to ensure that all the Government's policies were consistent with its constitutional limitations and theory of federalism. The committee also developed federal proposals to be submitted to the constitutional conferences and kept an eye on hundreds of federal-provincial negotiations.

Most important, the mandate of the committee on Priorities and Planning was extended from control of spending commitments to cover the broad objectives and long-term implications of all the Government's activities. Trudeau took the chair and limited the membership to about 10 of the ministers whose advice he most respected. Discussion ranged beyond immediate practical problems to such philosophical questions as the work ethic, the morality of economic growth, the shift of population from rural to urban society, and the extent to which modern government should intervene to direct changes in society.

To serve the committee, a new planning division of the Cabinet Secretariat with a staff of 47 was set up under the command of Michael Pitfield, a fast-rising young mandarin. The son of a wealthy Montreal family, he was a friend and sometime travelling companion of Trudeau, and a student of modern society and Byzantine history. He was said to have learnt from history that power lay not so much with the emperor as with those who controlled the flow of information to the emperor; in any event, he was widely regarded as one of the most influential men in Ottawa.

The committee on Priorities and Planning was not intended to be an Inner Cabinet wielding final power. Its decisions, like those of all other committees, were subject to debate and confirmation by the full Cabinet. But its membership obviously gave it unusual authority and it soon became known throughout the bureaucracy as the central planning agency of a Government which placed high priority on planning.

The fourth co-ordinating committee was the traditional Treasury Board which had been set up at Confederation to advise the Finance Minister but gradually became a power in its own right. In addition to managing the public service and overseeing departmental administration, it authorized government spending. Because it controlled the total spending program sent to Parliament each year in the Blue Book of Estimates, it effectively established government priorities. But under the Trudeau plan, its general financial authority was limited to implementing the guidelines established by the committee on Priorities.

The board, however, increased its influence in other directions. The Glassco Commission on the Organization of Government had urged the development of the techniques of scientific management in the federal service, and the chief among these was the Planning, Programming, Budgeting System. This was designed to force departments to think through and state their program objectives, weigh alternatives and monitor performance to ensure that objectives were achieved. At the centre of the system was the Treasury Board, as a committee of Cabinet.

In addition to the regular Cabinet committees described above, there were special committees which met as required. The committee on Security and Intelligence, for example, was convened to deal with the FLQ crisis in October, 1970.

The new Cabinet machine set up by Trudeau in 1968 was certainly shiny and it looked impressive. But the real test was how well it worked, and that was mostly a subjective political judgment. The objective measures were interesting but not particularly revealing.

The number of effective documents flowing through the Cabinet increased from 700 a year under Pearson to more than 800 a year under Trudeau. The number of full meetings of Cabinet dropped from 139 in 1966-67 to 70 or 80 a year. The number of meetings of Cabinet committees jumped from 120 in 1966-67 to more than 300 a year.

The Cabinet Secretariat had grown in 1971 to almost 70 officers with supporting clerical staff. It was divided into Planning and Operating sections and sought to blend the caution and experience of senior civil servants drawn in rotation from different departments with the bright ideas and enthusiasm of young technocrats, sometimes recruited directly from university, complete with beard, blue jeans and guitar.

Cabinet committees mixed ministers and officials and permitted probing exchanges in a way not possible in the full Cabinet. While some observers suggested that this increased the influence of the officials because they were experts while politicians were amateurs, Cabinet Secretary Robertson disagreed.

"Ministers have the opportunity to learn more of what their colleagues are doing and to be better informed about all aspects of government activities than under previous methods. Policies and programs are related more consciously and more constantly to the totality of problems and less to partial or sectional aspects. Ministers have more influence on the shape of policy as a whole and on its development and officials have proportionately less than they used to. This judgment is at variance with the conventional wisdom but, after 30 years in the operation of government, more than half of it at the centre, I feel confident it is correct.

"Finally, there is a more planned attempt to assess in advance the probable nature of developments of broad national and social moment before they arrive as immediate problems for urgent action. Such things rarely fall within the boundaries established for administrative convenience and when plans were confined within these tidy limits, some quite major questions remained neglected."

Robertson might have been a prejudiced witness. He was the principal architect of the new system and Ottawa's top civil servant, a pleasant but reserved man, with greying hair, the tanned face of a skier and a shy smile. He briefed Trudeau every morning on the day's official business and, as head of the PCO, exerted considerable influence over the work of Cabinet by managing the flow of paper and preparing the agenda. A wise minister sought his understanding and support for any major proposal he wanted to steer through the Cabinet machine, and every ambitious bureaucrat was aware of Robertson's influence, and of his comment: "Any civil servant above clerical or stenographic grades who has spent any substantial time in a job without contributing to some degree to the policy he administers should be fired . . ." In what could almost be the creed of the mandarin, he said: "The agenda of Cabinet, week by week, reflects the problems, interests and aspirations of the Canadian people. To understand, to inform, to advise and to share in the discussion of such meetings is a reward in itself. For an official to feel that he has contributed, however modestly, to constructive decisions for a better country in a better world brings no glory, but a great sense of participation in events that count."

In a paper presented to The Institute of Public Administration in 1967, Robertson suggested many of the changes in parliamentary procedure and Cabinet organization which Trudeau implemented when he came to power the following year. So Robertson could hardly be expected to be critical of the results. But, in fact, few informed people did dispute the judgment that ministers' time was better used, policy decisions more carefully considered and the total government program better co-ordinated and controlled. The high-powered committee of business experts and provincial civil servants appointed by Premier Robarts to advise on the reorganization of the Ontario Government studied the Ottawa model and cited it admiringly when recommending, in 1970, a similar system of Cabinet committees and support staff. Trudeau himself boasted that he had restored stability to government and ended administration by emergency action in response to unforeseen crises.

It was hard to refute this claim and criticism usually took the opposite tack, suggesting that Trudeau built a machine which was too slow, too centralized and which produced coldly technical rather than warmly human answers to problems.

The most common complaint from ministers was that they spent too long in Cabinet commitees and had too little time in their departments or in the House of Commons. Robertson conceded that this might be right: "It is quite possible that the improvements in the Cabinet system may have been at too high a cost in the time ministers can devote to the total political role that they fill. The right balance will never be final or certain . . ." he said in 1971.

The most perceptive criticism, however, was that the end result of the whole elaborate participatory machine might be to make the Prime Minister more powerful than ever. He was the only man who saw the complete picture, who was in touch through the Privy Council Office with all developments. While all other ministers were bogged down in the endless committees, swamped with paper from the PCO and handed a file of reports three inches thick before each Cabinet meeting, Trudeau was briefed daily by Robertson and advised of conflicting opinions and policy implications.

He went into Cabinet vastly better informed than his ministers and thus enjoyed essentially the same advantage as all those old-time Prime Ministers who ran things out of the hip pocket, without agendas or official records.

The PCO operated with the customary discretion of the civil service, and the Cabinet and its committees met in private, so this important branch of administration attracted little public attention. The power struggles burst into the open only occasionally. Politics, however, are very much a public affair, and most of the complaints about Trudeau's establishment in the East Block centered on his personal staff — the Prime Minister's Office.

The chief of staff was Marc Lalonde, Principal Secretary to the Prime Minister. A bony, bald-headed, hurrying man with a wary smile and aggressive good humor, he was an old friend and political ally of Trudeau. Before either made a name in Ottawa, they fought the same battles in Quebec, shared the same views of federalism.

Lalonde first came to Ottawa as assistant to Conservative Justice Minister Davie Fulton, later handled occasional study assignments for the Government, and then was recruited by Pearson as his policy secretary in 1966. He was planning to return to Montreal and open a law office when the possibility suddenly emerged that Trudeau could become Prime Minister. Lalonde pushed enthusiastically from behind the scenes, and as the delegates roared their acceptance of Trudeau at the Liberal leadership convention in 1968, Lalonde left Pearson's side and moved discreetly behind the new chief.

When Trudeau moved into the PMO in the East Block, Lalonde knew from experience what should be done about staff. Every Prime Minister since Confederation had had some private aides, and by King's time, the staff had increased to 30. It stayed at that level until Pearson increased it to 40, with a salary and travel budget of $330,000 a year. Even so, Pearson's staff were overworked and the office was sometimes in a state of barely-controlled chaos.

Pearson's time was not always well used and he was sometimes placed in acutely embarassing political situations by poor planning, as when he was visiting a town in Quebec and had to dodge through the streets to avoid becoming entangled with a separatist demonstration. Lalonde was determined that those sort of things should not happen to Trudeau.

He was aware also of the new style of politics then emerging. It had been apparent that in the age of TV and the jet, people would expect more direct contact with their national leader. Trudeau's intriguing personal style suddenly accelerated the trend and it was obvious that he would be in enormous public demand.

Trudeau himself was anxious to establish channels of communication to the public and the Liberal Party. Unlike most Prime Ministers, he had only a brief political apprenticeship and few personal political friends outside Ottawa and Quebec on whose advice he could rely. If he wanted sources of information and guidance outside the bureaucracy and the Cabinet, he would have to organize an intelligence network.

These were all the functions of a political staff and the PMO more than doubled in size, to 85 people with a budget of $900,000 in 1970. There was an outcry in Parliament and the criticism in the press, mostly based on the fear that Trudeau was bypassing MPs and establishing some form of direct democracy through a team of cold-eyed manipulators, poll-takers, political organizers and press agents — and probably French Canadians at that.

In fact, Trudeau took over most of Pearson's staff and many of his additions had formerly worked for Liberal Ministers and were familiar figures on Parliament Hill. His chief press officer, for example, was Roméo LeBlanc, a shambling, sardonic but usually helpful Acadian whom Pearson had recruited when he was CBC French-language correspondent in Washington. LeBlanc sometimes operated as a lightning rod for Trudeau, apparently on the theory that if the press got mad at him, they wouldn't take out their frustrations on the Prime Minister.

But to be spokesman for the Prime Minister is a wearing job at best, and nobody can take it for too long. When LeBlanc left in 1971 to join the new University of Moncton in his home province, he was replaced not by a professional image-maker but by a diplomat, Peter Roberts, who had been interested in a discreet job in the Cabinet Secretariat but wound up in the hot seat. One of his aides was Al Donnelly, formerly financial reporter for the Canadian Press news agency who later worked in the Finance Department. Another was Vic Chapman, a former football star who came to Trudeau from John Turner's staff and was responsible for logistics, such as planes, hotels, working quarters and the bar, when newsmen travelled with the Prime Minister. He also tried to teach Trudeau to kick a football properly for the opening of the Grey Cup game — an exercise in image-making which was less than a brilliant success.

Mary Macdonald, who was Pearson's devoted executive

assistant and looked after the problems of his riding, became manager of Trudeau's paperwork and problem-solver for his Montreal constituents.

Gordon Gibson, who was executive assistant and later trouble-shooting special assistant, was the scion of a famous and wealthy Liberal family in British Columbia and he originally came to Ottawa to work for BC Minister Arthur Laing during the Pearson years. Gibson careered around Parliament Hill on a motorcycle until he had an accident which left him with a limp. He resigned from Trudeau's staff in 1972 to become a candidate for Parliament in Vancouver, contradicting the theory that real power had shifted from the Commons to the PMO.

Ivan Head was a law professor who came to Ottawa from Alberta to help Trudeau, when he was Justice Minister, prepare his proposal for a constitutional charter of freedoms. He later became Legislative Assistant, briefing the Prime Minister on his House of Commons duties, and special emissary to foreign governments when personal contact outside diplomatic channels was desired. His next job was speechwriter and he edited a selection of Trudeau's sayings called *Conversations with Canadians* (University of Toronto Press). When he quoted in the foreword an Australian judgment that Trudeau's speeches were "so beautifully worded they almost sound like poetry," he was rebuked for immodesty. Although retiring rather than conceited in private conversation, he exercised considerable influence and took pleasure from it.

Trudeau's French-language speechwriter was Jean LeMoyne, a long-time friend, former journalist and author of a book of essays entitled *Convergences* which won a Governor-General's award. It included an eloquent statement of the rights of women to equality with men before the cause was fashionable and was noted in the report on the Royal Commission on the Status of Women. LeMoyne was the source of some of Trudeau's better passages questioning the role of technology in human affairs.

Jim Davey, the Program Secretary, was a new type of political aide in Ottawa in a new sort of job, and he was the reason for much of the suspicion about the Trudeau staff. A slight man, with fair hair and pointed, worried face, Davey was trained as a physicist but became a programmer and systems expert. He worked on the Arrow interceptor aircraft project at Malton, near Toronto, until it was cancelled by Diefenbaker, and when the design team scattered, Davey went to Montreal and became a project manager for Chemcell Ltd., specializing in systems analysis. He had ideas about the use of management techniques in politics and tried them out in John Turner's riding, somewhat to the alarm of Turner and his more conventional campaign staff. But Davey was one of the small group of Quebec Liberals who planned Trudeau's leadership campaign and then the general election campaign. Joining the PMO, he was charged with "ensuring that the Government and the party have and maintain a comprehensive and coherent program." This broad mandate stretched in the early days to include a visit to the Hudson Institute outside New York City where Herman Kahn and other thinkers were trying to forecast the shape of the world in the year 2,000, trips to Rochdale College to look at the counter-culture life style (Davey was sympathetic and tried to round up more federal funds for the project), and experiments with business techniques for managing Trudeau's time. Davey tried to maintain an overview of the Government's program to make sure it was in tune with a changing society, and intervened when serious problems seemed to be developing.

He is now a much less mysterious figure than he was, and lives in the heart of civil service Ottawa, where his neighbors include External Affairs Minister Mitchell Sharp and Auditor General Maxwell Henderson. He jogs for health, walks briskly to work in the East Block every day, and obeys Trudeau's instructions to his staff to "keep a low profile."

Another of Trudeau's innovations which caused misgivings were the so-called Regional Desks. One of the standard criticisms of Prime Ministers had been that they were out of touch with opinion beyond Ottawa and their own region of the country. Trudeau was particularly vulnerable as a Quebecker who had never worked elsewhere in Canada, except in Ottawa, and who had few personal ties with other regions.

Regional desk officers for the West, Ontario, Quebec and the Maritimes were supposed to fill this gap by establishing a network of private contacts who would keep the PMO alert to what the people "out there" were thinking and what regional problems were on the horizon. As part of this political intelligence operation, there was to be a national panel of 150 people to report reaction to government policies. MPs, including many Liberals, were alarmed at this apparent challenge to their own responsibilities, and were not at all reassured when the Chief Desk Officer, an abrasive and broadly experienced Quebecker called Pierre Levasseur, remarked that many Members were so complacent that 90 per cent of their job could be done by business machines. Responding to concern and press criticism, Trudeau modified the Regional Desk concept — the idea of the national panel was dropped — and when Levasseur eventually left, he was replaced by Dave Thomson, a tall, smiling, tactful Albertan who specialized in Western Affairs and had worked in the Agriculture Department.

The desk officers proved to be quietly useful. They kept in touch with aides in the offices of some provincial Premiers, providing an informal link between heads of governments; visited university campuses to listen to academic and student opinions; lunched with business leaders and met labor organizers; and often represented the Prime Minister in private political talks among Liberal leaders in the regions. They were also a new channel of communication to the busy Prime Minister which could be used by enterprising MPs, and it was not long before the Liberal MPs from Ontario who had prevented the appointment of an Ontario Desk Officer for fear he would undercut them, changed their minds and asked Trudeau to give the job to Colin Kenny, former director of the Ontario Liberal Party.

A major duty of the desk officers was to plan Trudeau's trips to their regions. Instead of flying out to make a speech and returning the same day to Ottawa, Trudeau liked to make the maximum use of travelling time by filling several engagements.

The desk officer would know who wanted and deserved

to see the Prime Minister, what issues he should hear about firsthand, how he could get the best public exposure. He also knew the limits of the Prime Minister's endurance and such operating rules as Trudeau's need to eat supper alone to gather his resources for the evening's engagements.

It was Thomson who conceived the Great Plains Project, a panel of 32 businessmen, scientists and Arctic experts to feed Trudeau ideas on Western and Northern development, such as an all-weather highway to the Arctic, a new port on Hudson's Bay and giant aircraft to bring northern oil and other resources to markets in the south. Thomson thereby fulfilled the duty of the Regional Deskman to give Trudeau contact with information and ideas from outside the bureaucracy.

Although patronage is no longer a factor in filling most public service jobs, the Prime Minister and the Cabinet still make about 400 appointments a year to boards, commissions, Crown Corporations, tribunals and other public bodies. Some can be very important, such as a new President for the CBC or a boss for Air Canada. The Prime Minister also makes appointments to the Senate and recommends a Governor-General to the Queen. This was a neglected area of administration for years, and appointments were often made in a hurry without adequate study of available candidates. Again perhaps because Trudeau had so little personal experience on which to draw and no network of political friends, he appointed an officer to specialize in appointments. Francis Fox, a lawyer who had previously worked for Ron Basford when he was Minister of Consumer and Corporate Affairs, was chosen for the PMO position and later acquired an assistant. They searched out possible candidates for public appointment, checked on names submitted by ministers, talked to groups who might have an interest in appointments, and advised Trudeau.

By far the largest division in the PMO, with 44 staff early in 1972, was the Correspondence Section, headed by Henry Lawless, a precise and stylish young man who was formerly director of the Canadian Federation of Mayors and Municipalities. When Pearson was Prime Minister, the mail averaged 185 letters, cards and wires a day; when Trudeau took over, it jumped as high as 550 a day but then settled back slowly to an average of 275 in the early months of 1972. But while most Prime Ministers have been content simply to acknowledge receipt of routine letters, Trudeau insisted on effective answers, and this required a sophisticated organization. Mail from Ministers, MPs, Provincial Premiers and other VIPs was directed from the Correspondence Section straight to Trudeau's desk. Other letters which were of particular interest — they might be wise, witty or warmly appealing — went to Trudeau with a draft answer which he could accept and sign or reject in favor of his own reply.

The routine mail was handled by the staff without reference to Trudeau. A research unit provided standard answers to standard questions and complaints and these were coded onto special cards. By selecting a combination of cards appropriate to the points raised in a letter, an official could compose an individualized reply. The cards activated an electric typewriter which produced the letter, leaving space for name and address and any additional information. While there were complaints about delays in getting answers from the PMO — it could take six weeks or more — the letters were usually persuasive when they arrived, and provided an important channel through which Trudeau communicated with the public.

The incoming mail, of course, could also be a sensitive barometer of public opinion, and Lawless and his staff provided a careful computer-style analysis to Trudeau every month.

It ran to seven large sheets of statistics and a written summary which translated them into human terms. Thus the summary for February 1971, for example, began by noting: "The mood of our correspondents seems to have been affected by the weather conditions of a winter which never ends . . . those who are not buried under the snow are dull, greyish, uniform (ugh!) ."

But the statistics were still interesting. There were 10,909 letters, telegrams and write-in campaign coupons that month. They dealt with a variety of current topics, from flooding of the Skagit Valley in British Columbia (11 critical letters) to concern for the Jews in the Soviet Union (94 rated as anxious) to unemployment (7 critical; 11 anxious; 1 favorable) to proposals to increase MPs' pay (58 critical, 1 anxious, 1 favorable). Scores of other subjects drew correspondence, and were classified by tone and compared with previous months to indicate trends in public concern.

But the big subject in February 1971 was abortion. Of 1,961 communications received on the subject, 1,914 criticized the proposition that the law should be eased, and only 13 were favorable to abortion on demand. A few were anxious, asked for information or offered ideas. The report to Trudeau pointed out that a considerable number of the letters opposing easier abortion came from French-speaking areas of Ontario, Manitoba, Alberta, and New Brunswick as well as from Quebec.

The new and strengthened PMO clearly helped Trudeau to do a better job as head of Government. Equally clearly, it increased his political influence outside Parliament.

Two months after his election, Trudeau appointed a Task Force on Information to recommend ways in which Ottawa could better communicate with the public. His objectives were to ensure that the federal Government would have a strong presence in the minds of all Canadians, particularly in Quebec, and to provide the basic facts about government programs without which participation would be impossible. The Task Force documented the appalling incompetence and waste in the existing information sections of many federal departments and proposed the creation of a new coordinating agency to be called Information Canada. There were at once fears that this agency would be a Ministry of Propaganda, managing government news, manipulating the media and brainwashing the people. But when Trudeau set up the agency, the real difficulty turned out to be quite different. It was given no authority beyond the power of persuasion over existing information sections, and the first Director, Jean-Louis Gagnon, was suspected variously of being a Communist, a time-serving Liberal and a poor administrator. The Deputy Director was Bob Phillips, formerly a PCO mandarin and an enthusiastic Canadian nationalist who had ideas about developing the agency as a continuation of the 1967 Centennial Commission which had succeeded briefly in making Canadians feel good about their country. Faced with the hostility of established federal information officers and the suspicion of politicians and the press, with little authority and confused direction, Information Canada went nowhere in particular.

Parties and the People

The political party organizations which had been accepted as the mainspring of the democratic process were sharply challenged during the sceptical Sixties, in the United States as well as in Canada. They were widely criticized as undemocratic and probably corrupt machines through which the rich and powerful manipulated the poor and the weak at election time.

An army of young people marched on Chicago in 1968 to protest that the Democratic Party convention to choose a presidential candidate was rigged and rotten. The demonstrations developed into confrontations with the police and compelled many Americans to recognize that all was far from well with the state of their democracy.

In Canada, much of the same idealism and energy flowed into Trudeau's organization. Thousands of those who wore his orange-and-white colors and helped him to win first the Liberal leadership and then the general election, had never before been involved in politics. It was almost a children's crusade for a new style of politics — the politics of mass participation — and the innocent expectations were so high that let-down was inevitable. The problem was how to prevent the let-down developing into bitter disillusion, and the answer was important not only to the survival of Trudeau and the Liberals, but to the welfare of the whole political process.

For while the party system had its defects and Parliament could not meet the demand for direct participation.

the alternatives were not attractive. The politics of protest and confrontation led to violence. Direct leadership by a charismatic figure in TV communion with the masses would be simply another form of dictatorship. In time, Trudeau might reform Parliament to make it more open to public pressure and participation and improve communication between the executive and the public, but the main vehicles for popular involvement would have to continue to be the parties.

The Conservative Party had gone through an extraordinary upheaval and renewal under the presidency of Dalton Camp. A blend of adman, image-maker, backroom-organizer, philosopher and idealist, Camp had led the Tory rank and file to remove Diefenbaker from the leadership and elect Robert Stanfield in his place at an exciting public convention in Toronto in 1967.

He had asserted the power of the party members over the leader which meant that the party could be a vehicle for the popular will. But this was only a beginning in making the party a viable political instrument, as one of the most experienced Tory organizers was saying urgently in a penetrating analysis of modern politics. Flora MacDonald, an ebullient redhead, had worked at Conservative Party headquarters, won election as National Secretary and become a key figure in Stanfield's leadership campaign. She also worked in the political science department at Queen's University in Kingston where she was in daily contact with student opinion and an active member of the Social Planning Council. "Many already feel that there is so little genuine radicalism inside the party system that anyone wishing to effect change must look elsewhere," she warned a Conservative Party policy conference in 1969.

"Unless parties adapt to meet the needs of changing society — unless party associations become more actively involved in the life of the community — unless we recognize that the time is ripe for the role of the constituency associations to evolve into something new and uniquely different — then the day may not be far off when the community will question the privilege of small groups bearing party labels to foist their choice of candidates on the electorate." Her fear was that "by their lack of action within the community, political parties will become increasingly irrelevant" — replaced by "pressure groups, protest movements, student activists, social planning councils as agents of social change."

The New Democratic Party had been formed only in 1961, a new social-democratic version of the old socialist Cooperative Commonwealth Federation, and aimed, like the other parties, at electing MPs and winning Cabinet power. But already the radicals and activists — eying the New Left in the United States — were urging extra-parliamentary political action.

Reluctant to make the policy compromises which electoral success seemed to demand, they wanted the party to create a popular socialist consciousness by radicalizing the trade unions and working through community organizations, such as groups of tenants and consumers, to bring about confrontation with the Establishment of employers, landlords and business corporations. This militant approach to politics gave rise in 1969 to the Waffle Group within the NDP.

The development of the Liberal Party had been succinctly described by George Grant, the brilliant but gloomy philosopher of Canadian nationalism: "Liberalism was, in its origin, criticism of the old Establishment order. Today it is the voice of the Establishment." Success had spoiled the Liberal Party; too long in office, it had become the vehicle of those who held power rather than of those grabbing for power to change the world. The shock of election defeat in 1957 and massacre in 1958 shook this complacency and Pearson began to rebuild and democratize the party.

But when Trudeau took over in 1968, it was still the party of the upper middle class. About 80 per cent of the adult delegates to the convention which chose him as party leader were earning over $10,000 a year; 53 per cent were professionals, owners or executives and only 2 per cent were classed as skilled laborers. In the bitter words of John Varley, a leader of the Student Liberal Federation, "the party has operated through most of its existence as a weak, off-and-on apparatus, stunted in its growth, cadre in style and dominated by Cabinet and Leader."

The middle-class character of the Liberal Party did not mean that it would necessarily oppose reform or even radical change in society. Most revolutions are led by the middle class. But it still sounded faintly absurd when Trudeau went to a dinner meeting of his prosperous, black-tied supporters in Montreal in 1969 and told them: "Our party must become the party of the people, because this is what is now being said — and many young people say it — the government is not in Quebec, not in Ottawa, but out in the street; the choice between trouble or order is being decided out in the street; the orientation to be given our society is going to be decided in the street. That means, therefore, that we too must take to the streets . . . We must be there, as Liberals, amongst the poor. We must be there in the slums of our large cities. We must be there wherever people are suffering, where there is unemployment and poverty."

The principal responsibility for transforming the Liberal Party from an instrument for preserving the privileges of the rich into a vehicle for reform and participation fell on Richard Stanbury, an unlikely revolutionary. A Toronto lawyer, he had been a party bagman and head of the national policy committee.

His brother, Robert, became a member of Trudeau's Cabinet, and by one of those cosy coincidences which a party in power can arrange, Richard was appointed to the Senate in February 1968 and began to draw a public salary just before he took over as party president in April. But Stanbury, like Tory president Dalton Camp, was a mixture of realist and idealist, and his analysis of the place of parties in modern politics was even tougher than Flora Macdonald's: "The political party has been seen by the public as a sinister machine," he wrote in a Liberal discussion paper in 1969. "Governments in the past have tended to treat it as a useful tool at election time and as a nuisance between elections. The elite have regarded it as being beneath contempt." Stanbury's prescription for the survival of the Liberal Party was that it would have to be open and democratic; representative of the whole community; skilled in the techniques of involvement; a channel for two-way communication between the people and the government; and made up of Liberals whose motive was public service and not patronage.

But the man nominated by Trudeau to be National Organizer of this new-look Liberal Party was an Establishment insider. Torrance Wylie had worked for Pearson in the Prime Minister's Office, become executive assistant to the president of Molson's Breweries in Montreal, and served during the 1968 election as liaison between Trudeau and his riding campaign committee in Mount Royal. Wylie obviously had more connections with the PMO than with the Liberal rank and file, but he had studied the party system while at Carleton University and had ideas on how to build a modern mass organization.

The principal program adopted by the new leaders for broadening the base of the Liberal Party was a three-phase exercise in policy-making, the most elaborate experiment in participatory democracy ever attempted in Canada.

Phase One was a giant teach-in, in November 1969, on the social problems likely to dominate the Seventies. Distinguished academics and experts of every variety, including representatives from 100 leading national organizations, were invited to brief Liberal leaders from provincial and constituency parties. There were seminars, small discussion groups, a book of 62 background papers placed beside the bed of every Liberal delegate, and a philosophical speech by Trudeau advising the party to serve as a radar for government and guide it to objectives 10 years ahead. The whole affair was typically Liberal in that it was highly organized and held in a luxury hotel in Harrison Hot Springs, a British Columbia resort where the fortunate delegates, who paid $100 a day including charter air fare, were able to relax in hot pools between policy debates. A student radical from Simon Fraser University was brought in to pour the scorn of the New Left on the heads of the guilty Liberals, and representatives of a poor people's community development organization were flown all the way from Montreal to explain that their first operating rule was to avoid party politicians.

The teach-in produced no sparkling new ideas and was viewed with amused contempt by the old school of Liberal organizers who described themselves as hardware men not much interested in policy software. Nevertheless, the Liberal delegates went away briefed, backgrounded, stimulated and stuffed to the ears with facts and opinions.

These delegates were now supposed to organize policy discussions in their own ridings, and this was to be Phase Two. The idea was to draw the public and not just Liberal Party members into this process. The how-to-do-it manual suggested inviting representatives of such organisations as union locals, parent-teacher associations and tenants' groups to discuss public policy and offer ideas. Party headquarters in Ottawa printed 300,000 copies of pamphlets describing basic issues and asking the reader to make his opinion known. Resolutions from these local policy debates were then to go to Phase Three, a giant national policy conference in 1970.

Unfortunately, Phase Two hardly got off the ground. Stanbury sadly confessed later that only about 25 local Liberal parties succeeded in involving the public; perhaps another 50 made a worthwhile effort; and almost 200 were content to keep policy decisions within their own narrow ranks. So when the 2,400 delegates and observers arrived in Ottawa in November 1970 for Phase Three, it was still essentially the same Liberal Party — bigger, better organized but inescapably middle class and unrepresentative of the poor and powerless.

There were new participatory techniques and symbols of democracy. Trudeau's leadership was approved by secret ballot and he went through the motions of accounting for his actions by answering unrehearsed questions from the floor, a situation which any moderately skillful politician can turn to his own advantage. Instead of holding up their hands to vote Yes or No on complicated issues, delegates marked a written ballot on which they could register a degree of support or opposition for each of scores of policy propositions. The participatory procedures were so elaborate, in fact, that they tended to defuse debate and blur differences. But where consensus did emerge, it showed that the party was a long way ahead of the Government in enthusiasm for social and economic change. The delegates, for example, clearly wanted a guaranteed income program, easier laws on marijuana, the removal of abortion from the Criminal Code, and firm progress toward greater Canadian control of the economy.

Trudeau never implemented any of these party policies, which raised the question of what participation was all about. "To participate doesn't mean that you're going to make the decision," he explained in a 1971 interview. "In our form of government, the parliamentary system, people are elected to represent the constituencies and there's an executive which is set up to make the decisions and if you don't want to change the parliamentary system, it will always be that way."

To Trudeau, participation by Liberal delegates meant being heard before the Cabinet and Parliament decided on policy. It went no further than the right to express an argument or an opinion and to demand an explanation if it was not accepted by the Government. After the Liberal conference, Trudeau met party officials and agreed to a system under which ministers bringing proposals to Cabinet had to show in the documentation if they were consistent with party policy, and if not, why not. While this gave some representation in Cabinet to decisions by the Liberal rank and file, it obviously was not influential in major policy areas.

All the delegates who attended the 1970 conference were constituted a continuing national policy council when they went home and occasionally consulted by mail. Asked in 1971 for their opinion on the best way to control inflation, they voted for controls — another piece of advice rejected by the Cabinet.

Trudeau and Stanbury also set up so-called Troikas in some provinces to act as links between party and Government. They usually consisted of the federal minister with political responsibility for the province, the president of the provincial party and an MP. Trudeau was often directly represented by his regional desk officer. They were supposed to be a channel through which the party leaders could raise issues with the Cabinet and the parliamentary caucus, and the Cabinet and the MPs could explain themselves to the party.

But they were also the pipeline through which Ottawa dispensed what little patronage remained under its control, and through which favor-seekers made their approach to Government.

Yet another new structure was the Political Cabinet. The agenda for its meetings was drawn up by Liberal Party officials and the Prime Minister's political staff, instead of by civil servants, and they provided an opportunity about once every two months for the party to lay its concerns before Trudeau and all his ministers.

A group of MPs, Liberal officials and others, appointed to study The Politics of Participation reported in 1970: "The elitist concept of democratic government envisages decision-making in an atmosphere of quietude and efficiency. The fact is, however, that this style of government, whatever its virtues, has been rendered an anachronism by a revolution in the minds of men — a revolution touching fundamental human values concerned with the dignity, status, personality, significance and power of individuals. Very simply, people want more say."

The report concluded: "We do not agree that traditionally limited participation is any longer possible in the world of the Seventies. This is the age of advanced communication, of increased individual confidence, of dissent, alienation and confrontation. Institutions are under attack and the demand for change is irresistible. People want more say and they must be heard. When they are not heard, they circumvent the traditional vehicles or cause them to crumble. Our task as Liberals is not simply to encourage participation — this would be irresponsible and unwise. We must carry our task through to its logical conclusion — we must imbue in ourselves and our fellow citizens the spirit of participation and most important of all, create the necessary tools so that participation will become real, relevant and the basis of peaceful social change."

It was a noble goal and Trudeau and the Liberal Party made some stumbling progress toward it. They would have been more credible, however, if they had taken effective action to control election spending and political party financing. Although Trudeau had promised to give such reforms a high priority, he allowed matters to drift until 1972. Then he rushed in a poorly prepared bill, to place ceilings on expenditures on political advertising and to reimburse a fraction of campaign costs to candidates. The legislation was not only inadequate, but too late to be implemented in 1972, which was expected to be an election year. So it remained much easier for the rich than the poor to participate in politics.

Public Personality, Private Man

Trudeau received more than 3,000 invitations a year to attend functions in all parts of Canada and was able to travel more widely and talk to more people than any of his predecessors. He was the first Prime Minister to be at home in the jet age, and he made full use of the Government's fleet of fast executive aircraft and helicopters.

His office added up his engagements between July 1970 and August 1971 and found he had spent 37 days in Western Canada, 13 in the Maritimes, 11 in Ontario outside Ottawa and 10 in Quebec. He also spent 36 days out of Canada on official visits.

Most of the travelling was done when Parliament was not sitting and his diary of engagements during the summer of 1971 gives an idea of his activity: June 8-9, Toronto and Hamilton, Ontario; June 13-16, Victoria, B.C.; June 22-23, Toronto, Bronte, Brampton, Sheridan Park, Aurora, Toronto, Ontario; June 30-July 2, Victoria, Kelowna, Cranbrook, Kimberley, Vancouver, B.C.; July 9-12, Medicine Hat, Lethbridge, Standoff, Watertown Lakes National Park, Blaimore, Calgary, Alberta; July 16, Smith's Fall, Ontario; July 30 - August 8, Yarmouth, Lunenberg, Cheticamp, Ste. Anne's, Louisbourg, St. Pierre, Grand Bank, Marystown, Swift Current, St. John's, St. Anthony, Corner Brook, Port aux Basques, Charlottetown, Dalvay National Park, touching all the Atlantic provinces; September 10-11, Toronto, Pickering, Oshawa, Peterborough, Port Hope, Belleville, Picton, Cornwall, Ontario; September. 17, St. Lin and Ste Adèle, Quebec.

In addition to cities and towns, Trudeau visited the remote outports of Newfoundland, canoed in the interior of British Columbia, toured the high Arctic and led his Cabinet on a safari to the Prairies. It was easy to make fun of his trips as enviable holidays or kiss-and-touch political expeditions designed to expose the glamorous Prime Minister to his fans. But they were also serious exercises in communication between the people and their Government.

Trudeau was a poor speechmaker and at his best in discussion, so his staff tried to arrange question-and-answer sessions wherever possible. They put him on hotline radio and TV shows, before local press conferences, in sessions with university and high school students and in town hall meetings where he listened to briefs presented by local organizations and then replied. These events were often teach-ins rather than conventional political meetings and when the questioning was tough or hostile an atmosphere of drama, almost of political theatre, developed.

These travels and forums made it possible for thousands of Canadians to attend discussions with their Prime Minister and this was a significant development in participatory democracy. But spontaneity did not always work to Trudeau's advantage and he was capable of confusing as well as clarifying issues. He sometimes replied to one question with another, a technique which was supposed to stimulate thought but could be maddening to someone who wanted a straight answer, even if it was "No". He prided himself on being honest but it sometimes amounted to being callous with people who knew there were no real answers to their problems and were looking to the Prime Minister for a little hope and encouragement. Despite his skill with the English language, he occasionally used a phrase in the wrong context, to everybody's confusion.

While in Ottawa, Trudeau received many official groups carrying briefs and requests and also entertained privately a surprising variety of people. He had quiet get-togethers at 24 Sussex Drive and at his official summer home on Harrington Lake, in the Gatineau Hills across the Ottawa River, with student leaders, newspaper publishers and editors, businessmen, visiting foreign correspondents, provincial politicians who slipped in and out of town for an informal talk, and every liberal MP, among many others. When Beatle John Lennon and Yoko were in Ottawa in 1969, it was typical of Trudeau to find 50 minutes to talk with them. It was not primarily a publicity gimmick, as many people suspected. Trudeau saw some parallels between his own position as pop politician with a young following and that of the pop musician. Lennon at that time was emerging from the counter-culture of drugs and revolution and trying to lead his fans in a serious quest for world peace. Trudeau was trying to hold onto his popularity while changing his image from swinger to responsible head of government.

They discussed the changing youth culture and the mood of young people and joked that they wouldn't really know where they stood on the charts until Lennon made his next record and Trudeau called his next election.

Political reporters necessarily remained one of Trudeau's principal channels of communication with the public. But his habit of engaging in informal dialogues at public meetings and making provocative or exploratory comments was confusing to newsmen trying to fasten on fact and not quite sure when the Prime Minister was speculating and when he was stating official policy. This caused mutual annoyance and I once asked Trudeau if he was aware of the difficulty he was causing himself and journalists by making ill-considered and extravagant remarks which we had to report as serious statements. He replied that he was aware of the danger and had a solution: he was going to stop reading newspapers. (He didn't, of course, because his staff prepared for him a daily digest of the press, concentrating on the critical comments.)

Relations between a powerful politican and the press are seldom easy, however, and they follow a pattern which has been well described by the U.S. writer, Leo Rosten: "Newspapermen greet (a newly elected leader) with the hope that here at last is the great man incarnate. The great man's talents are sung, oversung, in the struggle for journalistic existence.

"Then 'incidents' occur, a political compromise of not

admirable hue, a political setback, attacks come from the Opposition, the newspapermen begin to see the feet of clay. They have been taken in, their faith has been outraged. How did they ever 'fall for that stuff'? . . . Other newsmen, columnists, publishers cry that the press corps has been hamstrung by phrases. The correspondents are hurt. They are irritated. And they feel guilty. The breaking of the myth begins by the very men who erected it."

So it happened with Diefenbaker and Pearson and so it was bound to happen with Trudeau. The news media did not sell Trudeau to the voters in 1968, but it is certainly true that most political reporters — myself included — admired his style, enjoyed the excitement of his campaign and contributed to his image. Trudeau responded with flattering comments about the power of the press, although he was never as "matey" as previous Prime Ministers had been. When Diefenbaker travelled out of Ottawa with a press party in attendance, it was his custom to wander through the plane or train telling his incomparable anecdotes or answering questions.

Pearson frequently invited the press corps to his hotel suite for a chat and a nightcap. Trudeau preferred to hold himself slightly aloof, valuing his privacy and moments of relaxation.

After the election, Trudeau continued for a few months Pearson's custom of inviting groups of members of the Press Gallery to 24 Sussex Drive for an evening drink or dinner and an off-the-record discussion of current issues. But in January 1969, he had a furious row with pressmen who accompanied him to London for the Conference of Commonwealth Prime Ministers. Trudeau made an exhibition of himself by lunching at a fashionable restaurant with a woman friend who was only too willing to talk to reporters about their relationship. He acknowledged that he had nobody but himself to blame for the embarrassing publicity, but it did not make him feel any better about it. And when he was told that newsmen had been harassing another of his woman friends in London, he exploded with anger and upbraided the assembled newsmen for "crummy" behavior.

If, as his staff told him, a reporter had tried to get information from the woman over the phone by giving the impression that he was an official aide to the Prime Minister, it was "crummy". But Trudeau was quite wrong to tongue-lash the entire press corps, many of whom had written nothing of his social adventures, and they came back to Ottawa seething with anger. After that, there were never quite the same cordial relations between Trudeau and the press.

Soon enough, there were the inevitable incidents, compromises and setbacks to cause the newsmen to question their judgment of 1968. They began to wonder if in fact they had foisted a fraud on the country as their critics alleged. The imposition of the War Measures Act in October 1970 turned some journalists from admirers into bitter critics. Rising unemployment offended the social conscience of many others. When the newsmen began to chip away at the myth they had helped to create, Trudeau did not help his own case by appearing sulky and often contemptuous of reporters. There were few invitations to 24 Sussex Drive, formal press conferences became a rarity and he gave more interviews to visiting foreign correspondents — usually at the request of the External Affairs Department — than to Canadians.

As the time for another election drew near, the mood on both sides began to change again. One or two of the more extreme press critics took leave of journalism to enter partisan politics against Trudeau. Other well known reporters and columnists were asked by opposition parties if they would like to be parliamentary candidates but decided that partisanship was not for them, or that they did not feel that strongly about Trudeau. And while newsmen might have soured on Trudeau, there was no new "great man incarnate" on whom to hang their hopes.

Trudeau resumed the practice of meeting groups of Gallery members for a drink and a chat, normally in the working atmosphere of his office rather than the privacy of his home. And he began to give interviews at such a rate that they became a drug on the journalistic market.

Throughout the four years, of course, Trudeau encountered newsmen a couple of times a week when Parliament was sitting, outside the Commons after Question Period. He usually gave polite answers to good questions, but occasionally showed his irritation at what he thought unfair or hostile queries by snapping at newsmen or simply turning away and running up the stairs to the sanctuary of his office.

No statistics are available, but it is probably correct to say that Trudeau was at least as accessible to the press as previous Prime Ministers, and he made far more appearances before panels of questioners on TV.

He succeeded to a remarkable extent, however, in keeping his private life private. Newsmen originally argued that Prime Ministers have only a very limited right to privacy because there is a legitimate public interest in almost everything they do: where they are at any particular moment, because even on holiday they remain head of the government; who their friends are, because a man is known by the friends he keeps; to what influences they are exposed by movies, the theatre and sports. But Trudeau would have none of this. He insisted that only his performance as Prime Minister was of concern to the public. Reporters who persisted in prying into his private affairs were discouraged by one means or another. When Trudeau entertained Barbara Streisand, the American actress, newsmen waited hopefully outside 24 Sussex Drive for an interview. The Prime Minister emerged in a track suit, chatted with the newsmen as he crossed the road to the Rideau Hall, the home of the Governor General, and then started on a brisk evening run through the park, leaving newsmen half his age panting far behind, with no story.

Discouraged by his tongue-lashing in London or persuaded that there was no way to break through the wall of privacy, most newsmen eventually gave up. This enabled Trudeau to take holidays without being closely watched by the press and to move freely in Ottawa. He showed up occasionally at private parties, lined up for the ski tow and the movies with other customers and ate in popular restaurants. Members of the public sometimes asked for his autograph which he gave politely, and he had a politician's memory for faces. Having chatted to a party of Chinese Canadians in a Chinese restaurant one night, he remembered one of the men when they met some months later at a civil service social. At weekends he often slipped away, unknown to the press, to

Montreal or to a family summer resort in the Laurentians, and he entertained friends at his official summer home without publishing guest lists.

The proof of his privacy was that not even his friend and daily adviser, Marc Lalonde, knew until the last moment that he was about to be married. That was one decision in which participation was not invited.

Trudeau made substantial improvements in the machinery of democracy. He shored up Parliament, strengthened the executive, liberalized the Liberal Party, and opened himself to persuasion by public opinion. Far more Canadians were given an opportunity to influence decisions — which was to participate in the exercise of power. But serious deficiencies remained untouched.

All the final decisions were still made in the privacy of Cabinet and the party caucus, while party discipline stifled effective debate in Parliament. As a result, the people could not see their elected representatives exercising influence at the centre of national power, and this encouraged feelings of alienation.

Those who looked to Parliament for a true expression of national opinion were usually disappointed, and as a legislature, the institution was still trapped in archaic customs which ensured that it was neither fast nor thorough, but often irrelevant. Government remained secretive and political parties financed by private interests.

TV and the jet put political leaders into direct communication with the public, calling into question the whole tradition of indirect accountability through elected representatives. For example, the Commons continued with its stylized Question Period, but the effective exchanges which the public saw and the press reported often occurred when the leaders left the chamber to face the TV cameras.

In an age of increasing education and sophistication, adversary politics which let off steam at the cost of trivializing complicated issues seemed increasingly to be of doubtful value. There was a need to re-examine the processes of democracy and to design more modern machinery, but the task was barely begun.

4

THE ECONOMY

Confusion and Crisis

When Trudeau took command in Ottawa in April 1968, the indicators which point the direction of the national economy were confused and the official advisers hesitant. Output and incomes were still climbing merrily as the longest boom in history rolled on. But prices and unemployment were rising together in a worrisome way that just was not supposed to happen, according to the theory of the well-ordered economy.

The theory, in simple terms, says that when almost everyone has a job and money to spend and the factories cannot keep up with orders, the pressure of demand sends up prices. These higher prices for labor and goods then become costs in the next round of production and push up prices again. To prevent this spiral of inflation getting out of control, government should ease the pressure of demand in the economy. This is done by raising taxes to reduce the cash which people have to spend, and by tightening the money supply and increasing interest rates to make credit less attractive. As the economy slows down, unemployment begins to rise and profits fall. Workers do not press so hard for wage increases and businessmen cut costs.

The theory goes on to explain that if unemployment rises too much or profits fall so far that businessmen cannot invest for the future, government should stimulate demand in the economy. It cuts taxes and increases spending to put more cash in the pockets of the people and increases the money supply to make easier credit available.

But the theory does not really explain what to do when prices and unemployment are rising together, as they were in the spring of 1968. Should Trudeau have damped the boom to stop prices going higher and giving another twist to the spiral of inflation? Or should he have pumped more demand into the economy to create jobs and stop the rise in unemployment?

The correct policy, or mix of policies, to follow was far from clear. The experienced Governor of the Bank of Canada, Louis Rasminsky, began his annual report in February 1968, by saying: "Canada's economic and financial situation has been characterized by a number of cross-currents which have confronted the central bank with some unusually difficult problems."

The Economic Council of Canada said helpfully in September: "To sum up, we reiterate that there are no simple policy prescriptions for price and cost stability. Consistent, forward-looking efforts, in which many decision-makers must play some part, are required across a broad policy front."

The Deputy Minister of Finance was Bob Bryce, one of the legendary mandarins of the civil service. After a brief career as a flaming radical while a student in Britain in the Thirties, he had become an apostle in North America of the revolution in economic thought inspired by John Maynard Keynes. In Ottawa, he was one of the few senior civil servants trusted by Prime Minister Diefenbaker, who made him Cabinet Secretary. Now at the Finance Department, he was reputed to carry all the secrets of state in his high-domed bald head, to have the next budget in his brief case and to work out the national accounts on the back of an envelope. But in 1968, even Bryce was confused.

In a frank and confidential paper delivered to the Institute for Economic Research at Queen's University in 1970, he traced the problem back to 1965 when "we all recognize that many of us misjudged the situation." That year, he recalled, an expansionary budget included a 10 per cent cut in personal income tax. It was designed to ensure that the economy would grow fast enough to make jobs for the postwar crop of babies who were about to start entering the labor force in dramatic numbers. (It was helpful also to the Liberals who were planning an election that year.) But as 1965 progressed, pressure built up in the booming economy, and by 1966, Bryce was recommending a budget to cool things off: "We recognized the risk of inflation and were endeavoring to moderate the rate of expansion to avoid it." For a time in 1967, the policy seemed to be working, but then inflation started to gather strength again and a special budget was introduced in the fall to raise taxes and cut government spending. Even this did not work and by the end of the year, said Bryce, the Government knew that further action would be necessary. But the Government was just in the process of changing: Pearson had announced his intention to retire and major policy initiatives would have to wait for the new Prime Minister to be chosen. Then, just as the race for the succession was getting organized in January 1968, the Canadian dollar was hit by a hurricane of speculation on world money markets.

The U.S. Government took drastic action to strengthen its own world position and the speculators judged that this meant trouble for the confused Canadian economy. The Canadian dollar looked vulnerable and they gambled that by pouring hundreds of millions of Canadian dollars onto the unsettled and nervous markets, they could edge down the fixed price and start a panic in which everyone holding Canadian currency would rush to sell it. Unable to buy all the dollars offered at the official price, the Government of Canada would be forced to devalue to a lower price. Then the speculators would buy back their millions at a rich profit.

By January 18, the dollar had slipped to its lowest world price since 1951 and the Cabinet in Ottawa was engaged in a desperate struggle to save it. As the Bank of Canada paid out reserves of gold and U.S. dollars to buy the Canadian currency flooding onto the markets so that the price would not drop further, Finance Minister Mitchell Sharp hustled to round up foreign loans and credits. Interest rates were raised to attract foreign money into Canada and the U.S. Secretary of the Treasury was persuaded to issue a reassuring statement that Canada still had free access to U.S. capital markets.

The budget which had been introduced in the fall of 1967 to strengthen the economy by damping inflation was still before the Commons, and in February, the Conservative Opposition ambushed the Government one night when few MPs were in the House and defeated the tax measures by a couple of votes. The political confusion and fear that inflation might not be tackled after all touched off a new flurry of speculation against the dollar. The Government hurried back to the Commons with revised tax measures and had to bargain with the Créditistes on the Opposition side to get them approved. There could be no question at that moment of raising the taxes even higher, whatever Bryce and the Cabinet knew about growing pressures.

The Canadian dollar rode out the hurricane, but in March the speculators turned the attack on the British pound and the U.S. dollar. As the money dealers rushed to change their paper notes into gold, the world gold markets were plunged into chaos and had to close temporarily. In Toronto, the price of gold mine shares rose to record heights. It was now Canada's turn to help the United States and Britain by freezing the gold trade and extending credit, and by mid-March the storm was over — at least for the time being.

As Minister of Justice, Trudeau had no direct responsibility for economic policy, but the crisis made a powerful impression on him. When he became Prime Minister in April, merely weeks after the international storm had passed, he was resolved to put the Canadian economy in a strong world position so that the dollar would not in future invite frightening speculative attacks.

This was probably the main factor in his decision in the confused situation of 1968 to give priority attention to rising prices rather than rising unemployment. He thought it essential to keep Canada competitive in a tough world, and he argued that if he let prices get out of hand, exports would fall and there would be heavy unemployment anyway.

But when Trudeau declared his War on Inflation and squeezed the economy through 1968 and 1969, his critics could see only that unemployment was rising, and management of the economy became the most bitterly controversial issue in current politics. Trudeau's public image changed from that of a progressive devoted to change and reform to that of a rigidly orthodox conservative callously throwing thousands of Canadians out of work.

Almost any Prime Minister taking office in the troubled times of 1968 would have taken action against inflation. There was a consensus among the experts and the general public, in Canada and the United States, that rising prices were a serious problem which had to be tackled. The tools available to Trudeau were limited. The Economic Council had already examined the idea of an incomes policy and rejected it, and the labor unions were vehemently opposed to wage controls. All that remained were the traditional Big Levers of fiscal and monetary policy — and a theory on how to use them that no longer seemed to work. The basic questions are about how well Trudeau faced up to a difficult situation and whether he used the Big Levers with sufficient skill.

The War Against Inflation

For the first few months, it seemed as if the new Government might be able to handle the problem with stern words and token measures. The interest rates which had been raised during the dollar crisis helped to restrain demand in Canada in the first half of 1968, and while Trudeau and his ministers were away on the hustings fighting the June election, the Finance Department experts were studying the outlook — and coming to a spectacularly wrong conclusion. They thought that the U.S. economy was slowing down and that this would reduce pressure in Canada. Over at the Bank of Canada, Rasminsky agreed, and so monetary policy was eased. Production picked up and unemployment began to fall.

The black cloud in the sky was still inflation. The Economic Council had defined price stability as an average increase of not more than 2 per cent a year in the Cost of Living Index. From 1959 through 1964, the index had risen less than 2 per cent a year, but in 1965 it rose 2.5 per cent; in 1966, it rose 3.7 per cent; in 1967, it dipped slightly to 3.6 per cent. But in 1968, it was climbing fast, toward 4.1 per cent for the year.

The Government had promised a White Paper on a price and wage policy and Trudeau had private talks with business and labor leaders to urge restraint. Meantime, to set an example, the Cabinet was hacking away at federal spending estimates with theatrical flourishes: the Winter Works Scheme was scrapped and plans for the Queen Elizabeth Observatory in British Columbia shelved. But the new Government was finding it much harder to control spending than it had anticipated. It could manage its own priorities fairly well, but previous Governments had locked into a variety of shared-cost programs which meant in effect that Ottawa had to pay half of whatever the provinces wanted to spend. And as the provinces had to put up only 50 cents out of every $1 they spent on these popular social security schemes, they were not encouraged to be thrifty.

But even with the axe flying in Ottawa, few people realized how serious the inflation really was in 1968, and there was great interest in what economic line would be taken by Trudeau's new Finance Minister, Edgar Benson, as he prepared his first budget. Both men were regarded as progressives, Trudeau because he had previously supported the socialist party in Quebec, and Benson because he had been identified with the left wing of the Liberal Party. After the leadership convention, when Trudeau wanted to escape the spotlight, he slipped away under an assumed name to join Benson and his wife in Florida, so they were friends as well as colleagues.

A poor boy who had worked his way through school and university, Benson became an accountant in Kingston, Ontario, by taking a correspondence course while he worked for a firm of accountants during the day and as a janitor by night. He grew into an affable, informal pear-shaped man with a collection of 100 pipes and a private wine cellar in Holland — his wife's homeland. He refused to have a phone installed in his one-bedroom Ottawa apartment on the ground that he did not want to be disturbed at night on minor matters, and if the problem were important he would certainly get the message some other way. His idea of a night out on the town when his wife came up from their home in Kingston was to go ballroom dancing at the Château Laurier Hotel. Although he could be intensely partisan in the Commons which he regarded as a knock-about comedy show, he was at heart a hard-working technocrat — an accountant fascinated by the mechanics of taxation and the techniques of administration.

His first budget in October 1968 turned out to be more restraint than reform. While promising to move toward full employment, he said: "The most urgent need now is to check the continuing increase in prices and living costs." The strategy was to balance the budget in 1969, by severely restricting spending, freezing the size of the civil service, and raising taxes on insurance companies and personal incomes.

It was a stern budget, but not enough to contain the pressures on costs and prices. For far from slowing down, the U.S. economy was accelerating as Washington tried to win the war in Vietnam and have the Great Society too. Unemployment in the United States fell to the lowest level in 15 years and prices rose rapidly. The U.S. demand for Canadian goods climbed and pushed up prices in Canada. By early 1969, there was broad agreement in the Government that further action was necessary if inflation was not to get out of hand. The fashionable phrase was "the psychology of inflation," which meant that if people expected prices to rise, they would do so, almost regardless of the underlying economic situation. For example, if trade unionists expected the cost of living to increase by 10 per cent over the life of their next contract, they would add that amount to their wage claims, which would increase costs to the employer and cause him to raise prices, bringing about the expected increase in the cost of living. Or if investors expected costs to rise and the value of the dollar to fall, they would demand a very high rate of interest on their money, which would increase costs and prices. The Government's experts advised, therefore, that it was impossible to try to live with inflation at a low level because everyone would try to protect themselves against rising costs, and that would cause costs to rise even faster. As Rasminsky said in a speech in London, England, in February 1969: "The idea that a certain rate of inflation must be accepted more or less indefinitely as a price that has to be paid for keeping unemployment at some target level assumes that large numbers of people do not know what is happening to them when prices rise persistently. But people are not so foolish. They do observe what is happening and if it keeps happening they develop an expectation of continuing inflation and adjust their behaviour accordingly . . . The most important immediate objective of economic policy in many countries, from both the external and domestic points of view, is to break the inflationary expectations that exist and to restore respect for the value of money."

In his annual report later the same month, Rasminsky reinforced the message: "It is of a crucial importance to all Canadians that the problem of inflation be dealt with successfully, that we bring an end to the excessive cost and price increases which are threatening to undermine our prospects for durable growth in the future . . . Broadly speaking, our main public policies seem to be pointed in the right direction — but we shall need a consistency of approach and a deep determination to persevere until we are certain that we have dealt effectively with the problem. The stakes are too great to warrant anything else."

In June 1969, Benson brought in his second budget and tightened his screws on the economy. He extended the anti-inflationary surtax on personal incomes, cut tariffs to reduce the price of foreign goods coming into Canada, discouraged commercial building in the cities of Ontario, Alberta and

British Columbia where pressure of demand was thought to be highest, and predicted the first surplus in years. The message should be loud and clear, he said: "We really mean business in the fight against inflation. We must not give way to the temptation of letting prices go on rising with all the injustice that will cause and the hardship it will cause to the people who have the least opportunity in our society."

Trudeau followed up in August with a TV broadcast in which he announced a virtual freeze on government spending and a sharp cut in the size of the civil service.

Moving in step with tax and spending policies, Rasminsky squeezed so tight that the rate of increase in the money supply, which had been averaging 12 per cent a year, dropped drastically to 3.5 per cent in 1969. The Bank Rate, which is a signal to the chartered banks and other lenders to adjust the interest they charge borrowers, rose from 6½ per cent to 7 per cent to 7½ per cent to 8 per cent. The rates which business and consumers had to pay for credit rose to prohibitive heights and a prime home mortgage cost 10½ per cent.

But for several years, Rasminsky had been calling for an incomes policy to supplement the blunt weapons of tax and monetary policy. He argued that sensible restraint in times of stress would reduce the need to squeeze credit and cause unemployment. Back in 1965, the Government had asked the Economic Council to look at the idea, but the Council decided that a formal incomes policy would not be effective, except under emergency conditions. But as inflation became an increasing problem, the concept was re-examined and in December 1968, a Government White Paper announced the intention to create an independent Prices and Incomes Commission to "... discover the facts, analyse the causes, processes and consequences of inflation, and to inform the public and the Government on how price stability may be achieved." A few months later, Dr. J. H. Young, an economist and Dean of Arts at the University of British Columbia, agreed to be chairman. Although economics are known as the dismal science, Young was a cheerful chap, always able to expect the best in the worst circumstances.

His mandate was basically to do research, but he soon decided to have a crack at the current problem. In August 1969, the commission began a series of meetings with labor leaders, employers and the federal and provincial governments. The unions were asked to hold wage demands to 5 per cent with a provision that if the cost of living index rose more than 2½ per cent, wages could keep pace. There were to be special provisions for the lower paid, such as hospital workers, who had to catch up. But the Canadian Labor Congress and the Confederation of National Trade Unions in Quebec were deeply suspicious and refused to co-operate. During the early years of the boom, profits had raced ahead; now labor was intent on catching up. But the commission, instead of doing research as instructed, appeared to be singling out wage claims as the cause of inflation and demanding restraint. The unions wanted prices controlled — but not wages.

By the fall of 1969, it was painfully clear that Canada was suffering the worst of several worlds. The rate of growth in the economy was slowing down. Unemployment was climbing toward 5 per cent of the labor force. But inflation was unabated — prices kept going up and up and up. Trudeau's management of the economy was coming under increasing criticism and suddenly the Economic Council added its prestigious voice to the chorus.

It was difficult to argue that the inflation in Canada was caused by excessive demand because there had been slack in the economy since 1967, said the council in its annual review, casting polite doubt on the Government's strategy of slowing the economy to ease demand pressure. On the other hand, the United States was obviously suffering from demand inflation, and "until some easing of price and cost increases takes place in the United States, Canadian policies to deal with domestic price and cost problems will be handicapped. Further fiscal and monetary restraint could conceivably result simply in higher rates of unemployment and economic slack with no more than marginal effects on current rates of increase in prices and costs." Moreover, said the council, if the United States did manage to get its economy under control in late 1969, the impact in Canada coupled with the severe squeeze already in effect might well "push the economy into a poor economic performance."

It was music to the Opposition and, indeed, to everyone who felt there had to be some better way to fight inflation than by raising unemployment, even if they were not sure what the better way was. The council seemed to imply that Canada might as well relax and wait for the United States to solve the problem. To Trudeau and the Finance Department experts trying to persuade Canadians that restraint was necessary and that inflation would be licked, the council's message was like a stab in the back and they reacted angrily.

But when the council's chairman, Dr. Arthur J. R. Smith, was invited before an excited committee of the Commons to elaborate on the implied criticism of Government policy, he modified the position. The council had not intended to say that policy should be changed immediately or that restraints should be eased, and the real problem was one of degree and timing. He explained: "It is clear that the essential need for slowing price and cost increases make it imperative that a general posture of at least moderate overall restraint be maintained."

As 1969 ended, Trudeau renewed his efforts to persuade Canadians that inflation would be beaten — to crush the psychology of inflation. "We can only get tougher, we can't get weaker," he assured a pre-Christmas press conference. "I'm afraid there are a lot of people who are bargaining that the Government can't act tough for too long because it will only get frightened if it sees unemployment go up to 6 per cent . . . But if people think we are going to lose our nerve because of that, they should think again because we're not." He repeated his familiar theme that inflation would destroy the value of the dollar, export markets and the savings of the middle class and said: "We just don't have any choice but to fight inflation, fight it fiercely."

The reference to 6 per cent unemployment became one of the political landmarks of the era. Critics took it as evidence of Trudeau's callous attitude toward unemployment. In fact, his intention was quite different. He believed that inflationary psychology was persisting despite all the tough measures because the idea had got around that democratic governments were too soft to squeeze long enough and hard enough to stop prices from rising. Businessmen and others thought that when unemployment rose too high and criticism got too loud, the Government would get frightened of unpopularity and relent, so they continued to expect rising prices and to build this into their own plans for the future. Trudeau thought it vital to restore the credibility of government. When a journalist suggested to him at a private lunch at 24 Sussex Drive that the price of such determination might be political defeat, he shrugged and said that perhaps it was his task to put the machinery in order for someone else to run. His remarks at the press conference were not a threat to raise unemployment to 6 per cent, but a warning that the figure could go that high, and higher, unless business, labor and consumers stopped acting as if continuing inflation were inevitable.

The campaign for restraint gathered force as it moved into 1970 behind a rolling barrage of conferences and communiques. Benson met the provincial Finance Ministers in Quebec City to ask for co-operation in controlling expenditures and to argue that if the rich provinces would take steps to cool their own economies, Ottawa would not have to be so severe in the use of national fiscal and monetary policies which hurt the poorer provinces, where recession rather than boom was the real problem.

John Young, at the Prices and Incomes Commission, undetered by labor's rebuff, had been working quietly with business leaders to win agreement to a program of price restraint. In February it was ready to be unveiled in public and some 300 top businessmen came to Ottawa to eat an austerity soup-and-sandwich lunch and take the pledge against inflation in an atmosphere reminiscent of a revivalist meeting. Some had taken the prudent precaution of raising prices just before promising not to do so, but the formulas worked out by the various sectors of industry in late-night sessions with the commission did have some teeth. In general, companies agreed to raise prices less than costs, which meant they would absorb some inflation by reducing profits, and they agreed that when they raised prices, they would open their books to the commission to prove that it was necessary and within the formula.

Trudeau carried the message of the conference to consumers, saying in a TV broadcast: "Be selective when you are buying goods or services. Make sure you are getting value for money . . . This is a test for Canada and Canadians which we must not, and which we will not, fail."

The following week the provincial Premiers came to Ottawa to be briefed on the dangers of inflation by Rasminsky and reminded pointedly by Trudeau: "If fighting inflation is a task for all Canadians, it is a special responsibility for governments — *all* governments. The fact that provincial and municipal governments currently account for some 58 per cent of total government expenditures means of course that this responsibility will have to be a shared one if we are to succeed."

Young asked the Premiers to be prepared to use sanctions against corporations which broke the price restraint agreement. He also urged that the provinces curb their own spending and borrowing plans, use their authority over doctors, lawyers and other professionals to discourage fee increases, and establish boards to review rent increases. The provinces were less than enthusiastic. While paying lip service to the war against inflation, they preferred to regard it as mainly a problem for the federal Government — particularly when unpopular measures were necessary.

The indefatigable Young then turned his attention back to the unions, and was again rebuffed. Unemployment was rising, bitterness increasing, the political struggle sharpening, and it was not an atmosphere to encourage co-operation and mutual confidence. Even inside the Liberal Party, the mood was despondent. The politics of optimism and happiness on which Trudeau had ridden to power were giving way to cynicism. Instead of setting a course toward a brilliant new era of government, Trudeau appeared to be turning the clock back to the greyest and most forbidding conservatism. A Just Society for the poor and disadvantaged, the attack on regional disparities and the federalists' response to Quebec's discontents were all taking second place to the iron hand on the economy. Rasminsky attempted to answer the rising storm of criticism in his annual report in February 1970: "There is not, as is sometimes alleged, one group who care about people and their employment and another group who care only about price stability. This is a false antithesis. Everyone wants to achieve increases in output, employment and standards of living that are as great as can be managed. The differences of opinion reflect, in large measure, differences in time perspective. Some concentrate their attention on the shortrun costs of anti-inflationary policies. On the other hand, those who stress as I do the importance of price stability believe that we shall have a better chance of maintaining a high rate of growth of employment in the future if care is taken to preserve the purchasing power of money. More than this, they feel as I do that there is no justification for risking the serious injury to our economy and our society which would occur if measures of restraint were insufficient and inflation were permitted to continue."

But behind the scenes, the Great Squeeze was already coming to an end. Although there were few signs that pressure on costs was declining, Trudeau and Benson and their experts knew that the tough measures taken in 1968 and 1969 were working through the economy and would bite deep in 1970. It was time to ease up, but for psychological reasons they did not want to appear to be giving up the fight against inflation. So the budget in March was something of a deception. "We must be resolute in continuing to restrain demand," said Benson and he announced his intention to impose controls on consumer credit to make it harder to buy on time-payment plans. But at the same time he eased fiscal restraints by budgeting for a smaller surplus and quietly gave the word to Rasminsky to loosen the money supply.

It looked like another tough budget, but it did not work out that way. Even before he told the Commons about the plan to introduce credit controls within a few weeks, Benson was pretty sure they would not be used, and soon the idea was scrapped. Within three months of forecasting a surplus for the year, he began to hand out spending money and revise his estimates. In June, he released $150 million to the provinces; in October, he announced another $60 million in spending; and in December, further measures including a $150 million load fund. The projected surplus had become a deficit of more than $300 million, and the policy was ". . . to impart as strong an impetus to the economy as we can without regenerating a spiral of price increases." The money supply increased by 11 per cent during the year, and the Bank Rate fell from 8 per cent to 6 per cent.

Year of Transition

Policy thus swung during 1970 from restriction to expansion, but it would be some time before the results would be felt in the economy. Meanwhile, the squeeze was at its most painful. Unemployment which had averaged 382,000 in 1968 and 383,000 in 1969, leapt to 495,000. The rate was almost 6 per cent of the labor force. The Gross National Expenditure, measuring the value of output after allowing for inflation, rose only 3.3 per cent, profits slumped and the growth of personal incomes slowed down. But pressure on prices was easing also throughout the year — although the cost of living still rose 3.3 per cent — and that was the object of the whole exercise.

There were other significant changes during 1970. Bryce, who had been seeking to retire from the demanding post of Deputy Finance Minister, was finally allowed to go. His replacement was Simon Reisman, a very different style of mandarin, younger, cockier, aggressive and even rude toward those who dared to disagree with him — including Cabinet Ministers and senior provincial civil servants. He had a tactic, according to detractors, of suddenly saying "bullshit" in the middle of a meeting and walking out, leaving the shocked survivors to wonder what flaw his superior intellect had found in their careful arguments. But obviously his reputation rested on more substantial achievements. He had, for example, organized the Industry Department when it was set up by the Pearson Government, and played a large role in negotiating the auto pact with the United States. While Bryce had run the Finance Department almost as a one-man show, Reisman set out to delegate authority and build a staff.

The Prices and Incomes Commission made its final efforts during 1970 to restrain incomes and prices. It first studied the idea of a special tax to withhold increases in incomes beyond a fixed level, but rejected it as impracticable. Chairman Young then turned back to persuasion and asked the federal and provincial Governments, in June, to use their moral leadership and economic muscle to hold pay increases to a maximum 6 per cent. Again the governments gave lip service to the idea, but took no effective action. When it became clear by fall that the provinces were not going to enforce rent restraints or limit professional incomes, there was clearly little hope of winning labor's co-operation. Young tried and failed. Understandably, business leaders refused to renew their lonely agreement with the commission, and the whole campaign to secure restraint by means short of legal controls expired with a wheeze. It had had some value. The commission reported that to its knowledge some 100 firms postponed or modified price increases during the campaign.

But Young and the commission had always lacked a certain credibility. They were constituted as an independent agency and could not speak with the full authority of the federal Government. And while Trudeau gave unqualified support to Young's campaign, it should have been the other way around: the Prime Minister should have been in the lead, with the commission giving support. As it was, the power and prestige of the Prime Minister were never fully committed to a program of voluntary restraints.

During 1970, also, Canada's exports boomed, earning a huge trade profit in foreign currencies, and high interest rates attracted foreign capital into Canada. There was a rising demand to change foreign money into Canadian dollars, and the speculators who had thought in 1968 that they could drive the value down, now gambled that it would go up, and added their demand. The Bank of Canada paid out over $1 billion in Canadian dollars at the official exchange rate, taking U.S. dollars in return which piled up in the reserves. Finally, the Government could hold the line no longer.

Trudeau, returning in May from a visit to the Far East, was met at the airport in the early hours of the morning and rushed straight to an emergency Cabinet meeting in his office at which the decision was made to remove the official price ceiling and let the value of the dollar float up to find its own level in world money markets. Communications Minister Eric Kierans, a distinguished economist and former President of the Montreal Stock Exchange, had been urging this move for some time but finding no agreement among his colleagues. At the Cabinet meeting, he asked Trudeau: "Do you remember when we last talked about this in your office?" Trudeau replied: "Yes, about six months ago." Kierans retorted: "No, it was $1.2 billion ago" — the amount of money which had been locked up in foreign reserves as the Government struggled and failed to hold the price down.

Expansion and Confusion — Again

The policy of expansion accelerated in 1971. Taxes were cut in the June budget and a large deficit forecast to signal to businessmen and consumers that the emphasis was now on economic growth. But in August came another international shock when President Richard Nixon suddenly reversed his economic strategy by imposing wage and price controls and slapping a 10 per cent surcharge on imports. The Government nervously forecast that if the surcharge lasted long it would do serious damage to Canadian trade, and although this proved to be a pessimistic view, it was unsettling to businessmen trying to plan ahead. Further, the U.S. actions had thrown money markets into confusion and it was clear that some new arrangement — probably devaluation of the U.S. dollar — would be necessary to restore stability. It was not clear what effect this would have on Canada.

Late in the year, during tough negotiations in Europe and Washington, it turned out that the United States indeed wanted Canada to pay a stiff price: revaluing of the Canadian dollar to be worth $1.05 in U.S. money, as part of an international agreement to fix new currency values. That would have raised the price of Canada's exports and reduced the price of U.S. goods, giving the United States a sharp competitive edge. But Benson refused to agree to the revaluation and there were critical hours at the Washington meeting when it seemed that Canda's stubborness might result in failure to reach international agreement. Alarmed, Rasminsky, who was on the Canadian delegation, wanted to telephone Trudeau for new instructions, but Benson held firm and at last the United States gave in. The Canadian dollar continued to float on the market, and when the United States tried to win trade concessions in direct negotiations, on the auto pact, for example, these also deadlocked, and economic relations became dangerously strained.

Even more disturbing, unemployment rose during 1971, instead of falling as the Government had confidently predicted. In October, as another depressing winter closed in, the figure for September was announced: a shocking 6.9 per cent, seasonally adjusted to show the underlying trend. Within hours, the Cabinet was assembling a package of measures which smacked of desperation: personal and corporation taxes were cut and winter-work spending programs introduced in a $1 billion dollar mixture of stimulants. As there were already signs of renewed price pressure in the economy, there was obviously a danger that Canada was off on another giddy round of inflation. Trudeau had in effect given up on his struggle to persuade the country that inflationary psychology would be smashed whatever the cost.

But he was unrepentant. When Tom Gould of CTV asked at the end of 1971 about his record, and challenged: "Would you do it again — knowing what the social cost was on the economy?", Trudeau replied: "I think I would take the same line of conduct. I rather think that other elements in the economy would realize the consequences of not co-operating with the Government's fight on inflation and would say, 'We'd better go along with it and show some restraint'; otherwise no government can be successful in keeping inflation down completely . . . having no cost to pay in terms of unemployment. So it's a choice."

In fairness, the record looked better from abroad, where other countries were having problems, than it did at home. On January 10, 1972, the Lombard column in the Financial Times of London handed out, rather casually, awards for economic management during 1971: "Best all-round performance. Canada wins the affluent group 'Oscar' for having achieved fast growth alongside an unusually low rate of inflation, simultaneously contending with the backwash of the U.S. dollar crisis in exceptionally competent fashion. Runners-up were Austria and France."

On that cheerful note, and no doubt with some relief, Benson left the Finance Department in January, to take a rest as Defense Minister. Trudeau asked John Turner to take over Finance, and made clear that while he did not think Canadians wanted a controlled economy, he had a plan ready to go into action if inflation grew worse. The trouble was that the economic indicators were again confused.

The Record

In his first budget in 1968, Benson accepted on behalf of the Trudeau Government the five broad economic and social goals set by the previous administration:

A high rate of economic growth.

Reasonable price stability.

A viable balance of international payments.

Full employment.

Equitable distribution of rising incomes.

The Economic Council, in its annual review in 1964, explored the meaning of these goals in detail and expressed them where possible in target figures. It has since warned repeatedly that the targets should be read as potentials for the future rather than probabilities for tomorrow. Obviously, also, progress within Canada depends to a great extent on conditions in other countries with which we do business, notably the United States. Nevertheless, the goals and targets are helpful in examining the economic record of the Trudeau Government.

GROWTH: Despite the War on Inflation and high **unemployment**, it is wrong to talk, as many critics do, as if there were a recession under Trudeau's management. The economy grew every year at an overall rate close to the long-term average.

As someone once said, there are lies, damn lies and statistics which can prove anything. But there is no way to avoid statistics in measuring the economy. So not counting the unreal increase in the figures caused by inflation, the Gross National Product (the value of all goods and services produced) increased by 5.8 per cent in 1968; 5.2 per cent in 1969; 2.5 per cent in 1970; and 5.5 per cent in 1971. Although, as we have seen, there was a deliberate policy of slowing the economy to ease demand, the average growth was 4.75 per cent, just below the average of about 5 per cent in the 20 years 1948-67.

However, in September 1971, the Economic Council estimated that the economy was producing at about $3 billion a year below potential. As business picked up and expanded into 1972, the rate of growth rose well above potential and some of the lost billions were being recovered.

Although Canada was having growth problems at home, it was doing better than many of its competitors abroad. The Organization for Economic Co-operation and Development (OECD) includes Canada, the United States, the major industrial countries of Western Europe and Japan, and regularly compares their performances.

It estimated the real rate of growth in Canada in the three years 1969-71 at 4.4 per cent. The rate in the United States was 1.8 per cent and in Britain 1.6 per cent. For all OECD countries, the average was 3.7 per cent. In the European Common Market, the growth averaged 5.6 per cent, but by 1971, Canada had caught up and was growing faster than the Europeans.

PRICES: Although Trudeau once bragged that he had licked inflation, his battle against rising prices was far from a complete victory. While the rate of increase in the cost of living slowed in 1971, cost pressures remained strong and some observers expected them to burst through into a new round of inflation.

The consumer price index increased by an average of 3 per cent a year in the 20 years 1948-67. In 1968, it rose 4.1 per cent; 1969, 4.5 per cent; 1970, 3.3 per cent; 1971, 2.9 per cent. But this rise and then fall as Trudeau squeezed the economy was exaggerated by the statistics. Food prices are influenced by factors such as the luck of the harvest and price wars between supermarket chains, so economists often take them out of the index to get a clearer look at the basic trends. When this was done, consumer prices for all other goods rose 4.4 per cent in 1968; 4.6 per cent in 1969; 3.8 per cent in 1970; and 3.5 per cent in 1971 — a change in the right direction, but not a dramatic one.

However measured, price increases were much higher than the target set by the Economic Council of about 2 per cent a year. But the council had warned that the target would be hard to hit in a period of strong demand in the economy, and Trudeau certainly inherited that problem.

According to the OECD, Canada was less successful than most of its competitors in holding down prices in the period 1965-68. The consumer index rose on the average by 3.8 per cent a year, compared, for example, with 3.7 per cent in Britain, 3.3 per cent in the United States and France, and 2.3 per cent in Germany and Italy. The record reversed in 1969-71, when the squeeze was applied. Consumer prices rose by 3.3 per cent a year in Canada; 3.7 per cent in Germany; 4.1 per cent in Italy; 5.3 per cent in the United States; 5.7 per cent in France; and 7.1 per cent in Britain.

In 1971, in fact, to Trudeau's pride, the rate of price increase in Canada was the lowest of all 17 OECD countries.

BALANCE OF PAYMENTS: Canada does business with other countries in a variety of ways. We are a major world trader, selling our products and buying foreign goods. Tourists come to Canada and Canadians flock abroad. We have borrowed a great deal of foreign capital to develop the country and we have to repay it with interest. Foreign corporations in Canada send profits home, and Canadian investments abroad bring profits here, and so on.

When our national earnings abroad equal the bills we have to pay, we have a balance in our payments on current account. When we make more than we have to pay, we have, in layman's terms, a profit to hold in reserve or invest for the future. But when we spend more than we earn, we have to pay the difference from the foreign money which comes into Canada on capital account. This money may come in as loans or as foreign investment to buy industry and resources.

The Economic Council has always considered that as a growing country needing to employ a rapidly increasing labor force, we shall require foreign capital for years ahead. And foreign investment can bring advantages such as new technology, access to foreign markets, better management. But to the extent that we pay our way on current account, we are less dependent on importing foreign capital.

In every year from 1953 to 1969, Canada had a deficit on current account and covered it with foreign capital. In 1970, when the squeeze slowed the economy, demand for goods from abroad fell, but export sales were high. The result was a huge trade surplus which more than paid all our bills, and left a surplus of $1 billion. When the squeeze relaxed and the economy began to grow fast in 1971, imports rose more quickly than exports. But the trade surplus was still over $2 billion — enough to pay the bills and leave us with a surplus of $227 million — only the second surplus in 20 years.

As a result of this dramatic improvement in the current account, Canadians were able to raise more capital at home and there was less need to import it from abroad. Thus the inflow of long-term capital dropped from $2.1 billion in 1969 to $750 million in 1970 to $478 million in 1971 — the lowest level since 1955.

But prosperity brings its own problems. The strength of Canada's balance of payments brought international pressure on the dollar and, as we have seen, it had to be allowed to float up in value. This raised the price of exports and reduced the price of imports, making it harder to achieve a big trade surplus. This of course is how a floating exchange rate is supposed to work to balance international payments over the years.

While Canada was strengthening its balance of payments, the United States was getting deeper and deeper into trouble, and suddenly, in August 1971, Nixon announced his New Economic Policy. One of the specific objectives was to improve the U.S. trade balance with Canada — for what is a surplus to us is a deficit to the United States. Washington demanded various trade concessions and Canada replied with a shopping list of its own complaints. Talks deadlocked until Nixon visited Ottawa in 1972 and he and Trudeau agreed to review negotiations to try to find grounds for a settlement.

UNEMPLOYMENT: The major flaw in Trudeau's economic record was unemployment. In his first year of power, 1968, the number of Canadians out of work averaged 382,000, or 4.8 per cent of the labor force — all the people who want to work. By 1971, the grim figure had grown to 552,000, or 6.4 per cent. And although the economy was expanding rapidly by late 1971 and into 1972, the numbers without jobs remained alarmingly high.

There is no doubt that much of the increase in unemployment was brought about by the deliberate squeeze on the economy, although Trudeau and his advisers argued that if they had not chosen to fight inflation, the final result would have been even worse unemployment — a might-have-been proposition which can never be satisfactorily settled. But in addition to the squeeze, there were other factors at work, some obvious and some merely suspected, which make it hard to analyze the figures.

The Economic Council originally set a target of 3 per cent unemployment and later adjusted it to the more practicable medium-term goal of 3.8 per cent — the figure usually used in the United States. The Council also pointed out that a low rate of national unemployment depended on a number of factors, including the major problem of relieving regional disparity. The caution was appropriate: Canada in fact has not enjoyed a rate of unemployment as low as 3 per cent for almost 20 years. When the Senate committee on National Finance conducted a major inquiry into the problems of achieving "Growth, Employment and Price Stability," and took evidence from leading economists from several countries, it concluded in its 1971 report that a target rate of 4 to 4.5 per cent would be a realistic objective in the foreseeable future.

In the five years 1955-59, the rate actually averaged 5.1 per cent. In 1960-64, it rose to 6 per cent. In 1965-67 it dropped to 3.8 per cent. Under Trudeau in 1968-71, it averaged 5.4 per cent. So it is clear that the problem of unemployment is more normal than abnormal, and despite Trudeau's squeeze, the percentage of the labor force without work was not out of line with Canadian experience.

Unemployment occurs when the number of jobs available increases less rapidly than the number of people entering the labor force to seek work. Government can influence the rate at which the economy expands and makes jobs. By studying population trends, it can foresee and prepare for normal increases in the labor force. But it has little control over social pressures or fashions which cause women to seek work instead of minding the home, or persuade youngsters to drop out of education and look for a job. All these factors influenced the unemployment statistics during Trudeau's management.

In the five years 1961-65, the number of jobs increased by 2.8 per cent a year and the labor force grew by 2.1 per cent. Result: falling unemployment. During the next five years, 1966-70, which included the Trudeau squeeze, the number of jobs still increased by 2.8 per cent a year, but the number of people seeking work grew by 3.2 per cent. Result: rising unemployment. In 1971, jobs increased by 2.5 per cent and the labor force by 3.1 per cent. Result: more unemployment.

As more young people and women entered the labor force, the quality of unemployment as a social problem changed. When a person of 20 living at home is without work, there may be hardship, but the situation is not as serious as when the bread-winner of a family is unemployed. Similarly, a married woman seeking a career outside her home may be be frustrated when she cannot find a job, but she is probably better off economically than the single woman who has to support herself.

The number of unemployed increased by 170,000 between 1969 and 1971, but more than 50 per cent were aged 17 to 24, and 17 per cent were married women. Only 50,000 of the total were married men.

So while unemployment remained a pressing social problem and a major political issue, there was a rising national debate about what the figures really meant and what could be done about them.

Stimulation of the economy to grow faster and make more work for the rapidly expanding labor force was the conventional answer from both the Government and its critics. But many of the people who took that view one day, could be heard the next warning about pollution, depletion of resources and the cancer of growth-for-growth's sake. The point was well made by one expert who pointed out that if jobs were the only objective, the solution would be simple: have two model changes a year in the auto industry to double the rate of obsolescence.

Some observers thought that the increase in the number of working women reflected shortage of income in homes where men were without jobs; others suggested it was a manifestation of Women's Liberation. Some said that the number of young people dropping out of university to live on welfare and show up in the unemployment figures represented a decline in the work ethic, while others argued that the youngsters really desired to work rather than waste their time in academic studies which no longer guaranteed a job.

Concern about the number of people unable to find a job in the factories was offset to some extent by worry about the alienation of educated workers condemned to mindless labor on the production line. Where the object of work had been production of wealth, it now seemed that the aim of production was to make work.

There was also the old problem of regional disparity lurking within the national employment figures. Stimulation of the economy would mainly benefit the industrial heartland of Ontario, where unemployment was hardly a problem. It would have a lesser impact in Eastern Quebec and the Atlantic provinces where the rate was well above 8 per cent.

By 1971-72, a new experimental approach to the problem of unemployment in the industrialized and increasingly automated society was emerging. Instead of trying to fit the unemployed into the few jobs available, the unemployed were being invited to create their own socially useful work. The basic idea was to redefine the nature of work and to pay for services to the community which previously would have been done on a voluntary basis, or not at all. The Opportunities for Youth program in the summer of 1971 was followed in the winter by the Local Initiatives Program, and the Government promised a similar self-help scheme for the elderly. The National Council on Welfare, urging guaranteed community work for all the unemployed who wanted it, argued in a 1972 report: "We have not yet adjusted our thinking to the notion that a job need not be unpleasant, that it need not involve the production of a commercial product. We still cling to the idea that activities such as undoing the results of pollution, providing services to senior citizens and improving the quality of neighborhood life are somehow unproductive forms of employment while putting the caps on bottles of underarm deodorant instead of letting a machine do it represents a contribution to the nation's economic growth."

As high unemployment continued into the Seventies despite rapid expansion in the economy, it seemed likely that more and more people would come to share that view.

This concept might be part of the answer also to achieving the fifth goal, equitable distribution of rising incomes, which is dealt with in the next chapter.

A JUDGMENT: It was Trudeau's misfortune to take over responsibility for the economy when it was in confusion and shock and when the pressures of inflation were already strong. He responded with policies which were not cruel or shocking or appalling, but simply conventional — well within the tradition of the past quarter-century.

Faced with the familiar problem of inflation, Trudeau battled it with the familiar weapons of fiscal and monetary restraint. It was one of the inescapable disadvantages of those weapons that they hit hardest at the powerless and the innocent on the fringes of the economy — the unorganized worker, the marginal businessman, the depressed region. But it was easier to reject restraints with high moral outrage than to suggest convincing alternatives.

To do nothing was never a realistic option. Although Canada imported some rising prices from overheated economies abroad and could do little about that, it had also generated a good deal of its own problem. In fact, the first and probably the most serious mistake of the Trudeau period was to be too complacent rather than too concerned in the second half of 1968 when monetary policy was prematurely relaxed. From then on, the expectation of continuing price increases was strong in all sections of the community, and if they had not been met by stern measures in Ottawa, they might well have escalated and become a much more serious problem.

There was no national consensus in favor of wage and price controls in 1968, 1969 or 1970 when the squeeze was at its height. Trudeau perhaps should have given more leadership to building such a consensus, but it is only fair to note that he had mixed advice. The Economic Council and the Senate study on Growth, Employment and Price Stability did not think much of the idea of an incomes policy; the Governor of the Bank of Canada and the Prices and Incomes Commission thought it would be useful, to support fiscal and monetary measures rather than to replace them.

When Trudeau turned from policies of austerity to expansion in 1970 and 1971, the economy failed to respond as fast as expected and unemployment remained high. To some extent, this may have reflected a lack of business confidence as a result of the Government's own measures: the long uncertainty over tax reform, the Competition Bill to make the law against combines more effective, the delay in producing a statement on foreign investment. But it also indicated that business and labor were more sceptical and less receptive to signals from Ottawa than they had been in less sophisticated times, and that new forms of unemployment were appearing in a less socially disciplined work force.

In short, there were no obvious or easy solutions to the problems of inflation and unemployment, and Trudeau's performance was what could have been expected from any conventional Prime Minister. The pity was that he was not able to rise above convention to produce the unorthodox solution.

But while the Government and its critics focussed on the short-run problems, potentially more serious difficulties rooted deep in the structure of the economy began to appear as Canada moved from the Sixties into the Seventies. The Science Council, the Senate's special committee on Science Policy and other analysts drew attention to the weakness of the manufacturing sector of industry. It was lagging behind in growth just when expansion was most needed to employ the growing and better educated work force. The trouble seemed to lie in an alarming backwardness in research and development in a world economy increasingly dominated by science and technology. There were differences of opinion about causes and solutions, but broad agreement that Canada was earning too much of its living by selling raw materials to more advanced economies.

The fear that Canada might sink into the slavish role of hewer of wood and drawer of water — or, rather, miner of metal and pumper of oil — was dramatized for the public when Communications Minister Eric Kierans suddenly resigned from the Cabinet in April 1971. An outstanding economist and former president of the Montreal Stock Exchange, he told Trudeau in his letter of resignation: "If Canada is to be an industrial force in the 1980s, we must be prepared now to husband our resources and to select those areas in which we can be internationally competitive and to manage and invest in the resources, physical and human, that will give us a compelling position." Outside the Cabinet, Kierans was free to challenge conventional wisdom about tax policies and industrial development in a series of sparkling speeches. As a minister he had been less than a popular success: under his management, the Post Office charged more and delivered less. But as a critic and gadfly he was brilliant and respected on all sides of the House.

While his facts might be open to question and his ideas sometimes contradictory, he stimulated political thought about the underlying problems of the economy and helped to prod the Government into starting work on a long-term strategy for industrial development.

Question period in parliament. By Macpherson, March 23, 1971,

5

THE JUST SOCIETY

The Skirmish with Poverty

The United States and Canada rediscovered poverty in the Sixties. The two richest countries in the world learnt to their dismay that despite economic growth, private affluence and huge expenditures on social security, there were still millions of people living in their midst in squalor and despair. President Lyndon Johnson declared "all-out, unconditional" war on poverty in 1964 and asked Congress to approve a massive new program to provide economic opportunities to the underprivileged. The Pearson Government declared Canada's war the following year, 1965, but the battle plan was less impressive: a Special Planning Secretariat to co-ordinate anti-poverty programs and, inevitably, a federal-provincial conference to discuss the problem.

The truth was that the Government was already over-committed to new social security schemes and out of its depth in projected expenditures. The Canada Pension Plan, the Canada Assistance Plan, the Health Resources Fund and Medicare were all in the works at the same time, and the costs would rapidly climb past $1 billion a year. The taxpayers were becoming restive and the Cabinet was struggling to get a grip on spending. Politically, it was a time for retrenchment and reassessment, rather than for radical new departures. Although Trudeau campaigned in 1968 for the Just Society, he was praised for making few expensive promises and applauded when he cried that there would be no more "free stuff" — welfare schemes which purported to provide benefits without costs. He told the provinces the federal Government would launch no more Medicares without their consent, and his priority on taking power was to get the budget under control in order to fight inflation and restore confidence in the dollar. In the drive for economy, the Special Planning Secretariat was quietly disbanded. As one wit commented, Canada had declared war on poverty, but poverty won.

The shortage of tax resources and the public mood could not, however, bury the bleak facts. In the fall of 1968, the Economic Council reported: "Poverty in Canada is real. Its numbers are not in the thousands, but the millions. There is more of it than our society can tolerate, more than our economy can afford, and far more than existing measures and efforts can cope with. Its persistence, at a time when the bulk of Canadians enjoy one of the highest standards of living in the world, is a disgrace." The Council estimated that one in every five Canadians suffered from poverty. After a three-year study, the Special Senate Committee on Poverty revised the figure upwards in 1971 to one-in-four: "Unless we act now, five million Canadians will continue to find life a bleak, bitter and never-ending struggle for survival," it concluded.

The Senators agreed with other studies that poverty could not be defined in modern society as simply a standard of living below the level of bare subsistence. As the Council put it, "To feel poverty is, among other things, to feel oneself an unwilling outsider — a virtual non-participant in the society in which one lives. The problem of poverty in developed industrial societies is increasingly viewed not as a sheer lack of essentials to sustain life, but as an insufficient access to certain goods, services and conditions of life which are available to everyone else and have come to be accepted as basic to a decent, minimum standard of living."

In short, poverty is relative. As the general standard of living rises, so does the poverty line. This means that governments cannot eliminate poverty by encouraging the national economy to expand and hoping that some of the wealth will trickle through to the poor. They have to redistribute wealth from the affluent to the poor if they are to narrow the gap. They have to ensure that as the total wealth increases, a larger proportion goes to the poor than to the non-poor, if relative poverty is to be gradually eliminated.

Massive social insurance and welfare schemes, and grand concepts such as a guaranteed income for all, are only one way in which governments can redistribute income. The tax system can ensure that the wealthy pay proportionately more than the poor for services which all share. Equalization grants can transfer resources from provinces in which most people are relatively well off to provinces in which many people are hard up. Regional expansion programs can subsidize industry to make jobs and pay wages in underdeveloped districts where the rate of unemployment is high. Special aid can be offered directly to impoverished groups in the population. Housing with rents partly paid from public funds can be provided to people with low incomes.

To obtain an overview of the Trudeau Government's record in the struggle for a Just Society, therefore, it is necessary to review a number of programs. We have already seen that the attack on regional economic disparity was a major policy priority and that Ottawa transferred increasing sums to the provinces to enable them to improve their services. Now let us look at some other programs.

The Munro Doctrine

Soon after he became Prime Minister, Trudeau asked the Deputy Minister of National Health and Welfare, Dr. Joe Willard, to re-examine existing federal social security programs: family and youth allowances, old age pensions,

Canada Assistance Plan grants to support provincial welfare schemes, and others. What had they originally been designed to do? How effective were they now? Where were the gaps in the system? Just what was Canada getting for over $3 billion a year? The Willard Report was more than a year in the making and filled three volumes. It was widely reported at the time to recommend a guaranteed income plan, but in fact it did not.

The study was an analysis of the situation, rather than a plan for action. It went to the Minister of Health and Welfare, John Munro, whom Trudeau had plucked off the backbenches at 37 to run the largest department in the Government. As an MP for Hamilton, the steel city, Munro had watched the affluent steelworkers moving out to the suburbs and a new class of people moving into the houses huddled around the mills. Among the newcomers who lined up at his constituency office were the disabled, the under-educated, the unskilled, the aged, the alienated — people with little opportunity, no security and a resentment of the welfare bureaucracy. He saw the dimensions of the new problem and he could make an eloquent speech about it: "Some years ago John Donne wrote, 'No man is an island entire of itself; every man is a piece of a continent, a part of the main.' Many years later Arthur Koestler offered a sad rebuttal, 'Every man is an island seeking to attach himself to the mainland.' The alienation to which Koestler was referring, the sense of aloneness, helplessness and impotence had, by the late 1950s, become the unhappy side of the shiny coin of modern, industrial, mass produced society. A thousand flashing neon signs shouted 'Smile' and bewildered man bravely forced a smile, seeing everyone else smile and being afraid to be so conspicuous as to be the only unsmiling face in the crowd. William Lederer wrote *A Nation of Sheep* and David Reisman wrote *The Lonely Crowd*, but the neon sign kept flashing 'Smile'. . . . But suddenly a thousand voices were saying that what we had built really wasn't the best of all possible worlds. The neon sign kept flashing its message, but instead of meek obedience, people — and particularly young people — were responding, 'I hate neon signs' . . . . I hope we will be open enough, flexible enough to admit that we have not built the perfect world and that with their help — the young people, the poor, the racial minorities, all those who haven't 'got it made' — we want to work to build a better one."

But what better world, and how? A creased, crumpled worried man, overweight and chain-smoking despite desperate efforts to stop, Munro worked fantastic hours in his penthouse office on the edge of the Ottawa River, but he was surrounded by problems and frustrations. The provinces were fighting the new Medicare plan and Quebec was demanding full control over social policy. The bills for the lavish new health and welfare plans introduced by the Pearson Government were pouring in at an alarming rate and driving up the budget just when Trudeau was demanding austerity to balance the budget. In the Cabinet committee on Social Policy, Labor Minister Bryce Mackasey was pushing his plan for a new unemployment insurance scheme. When whispers spread in late 1969 that Mackasey might quit the Government unless he got spending priority, Munro stormed into his office one evening and they had a blazing row. In the outcome, Mackasey won, and it was Munro who toyed briefly with the idea of entering Ontario politics.

The general political opinion in the Cabinet was that the taxpayers were in a resentful mood and not ready for any major new social security schemes. Munro half agreed because the opposition parties were not pushing, and when he invited some prominent journalists to dinner at the Skyline Hotel in 1970 to hint that he would welcome support for a more progressive attitude, he found that most of them shared the view that taxes were already too high.

When he produced his White Paper on Income Security for Canadians, in November 1970, it proved to be a cautious document, proposing in the main to redistribute existing spending, and adding only about $200 million in new funds. The strategy was to convert universal plans which had paid benefits to everyone into selective schemes which would support only those in need. Thus family allowances were to cut off when a family had an income of $10,000, but doubled for those in the lowest income brackets. Old age pensions were to be frozen, with supplements for those with no private income.

Munro estimated that a full guaranteed income plan would cost $800 million to $2.5 billion, depending on the level of the poverty line, on top of the $4.5 billion already being spent on income security plans by the federal and provincial Governments, which seemed out of the financial and political question. But his own plan was roughly received by the press, public opinion and the provinces. By June of 1971, he was back with an improved version which added an extra $150 million. But then it was held up by constitutional negotiations with Quebec, and it was not until spring of 1972 that Munro got his legislation before the Commons — a full four years after Trudeau had commissioned the Willard report, and still at least 12 months away from taking effect.

His Family Income Security Plan, proposed to raise allowances to $15 a month for children under 12 and to $20 a month for youngsters 12 to 17. As family income rose, allowances would taper off. For a family with an income of $5,500 a year and three children aged 7, 9 and 14, it would have meant that monthly allowances would have risen from $20 to $50 a month. Munro estimated that about 1,250,000 families would have collected the full benefit of the new scheme; 620,000 would have received some improvement; 580,000 would have stayed the same; and more than a million families in higher income brackets would have lost benefits. The overall result would have been to redistribute several hundred million dollars toward the lower end of the income scale.

It was a useful proposal, but far from revolutionary. Critics pointed out that rising living costs had already eaten into the suggested new benefits. Trudeau admitted that there was some danger that selective rather than universal plans would introduce an element of class distinction. And middle-class housewives grumbled that in losing the family allowance cheques which came addressed to them, they would lose the only bit of income which was not handed to them by their husbands.

Munro's White Paper had also proposed an improvement in old age pensions and the Government moved twice, in 1970 and again in 1972, to conciliate this politically potent group of almost 2 million voters. The basic old age pension was raised from $75 to $80, and later adjusted to keep step with the cost of living so that it reached about $83 in 1972. But the Guaranteed Income Supplement to the pension jumped from $35 to $55 to $70 for those without private income — again reflecting the selective approach to concentrate assistance on those in need. The effect was to guarantee a single person $150 a month and a couple, $285. There were also special tax allowances for the aged and, in most provinces, federal-provincial schemes to provide free medical insurance and drugs. Munro promised in 1972 a New Horizons program to provide seed money to pensioners' organizations wishing to start community development projects — an Opportunities for the Aged concept.

Munro's huge department also helped to finance the major health services operated by the provinces, and costs of medical and hospital insurance plans were escalating at an alarming 10 per cent to 15 per cent a year. His priority was to work out with the provinces a cost-control formula, and he offered a sweeping reform to (1) Repeal the federal legislation which set rigid standards for the plans, in order to give the provinces more freedom to design their own health-delivery systems; (2) Continue federal contributions toward health costs at a rate rising in step with the Gross National Product; (3) Provide a special $640 million fund over five years to encourage experiments with new methods such as community clinics and paramedical personnel. Munro hinted that when costs and budgets were under control, he would be ready to talk about denticare and drug insurance.

Aiding the Unemployed

With attention focussed closely on Trudeau during the first years of his administration, it was hard for ministers to emerge from the shadow as public and political personalities in their own right. One who did was Bryce Mackasey, the Minister of Labor and later of Manpower and Immigration. While his colleagues hired PR men to advise on image-building, Mackasey put on a topper and led the St. Patrick's Day parade through Montreal carrying a shilelagh, and he announced that he had settled a strike with the memorable communique: "Well, the old boss has done it again." Garrulous by nature, he was one of the few sources of political gossip at a time when Trudeau had ordered his ministers to be close-mouthed, and while his indiscretions sometimes caused difficulty and embarrassment, he more than made up by adding a splash of color and warmth to a Cabinet of technocrats. Trudeau obviously valued his political strengths above his weaknesses and treated him with affection, visiting him in hospital where Mackasey went from time to time when his heart rebelled against overstrain.

Behind the facade of the old-time Irish politician — the man of the people full of blarney about his years in the railway yards of Montreal and the boxing ring — Mackasey was intensely ambitious. He talked his way into the Cabinet by persuading Prime Minister Pearson that he ought to have some working-class representation from English-speaking Quebec, and then got a firm hold on Trudeau's flying coattails. Rewarded with the Labor Department, he built an impressive record as a shrewd judge of when to move in personally to settle a strike, and he pushed through Cabinet at a time of austerity one of the Government's major pieces of social legislation.

The old unemployment insurance scheme covered only workers who earned up to $7,800 a year, thereby including all the high-risk cases and excluding all the middle income groups who were most able to pay premiums and least likely to draw benefits. It also related benefits to contributions, which meant that new entries to the labor force and those who regularly suffered unemployment were entitled to the least benefits. Mackasey swept this away and brought in a new scheme with several progressive features. It broadened coverage to all employees, adding 1,200,000 people and making it possible to reduce premiums. Benefits were raised to two-thirds of regular earnings, up to a maximum of $100 a week. The length of time for which benefits could be paid was related not to contributions, but to the level of unemployment: when unemployment was high and the chances of getting work low, the pay period automatically stretched out. The new plan also paid benefits when employment was temporarily interrupted by pregnancy or sickness. Premiums paid by employees and employers financed the scheme when unemployment was low, but as soon as it topped 4 per cent, the Government began to contribute, at roughly $100 million for every 1 per cent climb in unemployment. Mackasey saw this as not only a way to carry the new plan through difficult periods, but also as a device by which the Government could pump money into the economy when it was slow and cut off the flow without difficulty as business and employment picked up. Statistics Canada reported that insurance payments were $74 million higher in April 1972 than a year earlier, "due mostly to the upward adjustment of benefit rates under the new Act."

The Tax Battle

In the heat of the 1962 election campaign, Prime Minister Diefenbaker made a bid for the support of the business community by suddenly announcing a Royal Commission on Tax Reform. It did him little political good, but it launched the country into a 10 year misadventure in social reform.

A distinguished Toronto chartered accountant, Kenneth L. Carter, was appointed to head the commission, and he recruited a research staff of 150 lawyers, accountants and economists. When the commission finished its task in 1967, it produced a 2,600 page report in six volumes which proposed not just tax reform, but tax revolution. The central principle was to be equity. Instead of different rates of tax on different sorts of income, a buck was to be a buck and taxed at the same rate, whether it was earned, inherited, taken in rent or profit, or received as a gift.

It was attractively simple and fair in theory, but the

practical implications bothered businessmen, tax lawyers and politicians. Mitchell Sharp was then the Finance Minister and announced in November 1967 that after receiving briefs and advice from interested parties, the Government would produce a White Paper offering its proposals arising from the Carter report. He was already backing away from the proposals, however, for he noted four reservations. The sweeping extent of the proposed changes made it difficult to predict the full effects. The new system would be quite different from that in the United States, with whom Canada shared a capital market. The plan might not generate enough savings for development. There was concern that it might affect regional industries, particularly mining and petroleum. Hundreds of briefs poured in. Tax lawyers and industrial lobbyists hovered anxiously around the Finance Department.

When Trudeau took over as Prime Minister, Edgar Benson became Finance Minister and inherited the task of tax reform. As an accountant in Kingston, Ontario, he had learnt a lot about loopholes in the law and he was enthusiastic to close them and to shift some of the tax burden from the low income groups, who were carrying a disproportionate share, to the rich.

The night he presented his White Paper, in a lively red and white design, to the Commons — November 7, 1969 — he set up a bar in his office and spread out the canapes for a celebration. I talked to him in a little room off his main office, in which there was a couch on which to rest in peace when pressures became too intense. But Benson was relaxed and happy that night, a whisky in one hand, the inevitable pipe in the other. "It's a very liberal document," he bragged about his policy paper. "It's all for the little man ... I'm going to get hell from the corporations, big and little. You see, I expect that and I'm not worried." The object was to remove 750,000 low-income Canadians from the income tax rolls, reduce taxes on 3 million more, and make up the revenue by higher taxes on the middle and upper income groups — including, for the first time, a sharp tax on capital gains. Although Benson had dropped many of the Carter proposals, he was advocating major changes in the methods of taxing business.

Benson presented the White Paper as a document for discussion rather than fixed policy, and he soon began to get hell from all quarters. In addition to the regular business associations and the professional lobbyists, there were special committees in Toronto, London, Vancouver and elsewhere organized to oppose the tax proposals as socialistic and a threat to small business and the middle class. The provinces joined the chorus of criticism and Ontario, in particular, claimed that when it ran the plans through its computers, the figures suggested that Benson was really trying to increase revenues under the guise of reform. The mail which had been running 20 to 1 in favor of the White Paper switched completely as the opposition campaign gathered momentum, and scare stories spread suggesting that officials would soon be tramping into everybody's home to value their possessions for capital gains tax. When a committee of the Commons began public hearings, Liberal members were swamped with protests and were soon siding with Conservative MPs to demand changes. The Senate committee holding parallel hearings was composed largely of elderly gentlemen who had done very well out of the system: between them they held some 150 company directorships and uncounted millions in assets. While it would have been quite wrong to suggest corruption, it would have been equally foolish to expect any great zeal for radical reform.

Benson's case was not helped by the fact that there were serious flaws in his proposals which weakened the credibility of the whole scheme. And when all the window dressing was stripped away, it turned out that only some $150 million of tax burden was being shifted from the low income groups anyway. That was a useful degree of reform, but it could have been achieved through the regular budget process without upsetting the entire tax system.

When Benson finally introduced his tax reform legislation in June 1971, he had accepted many of the criticisms and substantially modified his original proposals — moving even farther away from the Carter concepts. He still claimed, however, that the new system would take 1 million Canadians off the rolls and reduce taxes for another 4,700,000.

According to one calculation, the broad effect would be to reduce personal income taxes by about $300 million on incomes up to about $15,000 a year.

Parliament finally approved the legislation at the end of 1971, getting on for 10 years after Diefenbaker had first promised tax reform. The new system came into operation in 1972 with tax experts complaining that parts of it were so complex that nobody could be sure how they would work, and Benson promising to bring in many more amendments to clean up details.

He said the whole procedure had been a great exercise in participatory democracy and in some ways it was. But one of the lessons was that the political process is loaded in favor of the rich and articulate who know how to manipulate the levers of power, and that when taxes on corporate and personal incomes are involved, the levers will be used. Parliament did not really represent the poor and the voiceless. The second lesson was that the Carter Commission and then the Government tried to do too much at once. More progress could have been made more easily a step at a time.

Red Power

A year to the day after winning election on the slogan of the Just Society, the Trudeau Government produced the first of its major statements of new policy: a striking green and orange book proposing a radically different approach to the problem of Canada's quarter million Indians. The priority given to this particular issue was no accident. Trudeau had travelled in the North and seen something of the appalling conditions in which most Indians lived, and he had been made aware during the election campaign that new leaders were emerging from this depressed minority — angry men who warned that Red Power could explode with the violence of Black Power in the United States. He was advised also that the plight of the Indians was becoming an embarrassment to Canadian diplomacy. Foreign governments were telling Canada tartly to look after its own minorities before presuming to give advice on, for example, the treatment of the Ibo people in Nigeria.

Trudeau appointed two young ministers to tackle the Indian problem: Jean Chrétien to run the existing Department of Indian Affairs and Robert Andras to assist him to develop a whole new policy. It was a poor arrangement and the two ambitious men were soon at cross purposes. Chrétien had to carry final responsibility and the burden of entrenched bureaucracy, the law as it stood and the old way of doing things, while Andras was off drinking beer with Indians in sleazy hotel rooms, earning their sympathy, becoming radicalized by the process. When the conflict between the two ministers began to show in public, Andras had to be moved. But the Prime Minister's personal staff played a large role in drafting the new policy paper, and Trudeau himself spent more time on the subject than on any other single issue during his first year.

When it was published, the policy statement — delicately, it was not called a White Paper — included a candid admission that 100 years of federal administration of Indian affairs had been a disaster, and an eloquent description of the dependence to which Indians had been reduced: "To be an Indian is to lack power — the power to spend your own money and, too often, the power to change your own condition. Not always but too often, to be an Indian is to be without — without a job, a good house, or running water; without knowledge, training or technical skill and, above all, without those feelings of dignity and self-confidence that a man must have if he is to walk with his head held high. . . ."

The solution suggested was to abolish the system under which Indians were dependents of Ottawa, governed by special laws and separated from other Canadians by special school and health services. The policy proposed to repeal the Indian Act and close up the Indian Affairs department within a few years, and to turn over to the Indian bands the powers which had been exercised on their behalf by the minister. As full citizens, the Indians would draw their services from provincial governments, like everybody else, but would get special assistance from the federal Government to develop their economic resources. Eventually, each Indian would be in the position to make a practical choice between assimilating into white society or remaining on the reserve in a cultural minority which would be distinct but integrated into the Canadian mosaic.

The policy was admirable in every respect except one, and that one was fatal: it had been conceived and written by a white Government. Although there had been an elaborate attempt at consultation with the Indian people, the officials and the politicians were only beginning to understand how difficult it was to communicate across a cultural gap. The paper could not represent Indian aspirations if for no other reason than that the Indians had only begun to identify their grievances and formulate their goals. Soon the Chrétien-Trudeau policy was under fierce attack. The most articulate critic was Harold Cardinal, a 24 year old Indian leader from Alberta who had learnt political tactics in the Canadian Union of Students. With the help of a *TIME* magazine reporter, he wrote a compelling book called *The Unjust Society* (M. G. Hurtig Ltd.), in which he said: "Generations of Indians have grown up behind a buckskin curtain of indifference, ignorance and, all too often, planned bigotry. Now, at a time when our fellow Canadians consider the promise of a Just Society, once more the Indians of Canada are betrayed by a program which offers nothing better than cultural genocide."

Behind the searing phrases of the book, there was a revealing pattern of argument. Cardinal did not basically disagree with the proposals in the Government's policy paper: he simply did not trust the white man to carry them through in good faith. The same theme of mistrust ran through the Red Paper which the Alberta Indians, supported by the National Indian Brotherhood, presented to Trudeau and Chrétien in the historic Railway Committee Room on Parliament Hill in June 1970. If Cardinal and his colleagues expected to meet an arrogant white Prime Minister, they must have been surprised. After listening to their attack, Trudeau replied: ". . . We did our best to come to grips with this problem with the means and the minds and the tools and the assistance we had at our disposal. Well, now the next phase has arrived, the phase where the Indian people have looked at this and they have said, 'It's not good.' And I'm sure that we were very naive in some of the statements we made in the paper. We had perhaps the prejudices of small *l* liberals, and white men at that, who thought that equality meant the same law for everybody, and that's why as a result of this we said, 'Well, let's abolish the Indian Act and make Indians citizens of Canada like everyone else. And let's let Indians dispose of their lands just like every other Canadian. And let's make sure that Indians can get their rights, education, health and so on, from the governments like every other Canadian.' But we have learnt in the process that perhaps we were a bit too theoretical, we were a bit too abstract, we were not, as Mr. Cardinal suggests, perhaps pragmatic enough or understanding enough. . . . We will be meeting again and we will be furthering the dialogue, and let me just say, we're in no hurry if you're not. You know, a hundred years has been a long time and if you don't want an answer in another year, we'll take two, three, five, or ten or twenty — the time you people decide to come to grips with this problem. And we won't force a solution on you, because we are not looking for any particular solution."

Trudeau in effect shelved the Indian policy, and this was interpreted at the time as a defeat. But what it really proved was that the Indians were no longer powerless, no longer helpless dependents. They could come to Ottawa, confront the Prime Minister and win.

While the Indian provincial brotherhoods went off to prepare their position papers — and some were still not completed by 1972 — Chrétien developed new policies designed to assist them to gain experience and confidence. He reported to the Commons in November 1971 that spending on Indian programs doubled from $122 million in 1967-68 to $256 million in 1971-72. Federal contributions to Indian organizations, to pay office staff and other expenses, totalled $2.7 million in 1971. Indian bands and other local groups took over from Ottawa the management of $30 million a year of community development programs. The number of

Indians employed by the Indian Affairs department rose from 770 to 1,700.

Cardinal had made clear to Ottawa the vast importance which Indians placed on their treaty rights. While the Government had tended to regard them as out-dated and often obscure arrangements which could do little to solve real problems in the changed circumstances of the times, the Indians seemed to hold on to them as almost the last shred of dignity — the evidence that a trusting people had been cheated out of their birthright by the white men. Nothing could finally be settled until the treaty rights had been met. A major problem was that many Indians had been displaced from their lands without receiving a treaty in exchange. They had only aboriginal rights, which could mean nothing or that they still owned everything which stood on their historic lands, depending on legal and moral interpretations. The Government appointed a Claims Commissioner to help the Indians research treaty rights and formulate claims, and provided $500,000 to the National Indian Brotherhood in 1971 to conduct its own treaty research, but Trudeau would hear nothing of unwritten aboriginal rights. He explained to a questioner in Toronto in 1971: "We said, as far as aboriginal rights are concerned, we can't undo the past and we can't wish that our ancestors had not perhaps slaughtered Indians and in some cases been slaughtered by them, and had not pushed you out without signing the proper kind of treaties and so on. We're sorry it happened, but some of us are also sorry about the Plains of Abraham but we don't ask for compensation about that — and I don't say this in a frivolous sense. You know, if we were to try in any government, try to undo the areas of the past and buy back the past, we wouldn't have a nation, we wouldn't have a country." He added that a test case was before the courts and commented: "It may be that some court will decide that the aboriginal right has some kind of legal value, and if it has it will cost all of us one hell of a lot of money to buy this country back from the Indian at the price it's going today — and that's a good sign."

The flaw in the argument seemed to be that while the

concept of aboriginal rights might undermine the concept of nation and country, the Indians had never been encouraged to feel part of the Canadian nation and partners in the country. And while it would certainly cost vast sums to meet Indians claims, the money would probably have to be spent anyway to repair the neglect of the past and bring Indians to some sort of parity with other Canadians. The Senate Committee on Poverty reported in 1971 that Indians have a life expectancy of 36 years, compared with 62 for Canadians generally, and said: "The conditions under which they live — poor housing, sanitation, educational and health services — are worse than even the worst in the larger society. . . . their plight is a blot on Canada's record and a cause for shame for all Canadians."

Presenting his 1972-73 programs to the Commons committee on Indians Affairs, Chrétien said: "Over the last four years this Government has made a beginning in developing programs and policies which offer hope for a better way of life for the Indian people. It is only a beginning. What we have done is to start the process by which a better way of life can be found. . . . Only those solutions which involve Indians in basic decisions will have any chance of acceptance and long-term success."

It was a modest claim by a minister who survived four tough years in a department which had previously had eight ministers in eight years. And the more success Chrétien had in assisting Indians to organize and articulate their problems, the more abuse he received. He was able to live with it partly because he knew what it felt like to be in a minority. When he was first elected to Parliament in 1963 he spoke no English and almost quit in despair. Today he still likes to call himself "a damn pea-souper."

Housing and the Urban Crisis

Although Canadians have become accustomed to complaining about "the housing crisis," the truth is that the majority have better homes than ever before and the nation as a whole is probably the best-housed in the world. A research monograph prepared for the federal Housing Minister as part of an overall study of urban problems, and published in 1971, put the issue in perspective.

The nation had more basic housing facilities than ever before, and the construction industry was keeping up with the target set by the Economic Council. Incomes were abreast or ahead of housing prices, and only about 4 per cent of families were sharing accommodation.

But: "To the extent that there is likely a group of low-income families living or previously living in soon to be demolished or previously demolished core dwellings who cannot or will not be able to find satisfactory alternative accommodations, there is a housing problem — or more properly an income or poverty problem.

"To the extent that our transportation, servicing, zoning, taxing and building code policies remain unmodified, unenlightened, or non-existent, we will most certainly have a future housing crisis. We are not in such a crisis yet, however, and rational and concerted policy can prevent it."

The housing problem, in short, was partly one of poverty and partly an element in the larger and more complex urban crisis.

The Economic Council measured the poverty problem in its 1967 report when it said that about 1 million Canadians were living in sub-standard housing. The Senate report on poverty described the sour facts behind the cold statistic by printing a letter from a Toronto woman:

"We have moved six times in two years, constantly running from cockroaches and landlords with greedy hands. If I complained we got our notice. No one wanted four girls. . . . We nearly froze in one apartment and had to move in December. I took this place because it had a thermostat. We are nice and warm now. We are again on the third floor. The plaster is falling from the ceilings and walls. It needs painting badly. The toilet doesn't work properly. There is one plug in the middle room and we have to use about 200 feet of extension cord to all the rooms and trip over it constantly. The light in the bathroom doesn't work, so we have to use the extension through two windows to get around. The place is overrun with cockroaches. The landlord promised to redecorate before Christmas but hasn't touched it except to put in a sink."

The urban crisis was much more difficult to measure and describe in the Sixties. Everybody knew that the cities — Toronto, Montreal, Vancouver — were expanding at a furious rate, but was that good or bad? It promised jobs, wealth, sophistication — and status among the great metropolises of the world with New York, London, Tokyo. But it also meant suburban sprawl, traffic congestion, conformity, commuting, expressways, pollution, high-rise living, and the ruthless removal of the past to make way for redevelopment. Even the experts did not understand the dynamics of the urban explosion, and it was the end of the decade before the public really began to question the quality of urban life and to grope for some way to limit growth.

The man who set out to tackle the twin problems of housing and urban affairs for the Trudeau Government was Paul Hellyer. He had won election to the Commons in 1949 when he was only 25 and was a Cabinet Minister at 32. Out of power for a few years, he made a fortune in suburban housing in Toronto, showing more imagination and integrity than most developers, and then marched back into office with the Pearson Government in 1963. Assigned to the Defense Department, he decided that one unified force would make more military and management sense than three, and overcame the enormous influence of tradition to put his rationalization plan into effect.

The secret of Hellyer's successes was that he brought to public life the zeal of private religious conviction. He could see a problem in narrow focus and attack it with righteous energy and a sense of duty which left little room for doubt or hesitation. A fervent free-enterpriser in his own eyes, he nevertheless seemed offended by the outward chaos of the capitalist system and developed ideas about how the State could take charge and restore order and competition by controlling leading wages and prices. Concerned for the welfare of the little man, he was anxious personally to organize a massive housing drive. To obtain the power to carry through his ideas, he prepared to become Prime Minister, and was ready to launch his campaign as soon as Pearson announced his retirement. The campaign machine moved with power and precision, but suddenly, infuriatingly, Trudeau stepped into the race. Before Hellyer's disbelieving eyes, this recent convert captured the Liberal Party — took it clean away from Hellyer and the other legitimate heirs. Hellyer might have quit right after the leadership convention, like Bob Winters whom he finally supported for the leadership against Trudeau. He was half inclined to retire to private life, to give more time to his wife Ellen, who detested the limelight, and his children, to study, write and enjoy some of the pleasures of the theatre and the restaurant which a Puritan upbringing had previously denied him. But Trudeau moved fast to keep this capable, powerful man in his Cabinet, and perhaps Hellyer did not want to seem a bad sport by resigning at the moment of defeat. He agreed to become Trudeau's Deputy Prime Minister and to head a Task Force on Housing and Urban Affairs.

In the fall of 1968, he drove his task force across Canada with his customary energy and enthusiasm, striding through slum areas to talk to the poor, questioning developers and investors. By year's end, the report was ready for Cabinet.

"Every Canadian should be entitled to clean, warm shelter as a matter of basic human right," it declared with elegant simplicity. It said that public housing projects for the poor often degenerated into ghettos, deplored the way in which downtown developers were bulldozing more homes than they replaced and proposed to encourage rehabilitation, promised land-banks to hold down prices and envisioned new cities linked by high-speed transport to existing metropolitan centres.

That Christmas of 1969, Hellyer was home in bed with flu. He had nothing to read and he wandered into his daughter's room and picked up *Federalism and the French Canadians*, by Pierre Trudeau. As Hellyer read through it, the realization grew that he had little in common with this Prime Minister. He was an engineer, a nuts-and-bolts man, anxious to get things done, convinced that the real problems of Quebec were social and economic; Trudeau was an academic, a theorist, probably a socialist, preoccupied with constitutional problems and the division of federal and provincial powers.

Hellyer was not much concerned by the fact that the provinces had complete constitutional authority over the municipalities and, therefore, primary responsibility for urban affairs. He wanted the federal Government to exercise leadership to solve what he saw as a national problem. But Trudeau had a different priority. He was just about to resume constitutional negotiations with the provinces and he had promised that if they stayed out of federal affairs — foreign relations, for example — he would be scrupulous in respecting their rights. National unity was at stake, and he wanted to move cautiously.

In the Cabinet discussions, there were other objections to Hellyer's housing proposals. Jean Marchand, the former trade union leader, for one, objected to the attack on public housing and feared that most of Hellyer's proposed reforms would be of more help to the middle class than the poor. Officials of the federal housing agency, Central Mortgage and Housing Corporation, resented the way Hellyer had bustled in to teach them their business, and pointed out flaws in his arguments.

By April 1969, Hellyer was embarrassed and frustrated. He had joined the Trudeau Cabinet to tackle the problems of housing and urban affairs and he had committed himself publicly to the Task Force proposals — a most unusual position for a minister who has to be prepared to support the collective decision of the Cabinet. Now he was being held up in Cabinet and it seemed as if some of his ideas were not going to be accepted and he would have to back down. The alternative was private life and it looked increasingly attractive. So he went to Trudeau one morning and resigned. No ultimatums, no bargaining. He declined the Prime Minister's request to reconsider, and quit.

For a couple of years, it worked out well for Hellyer. He was a happy man when one met him, relaxed, enjoying new social experiences, writing a book on his economic ideas. But then, it seems, he began to brood about Trudeau and the other upstarts who had seized the Liberal Party. He worried about Communists infiltrating the administration and talked to friends about similarities between the writings of Pierre Trudeau and Mao Tse-tung. Rising unemployment re-awakened the conviction that he had the ideas and the ability to take hold of the economy and make it work better. The political fever was rising again, and he formed Action Canada in the hope of organizing a great mass movement which would return him to power. While undoubtedly well-intentioned, it was a disturbing organization in some ways, an alliance of the disaffected with little in common except admiration for Hellyer and his ideas. But it never seemed to get off the ground in any event.

Meantime, Trudeau was left without a housing minister or a policy. He gave the portfolio to Andras, who had just fallen out with Chrétien over Indian policy. An auto dealer from the Lakehead, Andras had arrived in the Commons in 1965 with the convictions of a typical small-city businessman. He had managed Hellyer's leadership campaign, which placed him on the right-wing of the Liberal Party, but politics were already teaching him that life was not the way he had imagined, back home at those Chamber of Commerce lunches. When Trudeau appointed him to the Cabinet, he chose as his principal aide Dan Coates, the scholarly former research director of the Liberal Party who seemed to have inherited from his father the qualities of the British civil servant: fierce loyalty to the interests and ambitions of his minister behind a screen of discretion.

Andras assumed responsibility for housing and urban affairs as a Minister without Portfolio. There was CMHC, a Crown corporation, but no regular department. There was also little money, because the spending squeeze was in force and Trudeau had just demonstrated in his clash with Hellyer that he considered urban affairs primarily a provincial problem.

It was not an encouraging outlook, and when Andras and Coates began to ask basic questions about the nature of the urban crisis, they were shocked to find that there were few answers. They did find a book called *Urban Studies: A Canadian Perspective,* edited by two young economists at Carleton University, Harvey Lithwick and Gilles Paquet. But Lithwick wrote in that book: "A discussion of urban policy currently being implemented in Canada requires little space. There is in fact no such thing." By July, Andras had convinced the Cabinet to authorize a new urban research program, but when he tried to contact Lithwick to persuade him to take the job, he discovered he had just moved to Israel on a year's sabbatical leave. Coates flew to Israel and talked Lithwick into turning his family in their tracks and coming home.

Lithwick commissioned a series of studies of housing, population, transportation, poverty and other aspects of the process of growth in the cities, and drew them all together in a report called *Urban Canada, Problems and Prospects.* The report was the first attempt in Canada to describe the process of urbanization as a whole rather than as a series of un-related parts, although Lithwick boldly acknowledged that little was known and much was misunderstood about some of the problems involved. The forbiddingly technical language of the report emphasized the complexity of the issues.

The real importance of the Lithwick report, probably, was that it convinced the Cabinet that the federal Government could not stand aside from the urban explosion and leave policy to the provinces. Even if it had no constitutional responsibility, 27 federal departments and agencies operated programs which directly influenced the quality of urban life; CHMC was a major mortgage lender and urban planning agency; Ottawa controlled air, rail and water transportation, and was a major landlord and property developer in the cities.

These federal activities in the cities were so widespread, in fact, that no new department of urban affairs could possibly take them all over, or even exercise co-ordinating authority. So Andras suggested a new and experimental type of department — a Ministry of State for Urban Affairs — to operate as a planning agency to provide leadership and guidance to the regular operational departments in their urban activities.

Although Trudeau announced in October 1970, the intention to set up such a department, action was slowed by an opposition filibuster against other aspects of the Government Reorganization Bill, and the new ministry was not legally established until June 1971. Lithwick was given a top job, but quickly decided that the Government was not moving fast enough toward full-scale involvement in the urban crisis, and he resigned.

British Columbia and Quebec in particular among the provinces viewed the new federal ministry with suspicion as a possible invasion of their powers. Although Andras had been working since June 1970 to convene a national urban conference, involving federal, provincial and municipal governments, agreement was not reached until 1972. The Urban ministry, meanwhile, had still to prove its worth; it was an impressive machine but not yet in production.

Andras had more visible success in working through CMHC to speed the housing program and concentrate federal funds where they were most needed. Housing starts rose to a record of 233,000 in 1971, well above the Economic Council target, and were still climbing in 1972. While changes in the law drew more private mortgage money into the market, CMHC funnelled 80 per cent of its funds into housing for low income groups, and 140,000 units were built in four years — twice as many as in the preceding 20 years.

New legislation was introduced in the Commons in June 1972 to encourage neighborhood improvement schemes instead of massive redevelopment projects; to assist in the rehabiltation of old homes; to subsidize low-income families to buy their own homes, and make other changes in the National Housing Act. Many of the proposals seemed to implement Hellyer's Task Force recommendations of three years earlier. The housing committee of the independent Canadian Council on Social Development commented that the proposed changes were the most significant housing legislation since 1954, but warned that they would be a deceit unless adequate funds were provided to make the new programs effective. It also emphasized that there should be no reduction in the intensity of the low-income housing drive.

Assessment

There were several problems in assessing in 1972 the Trudeau Government's record on social policy. The first was that the economic squeeze worked against every anti-poverty initiative. Unemployment rose precisely where incomes were lowest: to 8.6 per cent in the Atlantic Provinces and 8.2 per cent in Quebec in 1971. Families that might have been assisted in climbing above the poverty line were denied work and wages. As the Economic Council said in proposing a strategy for the War on Poverty, "The maintenance of high employment and strong and stable economic growth is crucial."

Second, participatory democracy was time-consuming. White Papers led to debate in Parliament and among the public, followed by legislation and more debate. Some of the major social programs were not in final form until 1971 and 1972, and two of them — the Family Income Insurance Plan and housing legislation — failed to clear Parliament before it adjourned in July, 1972.

Third, there are few up-to-date statistics with which to measure the poverty gap during the Trudeau years. As the 1971 census data becomes available, they may make clear if relative poverty was declining or increasing.

But one measure of a Government's priorities is how it spends its money, and the independent Canadian Tax Foundation analyzes the federal expenditure program every year. It shows that in 1962, the federal Government spent 25.5 cents out of every dollar on health and welfare, and this rose to 29.4 cents by 1969. In the next three years, 1970-72, the health and welfare share jumped to 35.3 cents, so it is clear that social spending was increasingly rapidly despite austerity.

Finally, the speed at which governments progress is controlled to some extent by public attitudes. For most Canadians, times were prosperous and income available to be spent after taxes continued to rise sharply — from $2,238 per head in 1968 to $2,715 in 1971. Despite this, complaints about taxes became louder and more menacing in the ears of the politicians. When the Gallup Poll asked Canadians in 1962 what they thought about the level of taxes, only 47 per cent said it was too high; in 1970, the figure was 75 per cent. There was talk of a middle-class backlash.

6

FOREIGN POLICY

The Internationalists

Canada emerged from the Second World War with military prestige and a modern economy, while countries potentially more powerful were defeated or exhausted and severely damaged. This was an exciting opportunity for a country with the enthusiasm and idealism of youth, and Canadian diplomats went to work with great skill to build a new and better world order.

Canada played a leading role in launching the North Atlantic Treaty Organization to provide not just mutual security in the Cold War, but the framework for an Atlantic community joining North America and Western Europe. In the United Nations, Canada saw beyond the debating society of the General Assembly and the Great Powers running the world through the Security Council, to a vision of a genuine supranational authority with the resources to keep order in the world. Whenever there was need, Canada was proud to commit armed forces to serve as UN peace-keepers.

The thrust was always toward internationalism and there were 20 fulfilling years. But by the middle Sixties, the era was ending and the foundations of Canadian foreign policy were crumbling. The Cold War was thawing, reducing the military importance of NATO, and the revived countries of Western Europe were more concerned with their Common Market and less with the dream of an Atlantic community. At the United Nations, the opposition of the Soviet Union and other powers made new peace-keeping operations unlikely, and Canadian public opinion suffered a traumatic shock when President Nasser abruptly ordered the UN Amergency Force out of the Gaza Strip in 1967, to clear the way for a new war with Israel, and home came the Canadian contingent. What sort of peace-keeping was that?

In addition to these developments abroad, there were forces stirring at home which were compelling Canadians to begin to re-examine the way they saw the world and their place in it.

As the connection with Britain had weakened — and not even Diefenbaker at the height of his popularity had been able to restore it — Canada had come to accept U.S. leadership and values. The U.S. economy, society and popular culture were models for many Canadians. U.S. security was Canada's security and U.S. wars were Canada's wars. But when Americans began seriously to question their own value system in the Sixties, Canadians had to look again. What they began to see, largely through the eyes of U.S. critics, was a wasteful economy, a violent society and an aggressive war in Vietnam. The U.S. model became increasingly unsatisfactory, but no alternative was readily available. Canadians would at last have to set their own standards and goals and define their relationships with the world.

The time was ripe for nationalism and it emerged in various shapes and degrees: the Centennial discovery of national confidence; Walter Gordon and the Watkins Report on foreign ownership; the anti-American rhetoric of the radical Left; even the appearance of Trudeau as a unique and hopefully superior type of politician.

Thus the crumbling of the old foreign policy and the rise of the new nationalism coincided in the Sixties to generate a lively debate about Canada's proper place in the world. It was not a great popular issue — foreign policy seldom is —

but politicians, diplomats, academics and the media were deeply involved. Articles and books about the issues and alternatives poured off the presses. Learned conferences were held. For the first time in a generation, foreign policy became a controversial issue at political party meetings.

Ironically, there was less discussion inside the Government than outside. External Affairs Minister Paul Martin's personal commitment to collective security went back to the League of Nations in the Thirties. He had been a Parliamentary Secretary in the war-time administration which forged the alliance with the United States and a member of the post-war Cabinets which took pride in the Canadian record at the United Nations and NATO. Now, in the Sixties, he was too busy trying to shore up these policies to want to undertake a radical reappraisal.

Martin discouraged discussion on foreign affairs in the Cabinet and stoutly resisted urgent suggestions from Prime Minister Lester Pearson that it was time to invite an independent review of policy. He argued that he could not open the confidential files of the department, which included the secrets of foreign governments, to outsiders. When Pearson persisted, they compromised. Norman Robertson, who had been top man in the department before becoming Director of the School of International Affairs at Carleton University, worked with two senior but independent-minded officials to re-examine the roots of policy. They apparently concluded that no basic changes were necessary, at least for the time. This reinforced Martin's convictions that the old policies were the best policies and that to attack them publicly was irresponsible. He feared that if Canada weakened its commitment to NATO, other countries might follow suit, causing the Western alliance to collapse, and he argued that Canada had to remain a friend and ally of the United States if it was to be able to work behind the scenes for a settlement in Vietnam.

However, the old policies were being attacked, and by critics with substantial credentials. The President of the Progressive Conservative Party, Dalton Camp, suggested to a political thinkers' conference in 1967 that Canada should slash its defense program and switch resources into foreign aid, and align herself with the Third World of developing countries instead of with NATO. Escott Reid, who had been a leading architect of the old policies while a senior diplomat and adviser to Pearson in the Forties, now declared: "It is time for the establishment of new priorities. It is time for crusading leadership by the Government of Canada." He argued that Canada could do little to preserve peace by spending $1.8 billion on defense in the age of Superpowers and vastly expensive weapon systems, but the same amount of money spent on international development could have an important impact on world poverty.

The debate was growing hotter when Trudeau suddenly emerged as a leadership candidate early in 1968. Which side would he take? Not much was known of his views on the world, except that he had wandered widely as a young man with a pack on his back before it was fashionable, and had visited the Soviet Union and China when to do so was to invite suspicion of being a Communist. There was confusion also about his views on nationalism. At home in Quebec, he was a powerful opponent of French Canadian nationalism and he was assumed, therefore, to be an anti-nationalist in the larger Canadian context. But this was a misreading of his theory. He was an articulate critic of nationalism based on racial loyalty and emotionalism because it gave rise to hatred, wars and atrocities. But he was an admirer of the national state, particularly the federal state, based on reason and serving equally the interests of citizens of various ethnic groups and origins.

Trudeau had little to say about foreign policy during his leadership campaign, but as soon as he became Prime Minister in April he began energetically to re-order priorities. The first step was to dislodge Martin as External Affairs Minister and appoint Mitchell Sharp. Sharp was an executive of broad experience in government, a poor boy from Winnipeg who early set his red head and quick mind at success and rose through the war-time civil service to become a Deputy Minister. Entering politics, he served as Minister of Trade and Commerce and then of Finance in the Pearson

Cabinet and was thought to have a fair chance of winning the leadership. But when the dollar crisis interrupted his campaign and he calculated on the eve of the convention that he could not become king, Sharp made the typically cool decision to accept second best and be a king-maker. He suddenly withdrew from the race, switched his support to Trudeau and often claimed thereafter, probably correctly, that Trudeau could not have won the tight race without him. Sharp was always a manager rather than an innovator and never a powerful political figure in the Cabinet, but Trudeau admired his all-round competence and the steadiness of his advice, even when they disagreed.

Within a few weeks of taking over, Trudeau was ready with a number of important foreign policy decisions: negotiations to establish relations with China; steps to broaden contacts with Latin America and the countries of the Pacific rim; a bigger and better foreign aid program; increased efforts to project abroad the image of Canada as a bilingual country, which meant in practice closer relations with the former French colonies in Africa; a hard look at the military commitment to NATO in the light of changing conditions in Europe.

There was in fact to be a thorough and comprehensive review of foreign policy, so the great debate in the country was now becoming a debate within the Government, or so it seemed. But the world does not wait on policy reviews and Trudeau had no sooner won the election than he was in deep difficulties.

"Where's Biafra?"

As he came out of a Cabinet meeting on Parliament Hill one hot noon-time in August, Trudeau was tackled by a squad of reporters eager for any comment this newsworthy new Prime Minister would drop. The CBC's Ron Collister asked about the civil war in Nigeria, where the Ibo people were fighting to separate and establish their own state of Biafra. Taken by surprise, Trudeau countered with the first of the semiflippant answers which were to get him into trouble on many issues: "Where's Biafra?"

A shock-wave of dismay ran through the network of liberal humanitarians whose hearts were easily enlisted for every cause and who now had the first reason to doubt that Trudeau was one of theirs. Although the Nigerian war had begun more than a year before, it was only just coming to popular attention in Canada. There were haunting pictures of starving Ibo children on TV and rumors of hideous massacres and threats of genocide in the papers. Biafra was becoming an emotional issue and Trudeau was acting as if he had never heard of it and could not care less. When the new Parliament met in September, the first question to Trudeau was about Biafra and this interest soon blew up into a political storm which raged for almost 18 months.

There was incessant pressure on the Government, from Parliament, press and pulpit, to assist Canairelief, a consortium of church groups in Canada and part of the international effort to fly emergency relief through the Nigerian Government's blockade to feed the starving Ibo rebels. But Trudeau felt he had to be extremely careful about interfering in a civil war in another Commonwealth country. He insisted that humanitarian principles could not be divorced from political motives and that the Government could aid the relief effort only in ways approved by the recognized Government of Nigeria. Other countries, including the United States, were less cautious in sending aid and more enterprising in getting it into Biafra.

Critics suspected that Trudeau saw Biafra's attempt to break away from Nigeria in the light of what might happen if Quebec decided to separate from Canada, and recognized how strongly the federal Government would resent any foreign intervention. But he was probably more influenced by his dislike for states based on race, as Biafra was supposed to be an Ibo State, and his desire to support the federal principle in Nigeria. He also had to keep in the forefront of consideration the future of Canada's relations with Africa and the Commonwealth. Nigeria always seemed likely to win the war and remain a leading Commonwealth country, and other African states made it clear that they did not want Canada or any other white country intervening in Nigeria.

None of this convinced the humanitarians in Canada. Opposition MPs and journalists made adventurous flights into Biafra aboard relief planes running the blockade and hurried home with horrifying accounts of mass starvation and dramatic warnings that the Ibos feared they would be destroyed to the last child by advancing Nigerian troops. Protestors camped on Parliament Hill, occupied Sharp's office and chased Trudeau with angry signs, provoking him into foolish arguments and wild statements which got him into further trouble in the Commons and in Nigeria. A TV personality, Stanley Burke, became a passionate propagandist for the relief organizations in Canada. Canairelief, meanwhile, kept going by flying U.S. emergency supplies to Biafra.

The Government tried repeatedly, almost desperately, to work out some arrangement with the Nigerian Government for providing relief to the needy on both sides of the battle front. Trudeau's aide, Ivan Head, made three trips to Lagos to reinforce the regular diplomatic effort. The airforce in Canada devised a new system for dropping bulk supplies by parachute, and Hercules air freighters and lighter Caribous were despatched to relief bases around Nigeria. But the makeshift schemes always seemed to break down at the last minute — mainly because the Nigerian Government did not want them to succeed. If it had not been a tragedy, it would have been a comedy of mistakes, misunderstandings and red tape.

By the beginning of 1970, Canairelief was in a state of financial collapse, unable to pay its bills unless the Government made a last minute grant. The political pressure was amost irresistible and the Cabinet at last agreed to provide $1 million. Only two days later, Biafra surrendered and the war was over.

In his recent book, *The Nigerian Civil War*, British journalist John de St. Jore shows how starvation was a weapon ruthlessly used by both sides in the war: by Nigeria to force Biafra to its knees, and by Biafra to arouse world sympathy. The relief organizations were manipulated for political ends and St. Jorre seems to suggest that their humanitarian efforts actually extended the war by encouraging Biafra to hold out. On the other hand, the attention focussed on Biafra may possibly have ensured the good conduct of Nigerian troops when they at last took control.

But if the humanitarians are to be given the benefit of the doubt, so also should Trudeau. He was never faced with a simple choice between right and wrong, but with questions of judgment about lesser and greater evils. He decided that the preservation of Nigeria as a viable state would be more important to Africans in the long term than the relief of short-term suffering in Biafra. Historians may one day decide if he was correct, but in the meantime it is probably fair to say that Canada's influence in Africa is the stronger for his stand, almost until the end, in the face of enormous pressure.

The NATO Debate

A second urgent issue which could not wait for the general policy review was the question of what armed forces Canada would continue to station in Europe as part of NATO defenses. NATO planners needed an early answer, and the Trudeau Cabinet, struggling to control total federal spending, had to make a decision about the 1969 defense budget. But before it could decide how much money would be needed for men and equipment, the new Government had to have a general policy toward NATO.

This opened up the central questions about foreign policy. Should Canada withdraw completely from NATO and align herself with the Third World? Should she bring the forces home from Europe but seek to remain in NATO and contribute to the political discussions of the Western Alliance with the communist world? Was the military contribution the price for having influence in Europe where the decisions about peace and war might have to be made?

To secure answers to these questions, Trudeau geared up his new machinery of participatory democracy. He gave leave to his ministers to forget about Cabinet solidarity for the time being and express their personal opinions to help stimulate public debate. While Sharp and Defense Minister Léo Cadieux spoke for the conventional wisdom of their departments that existing policy was fine and should be continued, Communications Minister Eric Kierans attacked "sterile military commitments" and urged greater concentration on foreign aid. When Trudeau met students in question and answer sessions, he seemed to move from side to side of the argument and had to explain to puzzled reporters that he was merely being provocative and not expressing official policy. Newsmen invited to 24 Sussex Drive for dinner found that instead of learning the Prime Minister's mind, they were being led to expose their own ideas on defense, and Trudeau also entertained a number of academic critics of policy.

Other Ministers organized their own sessions with knowledgeable critics, and senior civil servants from departments concerned with the NATO review held private seminars to explore differences of opinion with academics. The Commons committee on External Affairs and Defense took evidence from a variety of experts before going to consult European authorities and prepare recommendations.

Inside the Government, a Task Force of some 30 civil servants drew up a massive review of Canada's relations with Europe. But the section on NATO was not sufficiently a new look to satisfy the Cabinet, and the Ministers of External Affairs and National Defense promised a more specialized study. This also turned out to be a justification of the past rather than a fresh look at the future, which was understandable because the civil servants involved were for the most part these who had helped set the original policies. The Commons committee, when it produced its report in a scramble to meet the deadline for government decision, also took more or less a status-quo position. It proposed that the existing military commitment should be continued pending another review and changes in the Seventies.

This was not at all the advice which Trudeau needed. As a new Prime Minister promising change and reform, and employing all the shiny machinery of participatory democracy, he was reluctant simply to endorse existing policy. Perhaps even more important, he had to put a ceiling on the defense budget at about $1.8 billion if he was to meet his other priorities, and the military experts advised that to carry through all existing defense programs would eventually cost about $2.5 billion a year.

Yet another study was needed, and this time it came from a source on whom the Prime Minister could rely: his personal aide, Ivan Head. In secrecy, Head assembled a group — known jestingly as the Nongroup — of known critics within the federal departments of the existing policies. They provided the fresh look and the justification for change which Trudeau and his supporters in the Cabinet had been seeking. It was not the radical realignment which Camp, Kierans and most of the academics had proposed, but it did expose the flaws in the current position in NATO.

The arguments were hardly original. They had been current in some offices of the departments of National Defense and External Affairs for years, but had never before received official recognition. Thus the Nongroup pointed out that Canada's force of CF-104 nuclear bombers in Europe was essentially offensive rather than defensive. With their airfields dominated by Soviet missiles, they would be destroyed in the first few minutes of war without getting off the ground — unless they attacked first. The Soviet Union could therefore regard NATO as a sword at its throat rather than a shield for the West, and the threat of the CF-104s should be removed as a gesture of good intentions. A second important argument was that the number of Canadian soldiers in Europe was not particularly significant: One man, preferably with his wife and children in married quarters in the line of Soviet advance, would be a sufficient guarantee that Canada would send more help in time of war. Meanwhile, forces could be stationed in Canada and used on other duties.

The Nongroup accepted the proposition, however, that Canada should remain in NATO to make its voice heard in the Western alliance as it sought a new relationship with the Communist bloc. This seemed to require maintenance of some Canadian forces in Europe.

The Nongroup report came as a shock to Sharp and Cadieux who had previously had all the expert opinion on their side. But they had to face up, in any event, to the need to cut the defense estimates for financial reasons. After several days of hot and sometimes confused debate in the Cabinet, the practical decision was no longer whether to reduce the forces in Europe, but when and by how much.

The new policy announced on April 3 rejected neutralism and reaffirmed Canada's intention to remain in NATO and assist in a political settlement in Europe. But it also declared that there would be a planned and phased reduction in the Canadian forces stationed in Europe. The details remained to be worked out in negotiation with NATO.

The Nongroup report apparently proposed cutting the forces in Europe from 10,000 to 3,000 men, and the Cabinet accepted this target. But Britain and other allies complained loudly that Canada was passing the defense buck, and after some angry months of haggling, the final decision was to reduce to 5,000 men. The CF-104s were converted from nuclear to non-nuclear weapons, and the army contingent gave up their Honest John nuclear missiles and heavy Centurion tanks to be re-equipped as a highly mobile tactical reconnaissance force. Air and land forces stationed in Canada remained committed to NATO in the event of an emergency and Canada continued to contribute to NATO naval forces in the Atlantic.

When he disclosed the NATO policy decision in April 1969, Trudeau also announced a new order of defence priorities: (1) Surveillance of Canadian territory and coastlines to protect sovereignty; (2) Defense of North America in co-operation with U.S. forces; (3) NATO commitments; (4) International peacekeeping. It was probably this approach to defense and foreign policy rather than the NATO decision which most worried the critics. Reduction in the number of forces in Europe might have been accepted as a reasonable economy, particularly when the European countries were enjoying rapid economic growth and could provide more of their own defense. But the new priorities seemed to suggest that the troop reductions were merely the first step in a withdrawal into national isolation, or at best, continentalism. The downgrading of commitments to NATO and the United Nations which had been the twin pillars of postwar policy, appeared to mark the end of Canada's internationalism and idealism.

The New Priorities

There were other reasons to fear that Trudeau was turning Canada in upon itself. When he went to London for his first conference of Commonwealth Prime Ministers early in 1969, he appeared more interested in escorting glamorous women to lunch and the theatre than in work, and a British newspaper dismissed him as a "trendy prig." Trudeau's own view was that as a newcomer and a French Canadian who knew little about the British Commonwealth, he should listen and learn rather than attempt to make a major contribution. He came home in fact much impressed by the opportunities the Commonwealth offered for multiracial co-operation and intrigued by some of the leaders he had met — including the Prime Minister of Singapore, Lee Kwan Yew, who first caught his interest when he left one frustrating meeting on Rhodesia remarking that if independence was important to the Africans, they could fight for it, and meanwhile he had more important things to do in London, and was off to see his tailor. But when Trudeau made a remarkably enthusiastic report to the Commons on the Commonwealth meeting, it was generally regarded as an official platitude and attracted little attention from the critics concerned with his isolationism.

At about the same time, Trudeau made disparaging remarks about diplomacy during a TV interview, suggesting that he could learn all he needed from a good newspaper without the benefit of a foreign service. Later, when the Government froze spending, the order fell with particular severity on the Department of External Affairs which spent most of its money on people and could economize only by staff cuts. Seven missions were closed and the staff reduced by about 7 per cent.

The Cabinet's rejection of the department's advice on NATO was soon followed by rejection of the first draft of the general review of foreign policy. Trudeau and other ministers regarded the analyses offered by the External Affairs officials as superficial. They demanded a thorough examination of the principles and objectives which should underlie current policies.

The department by now was thoroughly demoralized. The diplomats who had for so long, and with good reason, regarded themselves as an elite in Ottawa and abroad, were suddenly being rebuffed, rebuked and treated as second-class civil servants. What happened next is described by Bruce Thordarson in his brilliant study of decision-making, *Trudeau and Foreign Policy* (Oxford University Press). A senior officer, Geoffrey S. Murray, was recalled from London in August 1969 and given responsibility for co-ordinating the review, and "he began by reading everything Mr. Trudeau had ever written or stated publicly on foreign policy questions, including some of his *Cité Libre* articles and at least a hundred speeches the Prime Minister made between April 1968 and mid-1969. His next step was to summarize Trudeau's ideas, which he included in a draft memorandum on policy that he circulated to the heads of divisions within External Affairs in order to solicit their opinions and comments. Not all reacted well to what a few considered to be an overly subservient approach to the Prime Minister. One head of division reportedly suggested sardonically that they should request Ambassador Arthur Andrew, then negotiating with the Chinese over recognition, to find out from them how they extracted a foreign policy from the sayings of *their* chairman. Nevertheless most officials were of the opinion that the department's duty was to develop the kind of policy framework that the Prime Minister was seeking."

It was not surprising in the circumstances that when the White Paper review, entitled *Foreign Policy for Canadians*, finally appeared in June 1970, it closely reflected Trudeau's attitudes and priorities. But as he had announced two years earlier the newsworthy decisions to recognize China, broaden relations with Latin America and the Pacific countries, and expand foreign aid, and as the NATO episode had settled the broad alignment, little remained to be said in specifics. The paper was therefore something of an anti-climax, more interesting at first glance for the style of its presentation in six colorful booklets packed in a paper box, than for its contents. Critical attention centered on three statements in the paper because they tended to confirm the fear of a shift of emphasis away from internationalism and toward isolationism.

First, said the paper, Canada should not base its policy on reacting to world events by rushing around trying to be a "helpful fixer." This sounded suspiciously like a contemptuous rejection of 20 years of active and often successful intervention in international crises.

Second, foreign policy was "the extention abroad of national policies." This seemed to say that self-interest should replace the strain of idealism which had run so strongly through Canada's relations with the world.

Third, in the mix of policy themes and objectives, the highest priorities would be Economic Growth, Social Justice and Quality of Life. Of secondary importance were Safeguarding Sovereignty and Independence, Working for Peace and Security, and Ensuring a Harmonious Natural Environment. The emphasis here appeared to be highly materialistic, and to overlook the fact that Peace comes before Prosperity in the traditional prescription for a happy future.

The paper frankly conceded that there would sometimes be a conflict of policy priorities, and one of the most striking of these occurred in the discussion of Canadian attitudes toward Africa: "The reaction of Canadians has two main characteristics. One is a broad revulsion against the racial discrimination practised in southern Africa, and a general agreement that self-determination for Africans is a principle that cannot be denied. This reaction has been articulated by Canadian churches and other organizations, and by individuals. The other is the reaction of businessmen who see better-than-normal opportunities for trade and investment in the growing economy of the Republic of South Africa, or of those who are conscious of the practical limitations of effective outside influence on the pace of developments in South Africa. . . . The Canadian Government's attitude can be seen as reflecting two policy themes which are divergent in this context: (1) Social Justice and (2) Economic Growth. The first theme has been pursued in Canadian policy statements and in its actions against the illegal regime in Rhodesia, as well as the embargo on the shipment of significant military equipment to South Africa and Portugal. The second reflects Canada's basic approach, which is to trade in peaceful goods with all countries and territories regardless of political considerations."

The paper looked briefly at alternatives, but concluded that the best policy for Canada would be to continue to "balance" the two policy themes — that was, to continue to advocate Social Justice at the official level while permitting private Economic Growth. For example, the Government decided that the Crown-owned Polymer Corporation should get rid of its subsidiary in South Africa, but declined to interfere with much larger private investment and trade.

Here again, material advantage seemed to have preference over idealism, and the Committee for a Just Canadian Policy Toward Africa published its own Black Paper in which it said: "Canada has a unique opportunity and, indeed, an obligation to take up the challenge proposed by President Nyerere of Tanzania when he told a Toronto audience last year: 'We believe that this country (Canada) has both the opportunity and the willingness to try to build a bridge across the chasm of color.' Canada has the opportunity at a time when many of the independent nations are looking to us as one of their few trustworthy friends in the white Western world. But does it have the willingness? The Government's White Paper shows a declining interest in Canada's role in preventing this destructive polarization."

While the critics worried about objectives and motives in foreign policy, the Government justified its choice of priorities in perhaps the most revealing passage in the entire White Paper. It pointed out that the emphasis which would need to be placed on Safeguarding Sovereignty and Independence and protecting Peace and Security was outside Canada's control, because it would depend on external events: "On the other hand, the survival of Canada as a nation is being challenged internally by divisive forces. This underlines further the need for a new emphasis on policies, domestic and internal, that promote economic growth, social justice and an enhanced quality of life for all Canadians."

In other words, Canada was threatened more immediately by disunity at home than by pressure from abroad. So strengthening internal relations had a higher priority than external relations. In terms of foreign policy, this meant emphasizing trade relations which would promote economic growth in Canada and encouraging cultural contacts which would enrich Canada's bilingual and multicultural society.

A Key Decision

There were many Canadians who did not accept this new priority for foreign policy. Apart from those who held true to the old faith of internationalism, there were the new nationalists who insisted that the greatest threat to Canada was not internal, but external — the threat of U.S. take-over.

During the Fifties, Canadians were generally happy to receive all the U.S. capital and know-how they could get. During the Sixties, they became increasingly aware of the extent to which this flood of investment had taken control of their industries and resources: some 60 per cent of all manufacturing, 65 per cent of mining and smelting, 75 per cent of petroleum and natural gas.

By 1970 there was widespread concern that foreign ownership on this scale implied foreign control of vital decisions about the national economy, foreign influence in politics financed by business corporations, foreign pressure on government and the importation of foreign life-style.

The changing national mood was described by Joe Greene, then Minister of Energy, Mines and Resources, when he spoke to surprised U.S. oil men in Denver, Colorado in 1970: "Those Canadians who are candid will admit that we were, until recently, quite satisfied to be but a small microcosm of America. Our only complaint was that we were not more so. You had more money — higher wages and incomes — than we did. This was the only beef, and the remedy of this defect was our chief aim. But now the scene has clearly changed. Canadians are determined that they will build something which is clearly their own, and not the pale and small image of the great and powerful civilization to our south." Greene confessed that he had only recently been converted to the view that a growing degree of Canadian ownership of industry and resources was essential to independence, and he added insult to injury by telling his American audience: "A part of the cause of the rise of that new Canadian nationalism and determination to build something unique rests in the malaise that exists in your land — what appears to many as the sudden and tragic disappearance of the American dream which, in some ways, has turned to nightmare."

This was an accurate reflection of the feelings of many Canadians in all major political parties and in the non-partisan Committee for an Independent Canada formed to bring pressure on the Trudeau Government to take firm action to limit foreign control of the economy. But there were also pressures running strongly in the other direction — toward bigger businesses operating in bigger markets in response to economic imperatives with no concern for national boundaries. The Economic Council implicitly challenged the nationalists in its 1970 report when it noted that Canada was already about the only advanced industrial country without a consumer market of 100 million or more, and commented: "There is the more fundamental issue of how Canada will respond to the 'new generation' of big industrial markets, big international firms and the acceleration of technological change. Access to a large market for industrial products will undoubtedly be even more important in the future than it has been in the past."

The Council was not optimistic about the chances that Canada would find its larger markets through renewed world progress toward free trade, and it warned that if the United States turned protectionist, Canada would probably be forced to seek some special continental arrangement. It also forecast that multinational corporations might control as much as half the entire output of the free world by 1990 and implied that if Canada tried to control them too closely — as the nationalists were advocating — "... their future developments and even their present activities can perhaps be readily shifted elsewhere."

The protectionist trend which the Economic Council had feared was soon evident in the United States and took dramatic form in August 1971 when President Nixon suddenly announced his New Economic Policy, designed to improve the U.S. balance of trade and payments. The bad news reached Ottawa in a late-night phone call from Washington which woke up Acting Prime Minister Mitchell Sharp at home. "I thought it was a dream," he said; 'nightmare' might have been more appropriate.

The Government quickly calculated that the U.S. measures to reduce imports from Canada and increase exports would cost 90,000 Canadian workers their jobs in a year. To the disgust of the nationalists, but just as the Economic Council had forecast would be necessary, ministers rushed to Washington to demand special exemption. The ministers argued that although Canada was enjoying a big trade surplus with the United States, the money was largely returned in other payments. Washington was not impressed. "I don't think that they know much or care much about Canada," said Trudeau in a CBC interview. "I don't think they realize what they are doing. I don't think the U.S. is deliberately trying to beggar its neighbors and make this into a permanent policy. But if it is, we'll have to make a fundamental reassessment of our whole economy."

Trudeau saw more deeply and darkly that most Canadians, including nationalists, into the implications of the U.S. actions, and he explained them in an interview with Charles Lynch. For the first time in history, Canada was earning a trade surplus with which to pay interest and dividends on U.S. investment in Canada. But now Nixon was saying that the United States could not afford to allow Canada this surplus and was taking drastic measures to restore the balance. If this happened and Canada no longer had a trade profit, it would have to revert to the bad old habit of selling more industry and resources to earn the U.S. dollars with which to pay the bills on past investment. The result of Nixon's policies, therefore, would be continuing U.S. investment in Canada. Trudeau said he wanted to ask Nixon: "Are you saying that your economic system is leading you to try and buy up as much of the world as possible?" and he commented to Lynch: "I don't think they have thought this through. You know this is real Marxist theory about imperialism being the last phase of capitalism."

Trudeau had his opportunity to question Nixon when he visited Washington in December 1971, and he received the "fantastic" reassurance that it was not U.S. policy to gobble up Canada. More practically, the United States dismantled some, but not all, of its protectionist measures later in the month in return for a realignment of world currency rates. As we have seen in the chapter on economic policy, Canada was able to resist U.S. pressure to revalue its dollar upwards to give the U.S. a trade advantage.

When Nixon made a return call on Trudeau in Ottawa in April 1972, he made his assurance formal in a speech to both Houses of Parliament: "No self-respecting nation can or should accept the proposition that it should always be economically dependent upon another nation. Let us recognize once and for all that the only basis for a sound and healthy relationship between our two proud peoples is to find a pattern of economic interaction which is beneficial to both our countries — and which respects Canada's right to chart its own economic course."

A Canadian nationalist could hardly have written a more satisfactory statement for the President to deliver. It was licence for Trudeau to decide on a policy toward foreign ownership without fear of accusations that he was being anti-American. But if he was free from U.S. sensitivities, he was still subject to sharp pressures from within Canada.

The Cabinet had appointed one of its members, Herb Gray, in the spring of 1970, to study the whole question of foreign investment and make recommendations. When an early draft of his report leaked in the fall of 1971 and revealed that he was proposing a screening agency to decide what foreign investment should be allowed and what refused, there were angry reactions from several provincial Premiers and some business leaders. While some parts of Canada might have all the U.S. capital they needed and more, the slow-growth regions where unemployment and poverty remained the most serious problems were anxious for any investment they could get, regardless of nationality.

When the 523 page Gray study was officially published early in May 1972, it confirmed all the statistics of creeping foreign ownership and some of the suspicions that Canadian subsidiaries of foreign corporations tended to be cogs in international operations — truncated companies which took their orders and technology from abroad and did not provide complete career opportunities in Canada. The study also warned that "... the development of a Canadian nation with a distinctive indigenous culture will depend, in the main, on the encouragement of domestic talent and creative capabilities ... such Canadian capacities can be stifled if Canada is inundated with influences from other countries which are much larger or much more developed than Canada. The large volumes of United States direct investment in Canada constitute an important part of the massive American influence on Canadian society, although certainly not the largest portion of it."

However, the study concluded that foreign capital brought important benefits as well as costs to Canada, and it recommended a mechanism to screen each investment proposal to ensure that the terms were as favorable as possible — or to forbid the project if it seemed against Canada's interests. The Cabinet accepted the idea in principle, but decided to apply it only on a narrow front. Foreign investment to take over an existing Canadian company would be screened. But the much larger flows of investment to start a new foreign-owned company or to expand the operations of an existing foreign subsidiary would be exempt from control.

This meant that the Trudeau Government would continue to welcome foreign investment on a major scale, and that dynamic multinational corporations would probably continue to enlarge their share of business in Canada.

Trudeau told Jack Cahill of the *Toronto Star* that there were three reasons for the Cabinet's cautious policy: (1) Canadians were most concerned about foreign take-overs of Canadian companies so that was the problem the Government had chosen to tackle; (2) Take-overs of existing companies were often a matter of replacing Canadian capital with foreign capital and brought no new technology or employment; (3) The provinces "don't want the federal Government to prevent capital from coming in . . . to create jobs and economic progress."

Thus Trudeau was working out in practice the theory stated in the earlier review, *Foreign Policy for Canadians,* that Canada was threatened more by internal division and dissatisfaction than by external forces. He was saying that the Government gave a higher priority to meeting the provincial demand for economic growth and jobs than to resisting the encroachments of foreign capital on Canadian sovereignty.

This was probably the most important foreign policy decision made by the Trudeau Cabinet. It rejected nationalism and implicitly accepted that Canada's future lay in closer association with the United States.

The Trudeau Doctrine

While the nationalists anguished over the gradual surrender of sovereignty, Trudeau insisted that if Canada acted with foresight and resolution it could have the best of both worlds: economic integration and political independence. As *Foreign Policy for Canadians* put it, "Increasingly, the Canada-United States economic relationship will be affected by agreements between governments and arrangements by multinational corporations and trade unions. While such developments should be beneficial for Canada's economic growth, the constant danger that sovereignty, independence and cultural identity may be impaired will require a conscious effort on Canada's part to keep the whole situation under control"

Trudeau's tactics were (1) to resist direct challenges to Canadian sovereignty and identity wherever they arose, and (2) to offset the weight of U.S. influence in Canada by exposing the country to other foreign contacts and cultures.

When the U.S. ice-breaking oil tanker, the giant Manhattan, made an experimental voyage through the Arctic in 1969, threatening to establish the frozen sea as an international waterway instead of Canadian territory, the Government reasserted sovereignty by claiming a 100 mile pollution control zone in the Arctic. While it was doubtful under international law and drew a protest from the U.S. Government, the measure had the practical effect of causing insurance companies to insist that ships proposing to enter the Arctic must submit to Canadian regulation. The Government's new defense policy also emphasized military surveillance in the far North to establish Canadian jurisdiction.

To meet the cultural invasion of U.S. broadcasting, the Canadian Radio and Television Commission made tough Canadian-content rules to limit the amount of U.S. programming broadcast in Canada. Although book publishing was primarily a provincial jurisdiction, the Secretary of State devised a modest program to assist Canadian companies which might otherwise have to sell out to American corporations. However, the Government took no action against two important U.S. influences in Canada, *TIME Magazine* and *Reader's Digest*, which continued to enjoy a privileged position for foreign publications.

This was typical of Trudeau's cautious conduct of relations with the United States. While fending off new encroachments upon independence, he was careful not to open old wounds or provoke the powerful neighbor. He avoided public involvement in international issues such as Vietnam which might have brought him into collision with Washington, and his defense rhetoric emphasized continental security and the North American Air Defense Command — even when he was sending home the U.S. Bomarc anti-bomber missiles and making it clear that Canada would not participate in a defense against ballistic missiles.

Trudeau met Nixon four times in four years and valued the personal relationship. He always treated the President with deference and insisted that Nixon was a true friend of Canada when not preoccupied with bigger powers and more important issues.

Thus in his attitudes to the United States, Trudeau expressed the conventional diplomatic wisdom that Canada could exert more influence by the Quiet Diplomacy of persuasion in private than by public criticism and protest.

Foreign aid was one of the major instruments used to open new windows on the world and to change Canada's image abroad. The total program almost doubled from $253 million in 1967-68 to $491 million budgeted for 1972-73, although it was still far short of the international ideal of 1 per cent of Gross National Product. Within the total, there were important changes of emphasis. More money was channeled through international agencies, instead of being tied to high-cost Canadian supplies. And the amount of aid going to French-speaking countries in Africa rose from $12 million to almost $70 million. By 1972, there were 489 Canadian educators and 83 advisers working under the aid program in French-speaking Africa. While this helped to relieve unemployment in Quebec, it also made the federal Government more relevant in Quebec and promoted the image of Canada abroad as a French- as well as English-speaking country. Much of the improvement in the aid program was due to Maurice Strong, a restless, innovative man who believed it possible to use the methods of capitalism to achieve the humanitarian goals of socialism. A self-made millionaire, he left the presidency of Power Corporation, which managed one of Canada's largest pools of venture capital, to enter the civil service and run the foreign aid program. When he left in 1970 to become a UN Undersecretary and organize an international attack on pollution, he was replaced by a less effective leader, Paul Gérin-Lajoie, a former Quebec Cabinet

Minister whom Trudeau had brought to Ottawa earlier to help advertise the French-Canadian presence in the federal administration.

Trudeau himself led the campaign to establish overseas contacts to balance U.S. influence. In four years, he travelled officially in 14 countries: Britain, the United States, the Soviet Union, New Zealand, Australia, Malaysia, Singapore, Japan, India, Pakistan, Indonesia, Ceylon, Iran and Italy, where he opened Canadian relations with the Vatican.

The first major diplomatic initiative was to negotiate with Communist China for mutual recognition. Although Trudeau started out promising to continue recognition of the Nationalist regime on Taiwan and wound up completely disowning it, the arrangement with Peking caused little controversy in Canada. A year or two earlier and it might have been considered dangerously offensive to the United States, but now it was merely paving the way for Nixon.

Trudeau's visit to the Soviet Union and Premier Kosygin's return visit to Canada, both in 1971, aroused far more criticism — mostly because immigrant groups in Canada had bitter memories of communist oppression and were suspicious of any friendship with Moscow. Trudeau also invited attack, as so often, by a couple of incautious remarks. At a press conference in Moscow, he emphasized that the United States was a neighbor, friend and ally of Canada, but went on: "Canada has increasingly found it important to diversify its channels of communication because of the overpowering presence of the United States of America and that is reflected in a growing consciousness among Canadians of the danger (to) our national identity from a cultural, economic and perhaps even military point of view." The ambiguous reference to the military danger — did he mean the close defensive alliance with the United States or a possible U.S. attack? — raised startled eyebrows. Next, he managed to outrage the Ukrainian community in Canada by suggesting that their heroes, the Ukrainian nationalists in the Soviet Union, were revolutionaries who belonged in jail.

Nevertheless, Trudeau's Ostpolitik resulted in some potentially useful agreements. Canada and the Soviet Union established mixed commissions to co-operate in applying science and technology to industry; signed a protocol providing for regular consultation at the Foreign Minister level; and agreed to facilitate the exchange of scholars, musicians, artists, scientists, journalists and tourists.

Although *Foreign Policy for Canadians* had discounted Canada's usefulness as a "helpful fixer," Trudeau found himself in that familiar role at the Commonwealth Conference in Singapore in 1971. With the British Government determined to resume the sale of arms to South Africa and some black African members threatening to walk out of the Commonwealth if it did, Trudeau was able to act as a mediator, cooling both sides and emerging from the conference as probably the only white Prime Minister with credibility in black Africa.

The early decision to establish new contacts with Latin America was slow to take effective shape. But by 1972, Canada was ready to take observer status at the Organization of American States and to commit $100 million to become a full member of the Inter-American Development Bank. These were little-noticed but important initiatives to involve Canada in the political and economic life of the continent.

In Europe, the Government was able to restore the confidence which was shaken by the NATO decision and by the fear that Canada was turning isolationist, but had less success in finding a continuing basis for co-operation with the Common Market. After the departure of President Charles de Gaulle, who had encouraged separatism in Quebec, relations with France returned slowly toward normal.

In summary, it seems clear that Trudeau was interested in foreign affairs mainly to the extent that they could influence the internal problems closest to his heart, and it will be some time before the results of his initiatives are known. Meantime, I am aware of only one comprehensive review of Trudeau's foreign policy by a qualified observer, *Canada's Search for New Roles*, but Peter C. Dobell, Director of the Parliamentary Centre for Foreign Affairs and Foreign Trade (Oxford University Press, for The Royal Institute of International Affairs). In this excellent study, Dobell concludes:

". . . the modesty of the Trudeau Government may lead it to underestimate Canada's actual capacity for effective action in the world. The Prime Minister's reference to Canada as a 'smaller power,' and even more his remarks while returning from Russia to the effect that 'we're more interested in what is good for Canada, . . . we're not . . . trying to determine external events,' reveal a scepticism about Canada's capacity to influence its external environment which might inhibit the Government from undertaking useful international activity even where need, capability and opportunity might coincide. . . . These things having been stated, however, the concern is for the future. For to date, when opportunities have arisen for useful action abroad, such as during the period leading up to the Commonwealth Conference in Singapore, the Government has acted with intelligence and vigor. And since actions speak louder than words, it may be that there is no ground for concern."

7

MYTHS, MEN AND POWER

The French Canadians

Myths flourish in politics. Some spring from prejudice because it is tempting to believe the worst about opponents. Others are invented because it is simpler and more entertaining to describe the exercise of power in terms of a conspiracy by the few than as a diffuse and often obscure process of decision-making. Thus it was satisfying for many Canadians to believe that the Trudeau Government was run by a coterie of French Canadians, or to talk of a supergroup of politicians, advisers and bureaucrats who monopolized power and made all key decisions.

The myth that a Quebec mafia controlled the Cabinet had its origins in the fact that Trudeau came to Ottawa in 1965 with two friends and political associates, Jean Marchand and Gérard Pelletier. They were known as The Three Wise Men and it was easy to assume when Trudeau became Prime Minister that he would continue to give the closest attention to advice from his friends.

But this was a misunderstanding of Trudeau. He distrusted sentiment in decision-making and placed his confidence in elaborate systems of analysis. Unlike previous

Prime Ministers, he allowed himself no cronies. "I think I see less of Mr. Trudeau now than I used to see of him when he was not Prime Minister," said Marchand on a CBC-TV interview in March 1972. "Don't think that I spend my life at 24 Sussex. I haven't been there for six months. . . . And it's the same thing even for Pelletier, and we are friends. We don't have time. We're busy with our own departments. . . . Well, we see him (Trudeau) in the Cabinet. But privately? I don't see him more often than any other minister — and probably less." Pelletier said much the same. In the summer of 1971, when an irate Liberal backbencher called for his dismissal over the Opportunities for Youth program, Pelletier thought he ought to go through the formality of offering his resignation to the Prime Minister. When he asked for an appointment, he realized with a shock that it was a year since he had had a private talk with Trudeau.

The structure of the Cabinet confirmed that French Canadians wielded no special influence. In terms of numbers, in fact, they lost ground. The Pearson Cabinet in January 1966 counted seven French Canadians from Quebec among 26 ministers; in 1972, Trudeau had seven Québecois, including himself, among 30. Pearson had 11 ministers from Ontario, Trudeau 11.

At the centre of the Cabinet structure was the committee on Priorities and Planning. Trudeau was the chairman and Marchand and Pelletier were members, but the other seven ministers (in June 1972) were all English Canadians: Finance Minister John Turner, Treasury Board President C.M. 'Bud' Drury, External Affairs Minister Mitchell Sharp, Justice Minister Otto Lang, Transport Minister Don Jamieson, Urban Affairs Minister Ron Basford, and Consumer and Corporate Affairs Minister Bob Andras who was appointed after Trudeau had chosen him to serve with Marchand as joint chairmen of the Liberal election campaign committee.

French Canadians did make progress in terms of portfolio power — command of important departments. Traditionally, they had been appointed to the prestigious but immobile Justice Department and to ministries with control of substantial patronage. English Canadians held firm to the levers of taxing and spending power in the Finance Department and the Treasury Board, and supervised the country's business through the department of Trade and Commerce. Pearson continued the custom in general, but set change in train by apprenticing French Canadians, as it were, to learn the business of economic management. He placed Marchand in charge of Manpower; sent Jean-Luc Pépin to build up Energy, Mines and Resources; and placed Jean Chrétien under Sharp's tutelage in Finance.

When Trudeau took over from Pearson, he continued the process, but gently. Pépin became the first French Canadian Minister of Trade and Commerce, with Industry tacked on for good measure. His cheerful manner and refreshing frankness soon made him a favorite in the Commons. He was a tireless traveller and trade promoter, delivering pep speeches as if he were back in the university lecture hall and had to keep the sleepy students alert with punch lines and then drive home the message by constant repetition. He had the good fortune to preside over a period of trade in which exports were booming, and he worked hard to make the most of it. Marchand moved up to Regional Economic Expansion, which became a key department in the strategy of economic development. Chrétien was responsible for Northern development, as well as for Indian Affairs. But Finance and the Treasury Board, the two most powerful departments of government, remained under English Canadian command.

The Advisers

The myth of the supergroup started with this mistaken idea that Trudeau and a few political friends would form an inner cabinet. But it was associated also with the growth of Trudeau's personal staff, under the direction of another friend, Marc Lalonde, and the strengthening of control of the executive through the Privy Council Office. The senior civil servants in the major departments had always been recognized as influential figures — mandarins — but now they were mixed in with Trudeau's friends and staff to form the so-called supergroup.

The realities of power were more complex. In every government, senior ministers, aides who have access to the Prime Minister, and top bureaucrats, have the power to influence decisions. The fewer they are, the better they know each other and the more likely they are to work as a cohesive group. By enlarging the staffs and reorganizing structures of control, Trudeau did not create a supergroup, but rather the reverse: he set up checks and balances.

The growth of the Prime Minister's Office has already been described in an earlier chapter as not a new departure by Trudeau, but the continuation of a process. The main purpose was not to replace the traditional bureaucracy but to provide the Prime Minister with alternative sources of information and ideas. Most of the new staff, in any event, performed office services for Trudeau and rarely met him. The four who had more or less instant access and counted as senior advisers were Lalonde, a French Canadian; Ivan Head, the foreign policy specialist and speechwriter, from Alberta; Press Secretary Peter Roberts, also from Alberta; and Program Secretary Jim Davey, from Montreal and Toronto. Surveying these and other members of his staff, Trudeau quipped that he had been infiltrated by Westerners.

Some powerful officials have been mentioned in earlier chapters: Bryce and Reisman at Finance, Robertson and Pitfield at the Privy Council, and Al Johnson, from Saskatchewan, who became Secretary of the Treasury Board. Ed Ritchie was Ambassador in Washington before being called home and appointed Undersecretary at External Affairs with a mandate to pick the department up off the floor after its first, bruising encounters with the Prime Minister. Also at External, Allan Gotlieb was influential in launching the foreign policy review and then became Deputy Minister in the new Communications department. A brilliant lawyer from Winnipeg, he left Harvard when he found it insufficiently challenging, and was much admired by members of Trudeau's staff who regularly consulted him on problems outside his own department. He coined in another context the quip which Trudeau used with devastating effect against Claude Ryan and the provisional government rumors during the FLQ crisis: lack of power corrupts and absolute lack of power corrupts absolutely.

The Governor of the Bank of Canada is in a category of his own, with a large measure of independence in setting monetary policy and, therefore, influencing the economy. If the Government disagrees with what he is doing, it may issue to him a formal order to change course. But this has never happened, and if it did, the Governor might feel compelled to resign, touching off a first class political row and possibly a financial crisis. It is therefore essential for the Governor and the Finance Minister to work in harmony, and the sensational conflict between Governor James Coyne and the Diefenbaker Government was largely the result of lack of contact and understanding. Coyne's successor, Louis Rasminsky, did not make the same mistake. Every Friday, he stepped out of the bank to cross the road to the Finance Department for a chat. Rasminsky was frequently invited to meetings of the Trudeau Cabinet's committee on Economic Policy, and occasionally briefed meetings of provincial Premiers on the financial situation. Like all bankers, he took an extremely serious view of inflation and was a powerful influence on Trudeau. He was not well known on Parliament Hill. Many MPs would not have recognized the tall man with the snowy hair and impressive demeanor. But those who did meet him while travelling out of Ottawa reported that he sometimes carried a thermos of his own special martinis and a fund of amusing stories.

The Cabinet

All the aides and officials were, however, advisers, influential but not final decision-makers. The Cabinet remained the place where the advice had to be weighed and the political choices made. Here also, Trudeau's system tended to disperse power and responsibilty, rather than to concentrate it in a few hands.

No matter how a Cabinet is organized, there is a degree of conflict between the responsibility of the individual minister for his own department and the collective responsibility of all the ministers for all the policies of government. Under Trudeau's system, a minister's plans for his department were discussed and often amended in one or two committees before going to the full Cabinet. They became in effect committee proposals, lessening the power of individual ministers and increasing the collective power.

This helps to explain why a number of ministers who put through important legislation in the Commons and were highly visible in public, were never powerful personalities in the Cabinet. Some have already been mentioned: Pépin, Chrétien, Munro, Mackasey. Another in this category was Jack Davis, a cool and purposeful man with a slide-rule mind; he was in fact one of the few engineers in a Parliament of arts graduates. He set up the new Department of the Environment in 1971, employing a quarter of all the scientists in the federal service, and built up an impressive-looking battery of legal weapons against pollution: the Canada Water Act, the Fisheries Act, the Canada Shipping Act, the Arctic Waters Pollution Prevention Act, the Clean Air Act, the Motor Vehicle Safety Act, and others. It remained to be seen how well the weapons would work against entrenched business interests, and on a battlefield divided between federal and provincial jurisdiction. But Canada seemed to be well prepared compared with other countries when Davis led the national deputation to the UN conference on the Human Environment in Stockholm in June 1972, and scored a personal success.

Chunky, bald-headed Ron Basford was an aggressive Minister of Consumer and Corporate Affairs for more than three years and introduced much important legislation: the Hazardous Products Act to ban dangerous goods from the consumer market; amendments to food and drug and patent laws to create more competition in the drug industry in the hope of reducing prices; the Packaging and Labelling Act and the Weights and Measures Act to protect consumers; amendments to the Canada Corporations Act to compel disclosure of more information; and the controversial Competition Act designed to be a more effective law against combines. When Trudeau moved Basford to Urban Affairs in 1972, it was interpreted as a gesture to businessmen outraged by the Competition Act, and Basford himself was disappointed and appeared to have suffered a setback. But he enjoyed prestige among the insiders when Trudeau appointed him to the Priorities and Planning committee to succeed Arthur Laing, the veteran British Columbia minister who had decided to retire.

Basford was clearly one of the rising, younger politicians in the Government, along with Andras and Justice Minister Otto Lang.

At another level of influence in the Cabinet were the ministers with special knowledge and regional backing. Allan MacEachen spoke for Nova Scotia and for the Commons in which he was the Government's Leader. One of the few ministers with a feel for Parliament, he would interrupt a Cabinet discussion by saying softly: "They'll never go for that," meaning that the Opposition would not let the Government get away with whatever it was planning. The Cabinet learnt too slowly to take his advice. A bachelor and Cape Breton Highlander whose chauffeur doubled as a private bagpiper, MacEachen was something of a mystic among the technocrats.

Jim Richardson, the young business tycoon from Winnipeg and Minister of Supply and Services, was regarded at first with tolerance bordering on contempt when he warned of Western alienation and urged decentralization of federal operations. He won more serious attention when word began to filter back that he was perhaps the only Liberal on the Prairies to have made himself popular enough to have a safe seat.

The Power and the Influence

This review of the Trudeau Cabinet does not seek to assess every minister. Some were old men on the edge of retirement, and others fresh recruits at the time of writing. A few made no visible impression, and the activities of senior ministers such as Edgar Benson and Mitchell Sharp are discussed elsewhere in the book. But the men with the greatest influence throughout the period were, quite simply, those whose opinions Trudeau grew most to respect.

Treasury Board President Drury managed the public service and cut the spending estimates with a strong, impartial hand which enraged left-wingers in the Government but kept the finances under better control than they had been for years. With roots deep in English-speaking Quebec, he was educated at the Royal Military College and in his thirties he was a hard-driving army brigadier winning a string of medals for gallantry in Europe. He returned to a career of public service with the United Nations, the federal civil service and then in politics. He marched about Parliament Hill with a straight back, close-cut fair hair, cool blue eyes and suits like uniforms. In the Commons, he answered crisply, and in his department he tried to run the vast federal machine with the techniques and the smooth efficiency of a big business. His strength was his integrity. Other ministers might curse him heartily for cutting up their spending plans, but they never suspected him of political motives. And he gave Trudeau forthright advice from his point of view, which was conventional and conservative. He was related by marriage to Walter Gordon who once cheerfully offered to find out how valuable he was to Trudeau by arranging to have him kidnapped by Latin American guerillas and held for ransom — which was a joke before October 1970.

Donald Macdonald, a giant of a man who was nicknamed Thumper at school, had a delightfully frank explanation for his influence. "Why am I powerful? Because I'm close to Trudeau, that's why," he told Eric Malling of the *Toronto Star*. "I supported him from the beginning." He was indeed an early backer of Trudeau's leadership campaign, and he became the Cabinet's key political man in Ontario, solving problems, smoothing those that were insoluble, managing the limited patronage left in the system.

He also took on the thankless task after the election of forcing new rules of procedure on the Commons against cries of outrage and abuse, took over the Defense Department briefly to bring out the White Paper on new policies, and then moved to Energy, Mines and Resources to hard-bargain with U.S. interests for Canadian control of a gas pipeline from the Arctic. But Trudeau appreciated, in addition to his loyalty, his tough, independent mind. When the Cabinet was wrestling with the NATO policy decision, Macdonald conducted his own research and wrote and circulated his own position paper.

Don Jamieson first came to Ottawa from Newfoundland as a young radio reporter covering the negotiations which led to the entry of the island into Confederation in 1949. He had originally opposed the union, but went home converted, a convinced Liberal, and quickly achieved fame and fortune with interests in radio and TV stations. Canada's newest and poorest province always felt the need for special representation in the federal capital, and when Jamieson returned in 1966, it was as an MP preparing to become Newfoundland's Ambassador-to-the-Cabinet. A friendly, roly-poly man with a taste for bright shirts and the silver tones and easy fluency of a broadcaster, he charmed the House of Commons. But he was also in private an omniverous reader with a perceptive political mind. When Trudeau took him into the Cabinet in 1968, he quickly made his influence felt in two ways. He persistently challenged new spending programs, demanding to know the long-term costs and implications, which made him known as a right-winger.

But in the committee on Priorities and Planning, he became a social analyst, sympathetic to new trends and pointing out the implications for the Government. For example, in a long, privately circulated paper, he questioned the consumer economy with an analysis which began: "Conventional wisdom and experience maintain that expectations of economic bouyancy produce a predictable pattern of consumer spending. The argument goes that if governments and others create a climate of confidence large numbers of consumers can be persuaded to buy large quantities of goods, even if they don't really need them. That they don't need many of them is obvious.... The presumption, up to now, has been that most people have a latent desire to acquire these new possessions either because they offer greater convenience, are status symbols or simply because when prospects are reasonably bright people get a kick out of spending money on new possessions. . . .

"I believe many accept too readily the premise that history will repeat itself and that we have simply to follow precedent, with minor variations, in order to bail ourselves out of any economic slow-down. And even if they are right, this still leaves unanswered the basic question of whether we should be content merely to entrench a value system that is undoubtedly wasteful in many important respects and, perhaps, counter-productive in terms of other important though less tangible goals that we are seeking to identify and pursue." Trudeau appreciated Jamieson's blend of hard-headed realism and social curiosity, and also the way in which he took over the sprawling, sagging Transport Department bureaucracy and set about turning it into a decentralized, energetic and innovative force in national and urban affairs.

When Pearson was looking for a new Quebec lieutenant in 1965, Marchand was his choice, and Trudeau came along almost by accident. In 1968, many Liberals wanted Marchand to run as the French Canadian candidate for the leadership, but he insisted on pushing Trudeau forward. When Trudeau became Prime Minister, however, Marchand remained a personality in Quebec, and he put the source of his political power in a nutshell when he said: "He (Trudeau) relies on my judgment as far as the political situation in Quebec is concerned. This is the impression I have." It was the impression of others also because Marchand spoke in Cabinet about the interests of the workers of Quebec with the gut feelings of a former union leader, with a degree of political passion which was rare in that cool assembly.

Gérard Pelletier, the third of the Wise Men, was unlike both his friends, more analytical than Marchand and more sensitive than Trudeau, a quiet man with a high-domed head, hooded eyes and only the trace of a smile around his mouth. Diefenbaker thought he had a remarkable physical resemblance to Machiavelli, the Renaissance statesman whose name has become synonomous, unfairly, with political immorality, and he helped to establish the legend that the Secretary of State was really the sinister figure behind Trudeau's throne, the evil genius working to make the French Fact triumphant throughout Canada. To Pelletier's staff and colleagues, the caricature was grotesque. They saw an entirely different man, unassuming, fair-minded although strong in his convictions, open to argument and experimentation.

Pelletier had his own rational explanation for the violence with which he was attacked by Diefenbaker and others, particularly in the West. He believed that as a personal friend of Trudeau and the minister responsible for some of his most controversial programs, including bilingualism, he served as a convenient target when the Prime Minister was too popular to be seriously damaged by criticism. The Secretary of State is always vulnerable because he reports to the Commons for a number of controversial agencies over which he has no real control: the CBC, the National Film Board, the Company of Young Canadians, the Canada Council and others. Pelletier had in addition responsibility not only for bilingualism, but for youth policy and cultural support to ethnic minorities and community-action groups. It would be hard to devise a portfolio with more political booby-traps, but Pelletier moved serenely through the explosions, explaining that when he was editor of *La Presse*, he had learnt to live with crises.

He was quite unafraid of controversy. When considering a grant to *Guerilla*, the radical underground paper in Toronto, he made an unpublicized visit to the staff's commune to sip tea and argue politics — and then decided to offer the money. Gradually, much of the hostility toward him in the House and the press gave way to grudging admiration, almost affection.

The Heir Apparent

The minister in the Trudeau Cabinet who grew most in stature was John Napier Turner. For years he had seemed too good to be true: raised in the Ottawa establishment by a widowed mother who was a senior government economist;

a Rhodes scholar and an athlete named most popular student on campus at the University of British Columbia; a young lawyer who learnt fluent French in the Montreal courts; stepson of the millionaire Lieutenant Governor of British Columbia and son-in-law of a Winnipeg insurance tycoon; MP at 33 and junior minister two years later; handsome, energetic and handgroomed by Prime Minister Pearson for stardom; a credible candidate for the Liberal leadership in 1968 who made no deals and emerged as a man to be reckoned with in the party.

During his term as Justice Minister, Trudeau had begun to convert the staid old department into a vital agency of legal and social reform. When he asked Turner in 1968 to take over the portfolio and continue the work, it was a compliment and recognition of the power and quality behind the shiny good looks. Turner quickly convinced even the sceptics that he was a senior minister of skill and substance. He piloted through the Commons the controversial Omnibus Criminal Code bill which Trudeau had introduced before the election, reforming the law on abortion, homosexuality and a score of other matters, and took charge of the Official Languages Bill, negotiating a settlement with the Western provinces when they threatened a court battle to test its constitutionality.

Then Turner began to build a record of law reform which was one of the important but least known accomplishments of the Trudeau Government. "During my tenure in Justice, our thrust will be a three-fold one," he announced. "First, to balance the rights of the citizen against the State. Second, to give Canada a more contemporary criminal law — credible, enforceable, flexible, compassionate. Third, to promote equality of access and equality of treatment before the law for rich and poor alike."

A new Expropriations Act improved safeguards for the citizen whose land was taken by government for public purposes. The Federal Court Act broadened the power of the courts to review quasi-judicial decisions by boards and commissions. Another omnibus bill proposed to abolish flogging and the offense of attempting to commit suicide, among other reforms. A Law Reform Commission was established to keep all the laws of Canada under continuous and systematic review and recommend changes. A Bail Reform bill strengthened the rights of the citizen in dealing with the police before appearing in court, and a Privacy Bill proposed for the first time to ban wire-tapping except where legally authorized. Turner was negotiating with the provinces to organize a national legal-aid plan when he left the Justice Department in January 1972 to take over, at Trudeau's request, the Finance portfolio, the toughest job in the Government.

Although Turner and Trudeau were sometimes rumored to dislike each other, it was more gossip than truth. They were not close friends, but they respected each other and worked together with mutual confidence. During the Quebec crisis in October 1970, Turner made the leading speech in the Commons in defense of the War Measures Act and later put through the substitute Public Order legislation. His only major fight with Trudeau occurred when he insisted on allowing the legislation to expire on schedule in April 1971, restoring normal civil liberties, when Trudeau wanted to continue it at the request of Premier Bourassa.

In Turner's office on Parliament Hill, there was a picture of him with Trudeau. Both men were obviously under intense strain, frozen in grainy black and white by a news photographer at 3 a.m. as they emerged from the Prime Minister's office a few hours after learning of the murder of Pierre Laporte. The picture was inscribed: "To my colleague John Turner, Oct. 17, 1970, on an unforgettable moment for both of us and for Canada. With warm regard, Pierre E. Trudeau." Trudeau normally signs as P.E. Trudeau; Pierre is his intimate style and reflects the feeling which grew between the two men during the crisis that they were comrades in arms.

The Prime Minister

The relationship of a Prime Minister to his Cabinet used to be described as that of First Among Equals. He was head of the Government with powerful prerogatives, including the right to appoint and dismiss his colleagues in the

Cabinet. But he was still a member of a collective leadership and could not impose his views against a clear majority in the Cabinet without running the risk that he would be repudiated and removed from office. But as we have seen, the power of Prime Ministers increased as the party machines they controlled became stronger and politics became more a popularity contest between leaders.

The balance of power in a modern Cabinet depends to a great extent on how the Prime Minister wishes to run things. He can appoint strong or weak ministers, allow them more or less freedom of action in their portfolios, exercise his own authority or seek consensus.

Although Trudeau's public image was that of a Prime Minister who dominated his Cabinet and dictated all decisions, the reality in private was different. He was a consensus leader who appointed energetic ministers, encouraged them to be innovative, and insisted on full discussion of alternatives before decisions were made. Although he had the advantage of overview, of being the only man in possession of the complete picture of events, he presided over the Cabinet as a chairman rather than a leader. He was, for example, less prone than Pearson had been to arrive at a meeting, announce a decision and demand approval. Ministers grumbled more about the length of time it took to get decisions through the Cabinet machine than they did about lack of discussion, and far from viewing Trudeau as a tyrant, some of them complained that he too often witheld his opinion by indulging in Socratic dialogues.

The qualities of a leader, however, are best revealed in times of crisis, and a crisis is the subject of the next and final chapter.

8

THE OCTOBER CRISIS: A QUESTION OF LEADERSHIP

When the FLQ conspiracy of October 1970 was finally laid bare before the courts, it was seen to be the work of a mere handful of terrorists. With their disturbed personalities and naive idealism, they were more pitiful than terrifying. Poorly armed and unorganized, they obviously posed no direct threat to the security of Canada. But the extraordinary events they had set in train were, briefly, an explosive threat. Canada was hurled into a crisis which rocked the Trudeau Government and disrupted national priorities, shook the Quebec Government so severely that many observers expected it to collapse, and caused the suspension of civil liberties.

How was it possible for so few people with a smattering of revolutionary ideology to cause so much damage in the peaceable kingdom of Canada? Who was responsible for allowing events to run so wildly out of hand?

The story began when modern terrorism struck Quebec in 1963. A dozen adolescents and adventurers began a campaign for separatism by placing bombs in Montreal and Quebec City and hurling Molotov cocktails at federal armouries. They called themselves the Front de Libération

Québécois and were led by a Belgian immigrant who had learnt guerilla methods during the underground resistance to German occupation in the Second World War. The police soon broke up this conspiracy, but the seeds of violence had been sown. As the founders of the FLQ went off to jail, others were manufacturing the bombs with which to carry on their campagin. That was the pattern in the next few years, as wave followed wave of the FLQ — now the Front de Libération du Québec.

While the terrorists were always few in number, they attracted enormous publicity. Socialist revolution joined separatism as the goal. Fidel Castro became the revolutionary hero to emulate and Algeria provided the model of the successful movement for national liberation. Student radicalism became more violent in the United States and black ghettos were swept by riots. Trudeau remarked in 1968: "I am perhaps less worried now about what might happen over the Berlin Wall than what might happen in Chicago, New York, and perhaps our own great cities in Canada."

In Quebec, the escalation of violence continued through the Sixties. The bombs became bigger and better. Seven people were killed and several injured. New movements sprang up to demonstrate for popular causes and served as a screen and a recruiting agency for the FLQ. Montreal Mayor Jean Drapeau and Lucien Saulnier, chairman of the city's Executive Council, charged that a few members of the Company of Young Canadians were using federal funds to promote revolution.

Trudeau was so outraged by violence in the streets of Montreal in 1969 that he threatened to close down the French language network of the CBC if it appeared to be encouraging separatists. Early in 1970, police uncovered a plot to kidnap the Israeli consul in Montreal. A few months later, a raid on a cottage in the Laurentians turned up plans to seize the U.S. consul and hold him for political ransom.

So it should have been no surprise when the FLQ finally carried out its plan on October 5, 1970. Four men drove up to the Montreal home of British trade commissioner James Cross at breakfast time and carried him away at gun-point. It should not have been a shock, but it was — a numbing shock. Despite his prescience in 1968 about urban violence and his awareness of events in Quebec, Trudeau was not prepared for this emergency. A Government which prided itself on planning to deal with issues before they became crises, had no plan with which to meet this predictable crisis.

Because a foreign diplomat was involved, it was not a normal crime to be handled by provincial law enforcement agencies. The federal Government was responsible under international convention for the safety of Cross, and External Affairs Minister Mitchell Sharp was the natural spokesman.

Within a few minutes of the news of the kidnapping reaching Ottawa, a Task Force was formed. Officials from the External Affairs Department, the Prime Minister's Office, the RCMP and other departments concerned, gathered in the new Operations Centre in the East Block on Parliament Hill. This centre, developed by the External Affairs department for "crisis management," is essentially a briefing room and offices which can be immediately occupied, all linked by phone, radio and cable to missions abroad, the Prime Minister's switchboard, the news agencies and, for this crisis the Quebec Government. It was here that the first FLQ ransom note was received in mid-afternoon on October 5, with its extravagant list of demands: (1) No raids or investigations by the police; (2) Publication of the FLQ's manifesto on the front pages of the principal Quebec papers and broadcast on prime-time TV; (3) Freeing from jail of 20 FLQ members — the so-called "political prisoners" — so that they and three other men on bail, with their families, could escape from Canada; (4) A plane to fly them to Cuba or Algeria; (5) Jobs for the "Lapalme boys" — truck drivers who had lost their jobs when the Post Office changed contractors; (6) $500,000 in gold bullion; (7) The name of the informer who had broken up the last FLQ cell.

Sharp reported the abduction of Cross to the Commons but said cautiously that the reasons for it had not been conclusively established. Quebec Premier Robert Bourassa, meanwhile, was preparing to leave for New York to persuade the money-men that his province was a safe place to invest their capital, and was content to leave the Cross affair for Sharp to work out with Quebec Justice Minister Jérôme Choquette.

Neither Government knew what to make of the situation in those first hours. Was the kidnapping possibly a student prank? Did the demand for $500,000 indicate a criminal rather than a political enterprise? What would the British Government expect to be done for its diplomat? Another communique from the terrorists established that it was in fact the FLQ at work, and a new set of questions arose. As Secretary of State Gérard Pelletier has written in his book, *The October Crisis*, "It was necessary to evaluate the nature and extent of the threat which the FLQ and its sympathizers represented to the legitimate authority of the governments, to the confidence the people had in them, and, in a general sense, to the social and political climate of the province and the country."

The evaluation began when Trudeau called his senior ministers to a special meeting in the Cabinet room early on Tuesday morning, and then telephoned Prime Minister Edward Heath in London and Premier Bourassa in Quebec City. During the question period in the Commons that afternoon, he slouched moodily in his seat, fending off the Opposition and tapping impatiently with his glasses, and then hurried off to a full meeting of the Cabinet. The Government's basic strategy was being decided, but the decisions had to be made largely in ignorance. Pelletier confesses that there was in the Cabinet "a large measure of naivety" because "no one believed that such a thing could happen here." How large was the FLQ? Nobody knew for sure. How many weapons did it have? Well, some rifles had been stolen and thousands of pounds of dynamite had disappeared from construction sites over the past few years.

Three broad courses of action were open to Trudeau and the Cabinet:

(1) They could refuse to have any truck or trade with the terrorists. But that might be to condemn Cross to death when the Government was obligated to try to save him.

"From the very first moment, I was convinced that every care must be taken to avoid giving a reply of a humiliating and abrupt nature that could drive the FLQ to some desperate act," writes Pelletier.

(2) They could hope to save Cross by acceding to the ransom demands, including release of the so-called political prisoners from jail. But that would be to recognize the FLQ as a parallel power in Canada, able to reverse the verdicts of the courts. And it would tempt the terrorists or criminal groups to try the same tactic again.

(3) They could compromise. While privately resolving not to bow to the key demand for release of the FLQ prisoners, they could seek to negotiate terms.

The third course was the easiest course, particularly in an atmosphere of uncertainty, and it was chosen. By then it was too late to present the carefully worded statement to the Commons before the dinner adjournment at 6 p.m. and Sharp spoke to the opposition leaders to give them an idea of what was happening and to let them know he would make a statement at 8 p.m.

Curiously, the tension of crisis had not communicated itself to the Commons or to the public who usually swarm onto Parliament Hill when exciting events are afoot. It was an important night on Ottawa's social calendar: Trudeau was entertaining MPs and their wives at 24 Sussex Drive. When Sharp sauntered into the Commons Chamber a minute after 8 p.m., with an after-dinner cigar stuck in his breast pocket, he had to stand chatting and laughing with the Speaker until enough members straggled in to resume the sitting. Then Sharp read his statement in a firm voice, summarizing the ransom demand and adding: "Clearly these are wholly unreasonable demands and their authors could not have expected them to be accepted. I need hardly say that this set of demands will not be met. I continue, however, to hope that some basis can be found for Mr. Cross's safe return. Indeed, I hope the abductors will find a way to establish communication to achieve this."

The Government of Canada had officially opened negotiations with the FLQ. It was not taking the strong and unyielding position which many people later came to associate with Trudeau. It was offering to come to terms with a band of terrorists.

But was the offer to negotiate genuine or a ruse to buy time for the frantic police investigation already under way? Was Ottawa baiting a trap for the kidnappers? No: Trudeau has since said that the offer was genuine and Pelletier is specific in denying any Machiavellian purpose.

In the Operations Centre, the duty officers settled down to wait for the FLQ to respond, and in Montreal the next day, Justice Minister Choquette added his voice to the plea for negotiations. Denouncing terrorism in the name of the people, he added: "There is the case of Mr. Cross as a human being. The Governments are ready to investigate all practical means out of this impasse."

The FLQ was ready to negotiate. Another communique was issued demanding as evidence of good faith: (1) broadcasting of the manifesto; (2) an end to police raids. The demand for $500,000 was tacitly withdrawn. Sharp replied that Ottawa was prepared to arrange for the broadcast, "But we must have assurances that, without the imposition of unacceptable conditions, Mr. Cross will be delivered safe and sound. . . . As a first step, I invite those holding Mr. Cross to name some person with whom the authorities or a person representing the authorities can deal with confidence in making arrangements leading to Mr. Cross's early and safe release." The FLQ bluntly refused: a communique repeated the two demands and said: "We reject the idea of a mediator; we will continue to establish our communications in our own way, avoiding traps set by the fascist police." Ottawa backed down and ordered the manifesto to be read over Radio-Canada anyway.

Federal sources said it was a small gesture because the manifesto had already been published in the press and was a stupid document anyway. "The manifesto revealed nothing," says Pelletier. "All its propaganda was based upon well-known facts. But because of the dramatic circumstances surrounding the broadcast, the FLQ forced a large section of the population to listen to things that for the most part have been said for a long time." It was effective propaganda, couched in the language of the street and appealing to social and economic grievances rather than to separatism. "The Front de Libération du Québec is not a messiah, nor a modern-day Robin Hood," it began. "It is a group of Quebec workers who have decided to use every means to make sure the people of Quebec take control of their destiny." It named the "big bosses" of the capitalist system — Steinberg, Bronfman, Molson and others — and dismissed the politicians as of no account: "Drapeau the dog, Bourassa the lackey of the Simards, and Trudeau the fairy. . . ."

In the four corners of Quebec, may those who have been contemptuously called lousy French and alcoholics start fighting their best against the enemies of liberty and justice and prevent all professional swindlers and robbers, the bankers, the businessmen, the judges and the sold-out politicators from causing harm.

"We are the workers of Quebec and will continue to the bitter end. We want to replace the slave society with a free society, functioning by itself and for itself; a society open to the world."

Pelletier concedes that people identified with the manifesto: "Who does not long, when he receives a summons from the police or compares his gross pay with the net total of his cheque, to give the authorities a good going over or address a few suitable insults to some minister or other? The insolence of taunts addressed to public figures encouraged thoughts of this kind to come to the surface in the listener or viewer, who said to himself, thinking of Mr. Trudeau or Mayor Drapeau, 'They got it right in the eye.'"

The FLQ members certainly thought they had scored a victory. When the kidnappers of Cross finally departed to Cuba they left behind tape recordings in which they discussed their tactics, and the transcripts included a passage in which they gloated that the broadcast of the manifesto had attracted a lot of sympathy and: "For the first time, patriots of the Front managed to express themselves by entering every home, through Radio Canada. . . . They were in touch for the first time. . . . By making them read our manifesto, well let's say that stirred it up . . ."

It did stir things up. *The Last Post,* a radical news magazine published in Montreal, reported later:

"A survey of opinions on hot-line programs on popular French stations in Montreal showed that the vast majority of callers condemned the actual acts of the FLQ, but over 50 per cent supported the spirit of the manifesto. A CBC interviewer took a survey in front of a French Canadian church after 11 o'clock mass on Sunday and found that condemnation of the acts was almost universal, but that half the people he talked to expressed sympathy for the things said in the FLQ manifesto. Student newspapers came out in favor of the FLQ, some with grave reservations about the tactics, others not."

Liberal MPs began to realise that the FLQ was appealing dangerously well to the discontents among their working class constituents, with the help of radicals in the media who sympathized with the revolutionary objectives of the terrorists, if not with their methods.

Meanwhile, the FLQ had lost nothing. It still had Cross and negotiations were continuing. The Governments issued statements, the terrorists replied with communiques. Both sides were maneuvering for advantage. "There was a good deal of effort made to analyze very closely everything that came from them," said Claude Roquet, the External Affairs officer who led the federal Task Force. "There were signs in several of their communiques that the so-called 'Liberation Cell' was in no rush to kill Mr. Cross. The Government had already made certain gestures, such as brodcasting what the kidnappers called the manifesto. Deadlines put on Mr. Cross's life passed without mishap and gradually one saw that these people might wish to take advantage of an opportunity to get out of the predicament they had created for themselves."

Pelletier is even more complacent about this period: "In short the matter was not settled; far from it. But it could be hoped that, after a few weeks of shifting back and forth, a compromise could be worked out."

The compromise was soon offered. As the latest of the FLQ deadlines for the execution of Cross arrived at 6 p.m. on Saturday, October 9 — five days after the kidnapping —

Choquette appeared on TV with a conciliatory statement and a proposal: "The feeling within the person speaking is one of social reconciliation, of acceptance of change, of the abolition of ambiguity and distrust, and of the rallying of all Québecois, despite our differences of opinion, around a common ideal . . . I understand that it is by virtue of a particular conception of society that the authors of the abduction of Mr. Cross have acted. But this conception they cannot impose upon the majority of their fellow citizens by violence or by murder, which would in effect discredit it forever. Without giving in to undue pressure, even dangerous pressure, the 'ruling authorities,' as you say, are not unaware that there are areas of discontent and that injustice exists. . . . The Government of Quebec is a government dedicated to reform. It is deeply concerned with social justice for all its citizens, especially the most needy. Therefore, the proposal which I can put forward at the present time is to ask you to take account of our good faith, and of our desire to examine objectively the injustices of our society."

Choquette went on to offer several concessions in return for the freeing of Cross: (1) The so-called political prisoners could not be released from prison, but would be eligible for parole; (2) Alleged terrorists awaiting trial would be judged with clemency; (3) The kidnappers could have safe conduct out of Canada or, if they preferred, a guarantee of clemency before the courts. "Rising above all individual considerations, we must build a society which deals effectively with justice and liberty," said the Justice Minister in an emotional ending to his broadcast. "Gentlemen, you have your part to play in this matter if you so choose."

It was significant that a Quebec minister, instead of Sharp in Ottawa, was now speaking for the two Governments. Choquette was obviously talking to the people of Quebec as well as to the kidnappers. He was implicitly agreeing with all those who had sympathized with the FLQ manifesto that there were great social injustices waiting to be corrected in Quebec. He was tacitly recognizing the FLQ as part of the political process in Quebec and inviting it to change tactics and join in democratic debate and decision-making. It was a remarkable offer to forgive and forget, to legitimize a movement which had engaged in violence and murder.

The Trudeau Government, for its part, was agreeing to waive the criminal law and allow the kidnappers to go free out of Canada.

If the FLQ had accepted the compromise at this point, or been able to hang on for a few more weeks, as Pelletier hoped, and haggle for a few more concessions, it would have achieved a significant success.

In addition to spreading its propaganda and winning a good deal of favorable attention in Quebec, it had brought two Governments to terms, made the police look foolish, and proved that it was above the law. The federal and provincial Governments had not acted toward the terrorists with firmness at this point, but with a desire to compromise.

But the Liberation Cell which had seized Cross had no opportunity to appreciate the degree of its success. Another band of terrorists, the Chénier Cell, entered the scene. They had apparently had discussions with some members of the Liberation Cell months before about the possibility of a kidnapping operation, but had then split up and lost contact. When Cross was taken, the Chénier men were driving around Texas, apparently planning to buy guns with which to stage robberies to raise funds. They heard about the kidnapping on the radio and rushed back to Canada to get in on the revolution.

They chose as their victim Pierre Laporte, the 49 year old Quebec Minister of Labor and Immigration, and made plans to kidnap him. As soon as they heard Choquette refuse to release the FLQ men in prison, they drove to Laporte's home and seized him as he was playing ball outside.

The kidnapping of Laporte changed everything. Cross was British, a diplomat, a pawn for whom the average French Canadian might feel sympathy but not kinship. Laporte was a Québecois known to thousands of people, a popular figure in the Liberal Party, a member of the relatively small community of French Canadian politicians in which everyone knows everyone else, and relationships cross party boundaries.

For example, Michel Chartrand, the revolutionary

Montreal labor leader who never hid his sympathy for the FLQ, was a former school friend and political ally of Trudeau. They campaigned together for Jean Drapeau when he was a political candidate opposing conscription for the armed forces, and Chartrand tried to persuade Trudeau to become leader of the CCF socialist party in Quebec. Mrs. Chartrand, about that time, was sharing an office with Gérard Pelletier, then a Catholic youth worker. The third occupant was a young lawyer called Daniel Johnson, later to become Union Nationale Premier of Quebec.

Political differences divided the group and they were bitter opponents long before October 1970. But the lesson is that Quebec politics are almost a family affair, and when Laporte was kipnapped, it was suddenly civil war within the family.

Premier Bourassa was still in New York on business that Saturday, hoping for the fog to lift so that he could fly to Boston and have a publicity picture taken with Senator Edward Kennedy. But the fog was stubborn, so he flew home to Montreal and into the midst of the Laporte crisis.

At 9 a.m. the following morning, Sunday, the Chénier Cell issued its first communique: "In the face of the persistence of the governmental authorities in not complying with the requirements of the FLQ and in conformity with Plan 3 established earlier to provide for such a refusal . . . ," Laporte had been kidnapped and would be executed at 10 p.m. that night unless all seven of the original FLQ demands were met. It appears to have been a bluff in part: there was no Plan 3 and the Chénier gang were not in touch with the Liberation Cell. But to the public and the authorities, it looked like a major conspiracy. What would happen next? Who was next to be seized or killed?

Bourassa moved into the Queen Elizabeth Hotel where he and Cabinet colleagues could meet and operate under guard. Radio broadcasts were filled with excited speculation. Fear took hold of some. As Hugh MacLennan, the distinguished author of *Two Solitudes*, recalled later in an article in *Maclean's* Magazine, he and his wife were at their cottage and took turns sleeping, "as did several thousand others on that night, so that at least one of us would be awake should a car come up to the cottage filled with masked young men." Even the leader of the Parti Québécois separatists, René Lévesque, asked for police protection — according to Bourassa.

The most convincing evidence of the mood of uncertainty in Montreal that Sunday afternoon has been given by Claude Ryan, the nationalist editor of the influential paper, *Le Devoir*. He called his principal colleagues to a meeting to discuss the situation and they developed three main ideas about what might happen.

In the "dire confusion" felt by the political authorities, Bourassa might: (1) Succumb to pressure from Trudeau in Ottawa and Drapeau and Saulnier in Montreal to invoke the War Measures Act and given the federal Government responsibility for solving Quebec's crisis; (2) Lose control of his government and be forced to form a "provisional Government" team composed of the best people from the various provincial parties, backed up by a few political personalities from various milieus or, most likely; (3) Seek a negotiated solution with the FLQ and emerge from the crisis with a confident and united Government — although one that should still be "strengthened."

A week after the kidnapping of Cross, a day after the seizing of Laporte, the most influential editor in Quebec considered the situation so serious that an emergency coalition government might have to be formed. There was no thought of refusing to yield to blackmail. The concessions which had already been made to the FLQ were regarded as taking a hard line. The fear was that the Government of Quebec might refuse to make a deal with the terrorists to save the hostages.

There was never of course a conspiracy to set up a provisional government in Quebec. There was simply speculation that it might become necessary. When word of Ryan's theorizing reached Ottawa, it was not taken as evidence of a plot. It merely confirmed Trudeau's long-standing opinion that democracy had not yet taken deep root in Quebec. He had stated his view with brutal frankness in a 1958 article entitled *Some Obstacles to Democracy in Quebec*: "If I were to quote all the material proving that French Canadians fundamentally do not believe in democracy, and that on the whole neither the pulpit, nor the legislative assembly, nor the press is doing much to instil such a belief, I 'would exhaust time and encroach upon eternity.' "

Later in the crisis, it was suggested in a report in the *Toronto Star*, picked up elsewhere, that a plot to establish a provisional Government was the real reason the War Measures Act had been invoked. But this was not so. Investigating the story, CBC correspondent Larry Zolf, a student of political history as well as a reporter, wrote a script (it was never used) explaining what was going on in the minds of Trudeau and his advisers. Trudeau's Principal Secretary, Marc Lalonde, and his Press Secretary, Roméo LeBlanc, saw the script so it must be regarded as authoritative. Zolf wrote in part: "In a sense Prime Minister Trudeau sees Quebec democracy today facing the same dangers the Third Republic of France faced in the 1930s, when the Popular Front threat from the Left and the Fascist threat from the Right produced the collapse of the democrats in the middle.

"What people close to Trudeau seem to be reading these days is William Shirer's *The Collapse of the Third Republic* and Macmillan's and Eden's memoirs on the failure of will by the European democracies during the Munich crisis. The Trudeau people feel that this is the kind of context in which to view Ryan's activities. Ryan's mustering the Left elites in Quebec's labor and co-operative movements could have led to a countervailing mustering of Quebec's conservative authoritarian elites. In the middle, in an exorable bind, would be Robert Bourassa and the Quebec Liberal Government and the process of democracy in the province of Quebec. Then, too, there was some concern that the youthful Bourassa, and many of his young Cabinet ministers, not having lived through such crises of democracy as the Spanish Civil War and the collapse of the Third Republic, might perhaps be misled by the kind of confusion Claude Ryan was. perhaps unwittingly, sowing."

While Trudeau was at his summer retreat on Harrington Lake brooding about the political instability of Quebec and Ryan was speculating about provisional government, that Sunday — the day after Laporte had been taken — Bourassa was coming to grips with his Cabinet at the Queen Elizabeth Hotel. Naturally, ministers were divided; any group of people will begin a discussion with different ideas. And this was a particularly horrifying discussion. They were talking about the life of a colleague and friend. The question become even more dramatic and difficult when the FLQ released, at 4.45 p.m., a pathetic personal letter from Laporte to Bourassa. "You have the power to dispose of my life," Laporte appealed. "If this were the only question and if this sacrifice were to produce good results, one could entertain it, but we are facing a well-organized escalation which will only end with the release of the 'political prisoners'. After me, there will be a third one, then a fourth, and a twentieth. If all political men are protected, they will strike elsewhere, in other classes of society. One might as well act now and avoid a bloodbath and an altogether unnecessary panic." Presumably writing with a gun at his head, Laporte pleaded that he was solely responsible for the welfare of a large family and relatives, and the pitiful letter ended: "Decide . . . on my life or on my death. I rely on you and thank you."

Under this pressure, Bourassa decided that it was essential that his Cabinet should be unanimous, or close to it, on whatever action was taken, and he was prepared to take time to win full support. His broadcast that night, to meet the FLQ deadline, was essentially an effort to gain time. He pointed out inconsistencies in FLQ demands, asked for guarantees, before negotiations could begin, that the hostages would be released, and talked vaguely of setting up mechanisms.

Meantime, he had had a long talk on the phone with Trudeau at Harrington Lake. By his own account — confirmed by Trudeau and with no evidence to the contrary — he asked Trudeau to have troops available if necessary and to be ready to invoke the War Measures Act to provide emergency powers. "It was Quebec which had the power to decide, and we decided," said Bourassa later. Trudeau was certainly encouraging Bourassa not to yield to the demands for release of the prisoners, but he was not anxious to invoke the War Measures Act, with its sweeping powers to suspend civil liberties and impose, in effect, a police state.

The Quebec Cabinet continued to wrestle with its hideous problem until Wednesday, when it seems to have reached agreement. While the papers were full of reports of disastrous division in the Government, Bourassa has always denied any basic split. In any event, no minister resigned, which was remarkable given the atmosphere and the pressures of the crisis, and no politician has since come forward to tell a story markedly different from that of the Premier.

But if opinion was stiffening within the Cabinet, it appeared to be wavering outside. The two FLQ cells kept up a barrage of communiques, delivered mainly to radio stations — the medium which Marshall McLuhan would certainly have recommended as the most effective for stirring anticipation, excitement, and alarm. The press was in a constant state of excitement, piling headline on rumor. Robert Lemieux, the FLQ's chosen mediator, was holding almost daily press conferences. Labor leader Chartrand was doing his best to rouse the rabble, and Pierre Vallières, the FLQ theorist and author of *White Niggers of America*, was to the forefront with his partner in revolution, Charles Gagnon. The police were carrying out some 200 raids a day in the search for the captives or for clues to the conspiracy. FRAP, a coalition of left-wing candidates in the coming Montreal elections, declined to condemn the FLQ, and Québec Presse, the radical labor paper, endorsed the aims although not the methods of the terrorists.

Trudeau heard from an elderly family friend in Quebec City who was too frightened to go out to the shops and was locked in his apartment. Driving down from Harrington Lake through the Gatineau Hills of Quebec to Ottawa, he noticed that children waiting for the school bus were everywhere accompanied by parents, presumably standing guard against the unknown. From such observations opinions began to take shape. Liberal MPs were reporting distress and confusion among their constituents but also a disturbing shift in public mood. The terrorists were beginning to appear as Robin Hood characters, gaily outwitting the police, frustrating the bumbling governments and pursuing what, after all, appeared to be the just cause of social reform. In Toronto, Premier Robarts spoke for the mood in militant English Canada: "It's total war." Troops were already guarding Parliament Hill and the homes of politicians in Ottawa, as a precaution against kidnapping, and thousands more were preparing to move into Montreal at the request of Bourassa.

In this atmosphere of rising alarm edging on hysteria, Ryan the nationalist, Lévesque the separatist, union leaders who were already leaning to the radical Left, and several other Quebec opinion makers, suddenly emerged as a new and formidable force in political affairs. They called a press conference and issued a statement pledging full support to Bourassa if he would negotiate "an exchange of the two hostages for the political prisoners." Couched in terms of support for the Quebec Government, it was pressure on Bourassa to be more conciliatory toward the FLQ, and also a repudiation of any intervention by Ottawa in what was said to be Quebec's affair. If there had ever been occasion to create a coalition provisional Government to handle the crisis, the men who joined to sign the Lévesque-Ryan statement would presumably have been invited to take prominent roles.

Only two weeks earlier the FLQ had been regarded as merely a fringe of fanatics and Lévesque and his separatist Parti Québécois had been the extremists in the spectrum of Quebec politics. Now, with the FLQ forming a new extreme to be reckoned with, Lévesque appeared to be moving into the centre, a force for peace and stability. Or that's how it looked from Ottawa.

Trudeau had been keeping out of the way of the press; he complained that the "main thing the FLQ is trying to gain is a hell of a lot of publicity" and he didn't want to provide it with any more. But when he was caught by two

TV newsmen outside the Commons, he let himself be engaged in an argument about the use of troops for security purposes in Ottawa and snapped: "Well, there are a lot of bleeding hearts around who just don't like to see people with helmets and guns. All I can say is, go on and bleed, but it is more important to keep law and order in the society than to be worried about weak-kneed people. . . . I think the society must take every means at its disposal to defend itself against the emergence of a parallel power which defies the elected power in this country and I think that goes to any distance."

It went very soon to the distance of sending troops into Montreal at Bourassa's request, to relieve the harassed police in guarding public buildings and to offer a reassuring presence to the people. Ironically, the soldiers had been trained as peace-keeping forces to restore order in backward countries. Who had dreamed they would ever have to keep the peace in peaceful Canada? But their training paid off and there were few incidents between soldiers and the public.

The police had a few leads on the kidnappers, but the question now was whether they would be able to complete their investigations before violence erupted in the streets. Agitators were at work among students, with some success, and a mass rally and march were planned for the night of Thursday, October 15.

Pelletier, who spent most of the period in Montreal trying to keep in touch with the public mood, has explained his view: "One of my sharpest fears during this part of the crisis was that a group of extremist students, believing the great day had come, would go out in into the streets and create disturbances, which, with the police and the army exhausted, might have ended in shooting. I perhaps yielded to a tendency towards alarmism; yet this kind of scenario has already been played out too often to make it necessary to argue for its plausibility." The Kent State tragedy, in which panicky U.S. National Guardsmen fired on students, was in many minds; likewise the memory of the student revolt which had suddenly swept Paris in 1968 and almost toppled the Government.

As 3,000 people were gathering in the Paul Sauvé arena in Montreal to hear speeches in support of the FLQ and raise their clenched fists in salute (although reports differ on how serious or enthusiastic the rally really was), Bourassa met his Cabinet in Quebec City and issued a new statement.

"Faced with the deterioration of the situation and the need to ensure public order," he began, giving the Quebec Government's assessment of the problem, "the Government of Quebec has decided to give its final viewpoint in its negotiations with the Front de Libération du Québec". In return for the release of Cross and Laporte, two concessions were offered: (1) The FLQ men in prison would not be released but parole (technically a matter for the National Parole Board) would be "firmly recommended" for five of the 20 who had requested it; (2) A plane would be available to fly the kidnappers to a chosen country.

Bourassa demanded an answer from the FLQ within six hours, and steps were already being taken to meet a refusal. In Ottawa, Trudeau and the Cabinet had agreed to invoke the War Measures Act if necessary, and regulations were drafted outlawing the FLQ and making it legal for police and military to arrest without warrant, hold without charge and search without warrant.

When nothing was heard from the FLQ by the 3 a.m. deadline set by Bourassa, an Assistant Clerk to the Privy Council, J. L. Cross, secured his footnote in history by driving to Rideau Hall, waking Governor General Roland Michener and getting his signature on a proclamation that "apprehended insurrection exists" — the authority on which the War Measures Act could be brought into action.

Before dawn that Friday morning of October 16, police swooped on homes in many parts of Quebec to round up people who they thought might have connections with the FLQ. The prime suspects must have been checked during the previous 10 days, so now the police were operating only on suspicion and there is no doubt that injustices were committed. Before the great round-up finished, more than 400 people had been interned — a much greater number than Ottawa had expected. Most were released quickly with cursory interrogation, few charges were ever laid and there were a few cases of maltreatment by the police.

In the Commons on Friday morning, Trudeau tabled letters asking for the emergency powers from Bourassa, Drapeau and Saulnier in Montreal and Police Director M. St-Pierre. But whatever the advice from Quebec, the federal Government was finally responsible for the action, and Trudeau was almost apologetic in his language. He recognized that the massive powers available under the War Measures Act were overkill and promised to replace them with more limited legislation. He sympathized in advance with those who would protest the loss of civil liberties. And he acknowledged that he might be falling into a trap: "It is a well-known technique of revolutionary groups who attempt to destroy society by unjustified means to goad the authorities into inflexible attitudes. The revolutionaries then employ this evidence of alleged authoritarianism as justification for the need to use violence in their renewed attacks on the social structure. I appeal to all Canadians not to become so obsessed by what the Government has done today in response to terrorism that they forget the opening play in this vicious game. That play was taken by the revolutionaries; they chose to use bombing, murder and kidnapping."

There was one more vicious play to come. The following evening, the FLQ announced that Laporte had been "executed in face of the arrogance of the federal Government and its lackey, Bourassa." The body was found stuffed into the trunk of a car. Canadians were appalled. The fact that the terrorists were capable of cold-blooded murder seemed, in the moment of horror, proof that emergency powers were necessary to deal with them. Criticism was silenced.

But after a decent pause, the debate about the War Measures Act began in earnest. It turned around the central issue: what was the nature of the insurrection apprehended by the Government and had the evidence been sufficient to justify suspension of civil liberties?

When most Canadians thought of insurrection, they imagined an armed revolt or guerilla warfare at least. It was assumed that the Government had secret information of a conspirarcy. Government spokesmen in Ottawa and Quebec City talked loosely enough to encourage these ideas. Justice Minister John Turner said that some day the evidence would be published. Bourassa mentioned planned assassinations. Regional Expansion Minister Jean Marchand, always emotional and now overtired by the crisis, speculated wildly about plots to blow up skyscrapers in Montreal, infiltration of high places in Quebec, and thousands of terrorists armed with rifles and tons of dynamite.

But Trudeau insisted over and over again when he was questioned that the decision to invoke the War Measures Act rested not on private intelligence but on the facts known to the public. These were the official statements from Quebec and Montreal that insurrection was apprehended; the kidnappings and threats to commit murder; the belief that a large quantity of stolen dynamite and weapons was in the hands of the FLQ; and "the state of confusion" in Quebec. Other ministers were more specific. After talking of kidnappings and threats of violence, Turner told the Commons: "More disturbing, we have a type of erosion of the public will ..." Communications Minister Eric Kierans said action had been taken to stop a drift "into the self-fulfilling prophecy of terrorism ... The Government demonstrated that Canada is not in the classical pre-revolutionary stage where the authorities are so consumed with self-doubts that they are incapable of action."

Pelletier wrote: "I felt that the preponderant element was the presence in Quebec of a great number of conscious or unconscious FLQ sympathizers, as well as a body of facts and assumptions that lent credibility to the possibility of an insurrection — that is to say, grave civil disorders — in Montreal in particular. Just as I subscribe to the belief that the FLQ — or at least what we know of it as present — represented only a limited threat to our democratic institutions, I am equally convinced that there existed, and still exists in Quebec, as in most large North American cities, two or three thousand people who, without having direct organic links with the FLQ terrorists, can easily be drawn into violent action (spontaneous or organized demonstrations which turn into rioting, more or less serious crimes, looting, etc.). The presence of the army and the special emergency measures prevented a situation propitious to such potential violence from arising." It was a matter of judgment, he said, the least bad solution to a problem for which there was no good answer.

Such explanations were never acceptable to many critics and even Canadians who had given overwhelming support to Trudeau in the crisis, and applauded his strong leadership against terrorism, must have had doubts when Cross, after his release on December 3, was reported to have said of his captors: "It was a case of six kids trying to make a revolution." When the Chénier gang were captured on December 23, they were armed with a rusty shotgun and a blank pistol.

But if the Government had not really apprehended an insurrection, why had it acted? *The Last Post* declared: "The Government's tactic was the tactic of the pre-emptive strike. The suggestion that it was limited to terrorism stands pale. It was also aimed at separatism. It could easily be argued that it was aimed against Quebec nationalism of any color — against the maintenance of any strong national Government in Quebec City."

The theory that Trudeau had conspired to exaggerate the threat from the FLQ in order to attack and discredit the democratic separatist movement became the accepted truth on the Left, in English Canada and in Quebec. PQ leader Lévesque said Trudeau had "conducted himself like a fascist manipulator." Ron Haggart, a highly respected Toronto journalist, and Aubrey Golden, a lawyer and civil rights leader, pointed out in their book on the crisis, *Rumors of War,* that most of the people rounded up by the Quebec police under emergency powers were separatists with no known connection to the FLQ, and concluded: ". . . the War Measures Act was invoked only in small part to fight violence, and in larger part to surpress a legitimate political movement. . . ." *The Mysterious East,* published in Fredericton, N.B. and one of the best of the magazines produced by academics and others as an alternative to the regular press, said: "One can even interpret the Government's action as directed against the idea of separatism itself, as an attempt to make the idea of separatism so obviously dangerous as to frighten the vast majority of Quebeckers."

Peter Newman, the editor of *Maclean's* Magazine, wrote of "Pierre Trudeau's stifling of dissent at bayonet point." Many commentators in the *Canadian Forum* and elsewhere interpreted the federal use of troops and emergency powers to mean that even if Quebec made a democratic decision to separate, Trudeau would not permit peaceful disengagement.

The critical theories do not stand up to analysis. Far from trying to tar the Parti Québécois with the FLQ brush, Trudeau and other ministers went out of their way to warn people to distinguish between them and not to confuse democratic separatists with terrorists. The day after the War Measures Act was proclaimed, Bryce Mackasey, then Labor Minister, rebuked an opposition member for confusing the two groups: "When we try to equate the FLQ and the Parti Québécois we are equating bandits, terrorists and part of an international movement with a legitimate political party in this country."

Trudeau carefully distinguished between the two groups on French and English TV. "I would make every effort to make that distinction to make sure that there is no misinterpretation, no possibility of thinking that all separatists believe in violence because a few FLQ have used violence to promote separatism," he said on November 22, 1970. "I think that's a very fundamental distinction." Pelletier wrote: "It would of course be absurd to confuse the objectives of the FLQ and those of the Parti Québécois. . . ." These were not the words of a Prime Minister and a Cabinet seeking to confuse the public and discredit the PQ.

As to the theory that Trudeau gave notice that he would not permit peaceful separation, he said on November 10, 1970, while the country was still in crisis: "I've written often that the country is only held together by consent, not by force of arms, and if any part of our country wants to leave Canada, I don't think that force of arms will be used to keep them in the country. You can't hold a modern nation together by force. You have to hold it together by showing to the people that their lot, their future, their destiny is better within the country than without. Because if they think they will be happier outside of the country as individuals they will leave, but if a whole province decides that it is happier outside the country then it will leave."

A more pragmatic criticism of the use of the War Measures Act was that it proved quite unnecessary for tracking the terrorists. That was done by normal police work under the regular powers in the Criminal Code. But the criticism overlooked the fact that the decision to invoke emergency powers was never based on a declared need to find the terrorists and free the hostages.

In the letters which Trudeau tabled in the Commons, Bourassa asked particularly for powers "to apprehend and keep in custody individuals who, the Attorney General of Quebec has valid reasons to believe, are determined to overthrow the Government through violence and illegal means. . . ." Drapeau and Saulnier wrote of a "seditious plot and apprehended insurrection in which the recent kidnappings were the first step." Police chief St-Pierre reported: "An extremely dangerous subversive movement has progressively developed in Quebec in recent years with the objective of overthrowing the legitimate state by means of sedition and eventually armed insurrection." They appeared to be asking for powers to make arrests to prevent an escalation of violence.

If that was the intention, it worked like a charm. The night before the War Measures Act was proclaimed, Quebec was in a turmoil. The day after it was calm.

Perhaps Eric Hoffer, the longshoreman philosopher, was correct when he wrote in *The True Believer* that when masses are stirred to revolt, "it is not the wickedness of the old regime they rise against, but its weakness; not its oppression, but its failure to hammer them together into one solid, mighty whole. The persuasiveness of the intellectual demagogue consists not so much in convincing people of the vileness of the established order as in demonstrating its helpless incompetence." The War Measures Act demonstrated that the established order of government was not helpless and it certainly hammered the people into one mighty whole. The polls showed that 85 per cent of Canadians approved of the use of emergency powers and more than 80 per cent of the letters to Trudeau in October were favorable. He was widely praised as a resolute national leader who had stood firm against terrorism.

Yet that reading of events was as erroneous as the view of him as a conspirator and tyrant. The record shows that during the first part of the crisis he was ready to negotiate with the FLQ and offered no reassuring leadership to the country. The tactics of negotiation and conciliation confused public opinion and the silence encouraged a rising storm of speculation. After Laporte was seized, the initiative necessarily passed to Bourassa. Trudeau could encourage and aid him, but he dared not press the Premier to any step which would split the Quebec Cabinet. The collapse or even serious weakening of the Quebec Government in the atmosphere of growing uncertainty would have been disastrous. Bourassa set the pace during the second stage of the crisis and Trudeau did as he was asked: both men agree on that. It was while the Quebec Cabinet was taking hold of the situation that the uneasiness and insecurity of the first week grew in Montreal into fear and a dangerous feeling of instability in which anything might happen.

By the middle of the second week, it was a reasonable judgment, although not by any means certain beyond doubt, that riots could explode in the streets, leading to more violence and a further decay in democratic authority. The War Measures Act was a rough but effective way to cool the situation by taking possible agitators and FLQ sympathizers out of circulation and by assuring the populace that the Governments had firm control.

But that brings us back to the question at the beginning of this chapter: Who was responsible for allowing events to run so wildly out of hand? The responsibility must rest largely but not wholly on Trudeau. If he had been better prepared for a crisis which should have been predictable, if he had been better informed about the real strength of the FLQ, he could have offered firm and reassuring leadership early in the crisis and prevented much of the unnerving speculation.

If he had taken the hard decision not to negotiate with the terrorists but to treat them as a small band of criminals who had nothing to expect but to be hunted and caught, they would not have achieved their propaganda victory or provoked an enormous political uproar which has still to work itself out in Quebec. It is true that Cross might have been lost, but in time of war — and the FLQ had declared war — governments have to risk sacrifices.

The other parties who must share some responsibility for the crisis are the mass media. "We have learned to manipulate media," wrote Abbie Hoffman, the American Yippie leader, in his handbook on *Revolution for the Hell of It*. He described how a few radicals created a mythical Youth International Party and exploited the news hunger of TV and press to draw thousands of young people to Chicago at the time of the Democratic Party convention in 1968. There the young protestors clashed with the police and the media carried the Battle of Chicago across the United States and the world, stimulating a new wave of radicalism.

The media were manipulated during the October crisis. The FLQ poured out a stream of propaganda full of lurid threats and tension-building ultimatums and made skilful use of competing radio stations to ensure the fullest publicity. There were leaks and rumours from Ottawa, together with a lack of hard information, which helped to build excitement. And when there wasn't any real news, there was always speculation to keep the story alive.

The media did little to enlighten Canadians but served as the desired publicist for the FLQ, said John Saywell, Dean of Arts and Professor of History at York University and a TV commentator, in the preface to his book, *Quebec 70, a documentary narrative of the crisis*. Pelletier wrote: "We all remember that period when, with the press and radio in a state of hysteria, news was given out, denied, then officially corrected; discussions followed press conferences, speculations followed rumors. . . ." And we do remember. Cross's daughter, Susie, told an interviewer about her reaction to the crisis and commented bitterly: "None of us believes press reports anymore. If they could report little things I knew to be made up, why can't the big things be fabrications too?" Justice Minister Turner complained, ". . . all the action in terms of public opinion was left to a bunch of renegades and the Government was having a hard time sustaining its position," but, he added with satisfaction, with the War Measures Act in force, "All that has now stopped."

The media were not of course party to any conspiracy, although no doubt there were some FLQ sympathizers among the newsmen. But without the tendency of press, radio and TV to magnify and exaggerate, a handful of terrorists could not have brought Canada to one of the great crises in its history.

The consequences of the crisis cannot be fully measured. Who knows what changes have been made in the minds of men? But some things are known or can be deduced.

The federal Cabinet was diverted from its priorities for about six weeks. Some decisions were delayed. For example, the Opportunities for Youth Program plan was shelved for a time and when finally approved, it had to begin in a mad scramble which brought it much bad initial publicity. More significant, the desire to relieve political tensions in Quebec by showing economic and social progress influenced major policies. When the budget measures to stimulate employment were introduced in the fall of 1970, the emphasis was on increased spending in Quebec and other slow-growth regions rather than on tax cuts which would have had their principal impact in Ontario. But tax cuts would probably have been more effective in reducing national unemployment. In December, 1970, Montreal and neighboring districts of Quebec and Ontario were added temporarily to the regions in which federal subsidies were payable to encourage new industry. While this move was helpful to employment in Montreal, it diluted the value of incentives in the Maritimes and elsewhere.

The crisis may also have influenced the scope of tax reform. The federal White Paper had been severely attacked by Ontario which won support from Quebec and other provinces. Ottawa was prepared at one stage to take on the provinces and press ahead with its plans. After the crisis, there was less willingness to have a battle with Bourassa, and this seems to have been a factor in persuading the Cabinet to water down tax reform to meet some provincial objections.

In Parliament, there was talk of the need for permanent legislation less fearsome than the all-embracing War Measures Act to provide emergency powers in times of disturbance. This was a dubious proposition because the saving grace of the WMA was that it was a draconian measure which the government must hesitate to invoke. A handy little law for suspending just a few liberties might be too tempting. A better approach, perhaps, was suggested by Trudeau in June 1971 when he asked the provinces to agree to entrench basic political rights in the constitution. The draft charter provided that the government could limit these rights when necessary to protect public safety and national security, among other things. But according to Justice Minister Turner, it would then be open to the courts to determine if the government had reasonable justification for its action. If the charter had been in force in October 1970, the courts could have been asked to decide if the Government had reasonable grounds for suspending civil rights, and to restore them if there was insufficient evidence of an apprehended insurrection endangering order and security.

The charter was not accepted by Quebec for quite different reasons, but Trudeau's proposal should not be ignored by those who argue that the crisis stripped him of any claim to be a civil libertarian.

Montreal scene during crisis of October, 1970.
Reprinted with permission—Miller Services.

EPILOGUE

The October crisis was by far the most revealing event during the drama of the Trudeau years under review, and it provides the scene on which to bring down the curtain.

Shortly after he invoked the War Measures Act, Trudeau was asked if it had been a great struggle of conscience, and he replied: "In my own mind the importance of democratic movements not fearing to take extraordinary measures to preserve democracy, this importance has always been established, both intellectually and emotionally. So I didn't have to, sort of, weigh back and forth the kind of struggle that goes on between Creon and Antigone, in Sophocles' famous play about what is more important, the State or the individual. Democracy must preserve itself."

Trudeau was referring to the classical Greek tragedy, *Antigone*, in which Creon, the ruler of Thebes, speaks for the State. "Power shows the man," he says, insisting that he must at all costs uphold the law, even to the extent of ordering that his niece, Antigone, be entombed when she defies his authority. He thought that he was acting in the best interests of the State, but the gods disagreed, and he was swiftly brought to disaster. Creon is last seen in the play crying:

"... all that I can touch
Is falling — falling — round me, and o'erhead
Intolerable destiny descends."

It was a curious precedent for Trudeau to cite. But in our democracy, the gods are the voters at election time. It was for them to decide if by suspending liberty briefly in 1970, he best preserved it — if indeed the paradoxical quality of many of his policies revealed a truth or simply confusion.